Warwickshire Lime and Cement Works Railways

by

Sydney A. Leleux

THE OAKWOOD PRESS

© Oakwood Press & Sydney A. Leleux 2014

British Library Cataloguing in Publication Data
A Record for this book is available from the British Library
ISBN 978 0 85361 737 2

Typeset by Oakwood Graphics.
Repro by PKmediaworks, Cranborne, Dorset.
Printed by Berforts Information Press Ltd, Stevenage, Herts.

Title page: 'Hall' class 4-6-0 No. 4954 *Plaish Hall* hurries past Greaves Siding signal box with a down express, almost obscuring a 2-6-2T (bunker first) on a freight in the loop, while *Whitby* waits in the works' sidings, April 1958.   *R.C. Riley*

Front cover, top: The engine shed yard at Southam Works on Saturday 27th October, 1956, with all the locomotives outside for visiting enthusiasts (the several diesels were off to the right). *From left to right:* Triassic, Liassic, Mesozoic, Jurassic (partially obscured).
Photomatic, Author's Collection

Rear cover, bottom: Totternhoe Quarries No. 4 with a rake of empty wagons. The left-hand track in the foreground served the lime works and the right-hand one shortly split into the full and empty wagon sidings at the foot of the incline. The engine shed is obscured by the trees, the point giving access to it being level with the locomotive, 28th June, 1961.
Author

Rear cover bottom: Harbury Works No. 2 with a loaded train passing under an aqueduct carrying a stream as it leaves the quarry. Note the warning on the bonnet, 19th March, 1966.   *R.E. West*

Published by The Oakwood Press (Usk), P.O. Box 13, Usk, Mon., NP15 1YS.
E-mail: sales@oakwoodpress.co.uk
Website: www.oakwoodpress.co.uk

Contents

Introduction

At the Narrow Gauge Railway Society AGM in the spring of 1959, one speaker encouraged members to do research into individual systems. I spoke to him afterwards, and as a result I began to investigate the recently closed railway at the Southam works of the Rugby Portland Cement Co. (RPC), which was about 25 miles from my then home in Northampton. I was at this time a Rover Scout (for those aged 18 to 25), and I decided to work for the Baden-Powell Award. Amongst other things, this required me to

> ... choose, plan, and devote at least six months to a Project [which was] a self-imposed task demanding skill, application and care. The Rover ... picks the subject of his Project for himself. There is no restriction on his choice of subject ... but it should bear no direct relation to his means of livelihood ... (Policy, Organisation & Rules Boy Scouts Association, 1959, Rule 555).

For my project I chose to investigate the history of this industrial railway. It was not long before I discovered that there had been several other lime and cement works in the Southam area, some having links with 'my' works. Two years later, having 'completed' my research into the RPC Southam system to the satisfaction of my fellow Rovers, they agreed with me that it would be sensible to widen the project to include the other works before publishing anything. As a result, my research expanded until eventually it covered the county, and even further afield. (And, yes, I did gain the B-P Award.)

However, for various reasons, research did not proceed very rapidly. Periodically there would be a burst of activity before it was again left to gather dust on a shelf. Now, some 55 years after starting and following the closure of all the railways in the cement works, I feel that the material I have should be collated and published, although I am conscious of a number of gaps in the histories that follow. However, I also believe that one way to obtain more information is to publish what you have. The works are described in a generally north-easterly direction, from Stratford-upon-Avon to Rugby, a distance of about 25 miles.

Maps

A lot of information has been obtained from various editions of the Ordnance Survey maps, particularly the 1st Edition 1 inch (1834) and the 1st & 2nd editions 6 inch and 25 inch (around 1885 & 1905 respectively). These were made available by Bedfordshire & Luton Archives & Records Service and Warwickshire County Record Office. British Waterways Archives also provided a number of large scale maps.

When publishing its 6 in. maps, the Ordnance Survey divided each county into numbered rectangular areas. Each area was then subdivided into four parts, the individual sheets being referenced by the number and NW, NE, SW or SE as appropriate. The 25 in. maps had the same basic reference number as the corresponding 6 in. map, but the area was covered by 16 sheets, arranged in four horizontal strips, numbered 1 to 4, 5 to 8, 9 to 12 and 13 to 16. Thus the 6 in. sheet 23NW was covered by 25 in. sheets 23.1, 23.2, 23.5 & 23.6. Several works and their quarries extended over two or more sheets, so extracts have been joined for illustrations in this book, but there are a few discontinuities at the joints. As far as possible these were made to occur at field boundaries. Large maps are awkward to copy, and slight variations can occur in copying. A few maps are from microfilm images so their quality is poorer.

Money

Sums of money are given in pre-decimalisation amounts. Then, 12 pennies made one shilling, and 20 shillings made £1. Money was written as £2 12s. 6d. (two pounds twelve shillings and six pence). Due to the considerable changes in the value of money in recent years, where appropriate an approximate modern equivalent is given in brackets.

Abbreviations

AE	Avonside Engine Co. Ltd, Locomotive Manufacturer, Bristol
AP	Aveling & Porter Ltd, Locomotive Manufacturer, Canterbury, Kent
APCM	Associated Portland Cement Manufacturers Ltd
Bg	E.E. Bagulay Ltd, Locomotive Manufacturer, Burton-on-Trent, Staffordshire
BPCM	British Portland Cementn Manufacturers
BR	British Railways, formed 1.1.1948
BW	British Waterways
FE	Falcon Engine & Car Works Ltd, Locomotive Manufacturer, Loughborough, Leicestershire
GBL	Greaves Bull & Lakin, Lime & Cement Manufacturers
GKB	Greaves Kirshaw & Bull, Lime & Cement Manufacturers
GUCCCo.	Grand Union Canal Carrying Co., Canal Haulage
GWR	Great Western Railway
HC	Hudswell, Clarke & Co. Ltd, Locomotive Manufacturer, Leeds
HE	Hunslet Engine Co. Ltd, Locomotive Manufacturer, Leeds
HMRS	Historical Model Railway Society
IRS	Industrial Railway Society
JF	John Fowler & Co. (Leeds) Ltd, Locomotive Manufacturer, Leeds
KC	Kent Construction Co. Ltd, Locomotive Manufacturer, Ashford, Kent
KS	Kerr, Stuart & Co. Ltd, Locomotive Manufacturer, Stoke-on-Trent
LCLR	Lincolnshire Coast Light Railway
LMS	London Midland & Scottish Railway, formed 1.1.1923 and incorporated the London & North Western Railway, Midland Railway and others, became BR constituent 1.1.1948
LNWR	London & North Western Railway, became LMS constituent 1.1.1923
MR	Motor Rail Ltd, Locomotive Manufacturer, Bedford (formerly Motor Rail & Tramcar Co. Ltd) 'Simplex'; *also* Midland Railway
MW	Manning, Wardle & Co. Ltd, Locomotive Manufacturer, Leeds
NCB	National Coal Board, owned and operated British deep coal mines from 1.1.1947
NGRS	Narrow Gauge Railway Society
OCC	Oxford Canal Co.
OK	Orenstein & Koppel AG, Locomotive Manufacturer, Berlin
Oliver	Oliver & Co. Ltd, Locomotive Dealer, Chesterfield, Derbyshire
OS	Ordnance Survey
P	Peckett & Sons Ltd, Locomotive Manufacturer, Bristol
PO	Privately Owned - refers to wagons operated over the main lines but owned by the railways' customers, not the main line railways themselves
RCH	Railway Clearing House
RCHS	Railway & Canal Historical Society
RH	Ruston & Hornsby Ltd, Locomotive Manufacturer, Lincoln
RPC	Rugby Portland Cement Co. Ltd
RSHN	Robert Stephenson & Hawthorns Ltd, Locomotive Manufacturer, Newcastle-upon-Tyne
S	Sentinel (Shrewsbury) Ltd, Locomotive Manufacturer, Shrewsbury (formerly Sentinel Waggon Works Ltd)
S&H	Strachan & Henshaw Ltd, Locomotive Manufacturer, Bristol
SMJ	Stratford upon Avon & Midland Junction Railway, became LMS constituent 1.1.1923
TH	Thomas Hill (Rotherham) Ltd, Locomotive Manufacturer, Kilnhurst, S. Yorks
TLS	Totternhoe Lime & Stone Co Ltd, Lime Manufacturers
VCH	Victoria County History of Warwickshire

Note: Some firms described above as 'Locomotive Manufacturer' also constructed other equipment.

WB	W.G. Bagnall Ltd, Locomotive Manufacturer, Stafford
WDLR	War Department Light Railways – narrow gauge railways used immediately behind the front line in World War I
W&N	Warwick & Napton Canal

Locomotive Descriptions

The Whyte system of wheel classification is used for all locomotives having the driving wheels coupled by external side rods. The three figures give the number of unpowered carrying wheels (if any) at the front, then the number of driving wheels, and finally the number of unpowered carrying wheels (if any) under the cab, for example 0-4-2. If the driving wheels are coupled by gears or chains then the locomotive is described as 4w or 6w.

Steam locomotives are further described by the type of water tank and the position of the cylinders.

Water tank	T	side tank, mounted each side of the boiler
	ST	saddle tank, mounted above the boiler
	WT	well tank, mounted between the locomotive's frames
Cylinders	IC	inside cylinders, between the frames
	OC	outside cylinders
	VC	vertical cylinders
Drive	G	geared drive, otherwise the drive is assumed to use a connecting rod attached to the crank axle or a crank pin on a driving wheel

Internal combustion locomotives are further described by their fuel and transmission.

Fuel	D	diesel
	P	petrol, possibly changing to paraffin for economy when the engine has warmed up
Transmission	E	electric
	H	hydraulic
	M	mechanical

If the locomotive carried a name or number this is given, followed by the wheel arrangement and the details listed above. Then comes the abbreviation for the manufacturer (see list above) which is followed by the manufacturer's serial number and date of construction (reb is date of rebuilding). If the locomotive was supplied new this is stated, otherwise a letter refers to accompanying notes to give its origin. If there is a number in the disposal details refer to the accompanying notes, otherwise:

Scr	scrapped on (or by) the date given
s/s	scrapped or sold, disposal details not known

Much of the locomotive information is from IRS records, whose members often report details of the current locomotive stock after they have visited a firm. This accounts for notes such as 'after (date)' or 'by (date)'.

Acknowledgements

During the 55 years I have been investigating these railways all manner of organizations and people have provided me with information or facilities for research. I would like to thank the following companies and official bodies for their help:

Abelson & Co. (Engineers) Ltd, Aerofilms Ltd, Associated Portland Cement Manufacturers Ltd, W.G. Bagnall Ltd, Bedfordshire & Luton Archives & Records Service, Biffa Waste Services Ltd, Birmingham City Council – Archives & Heritage Services Central Library, Britannia Iron & Steel Works Ltd, British Cement Association, British Museum, British Waterways Archives, Cemex UK Operations Ltd, Companies House, John Fowler & Co (Leeds) Ltd, Historical Model Railway Society, Hunslet Engine Co. Ltd, Industrial Railway Society, Leeds City Council, Motherwell Heritage Centre, Motor Rail Ltd, Narrow Gauge Railway Society, National Monuments Record (English Heritage), Oxfordshire History Centre, Parliamentary Archives House of Lords, Peckett & Sons Ltd, Rail Management Service Ltd (RMS Locotec), Railway & Canal Historical Society, Rugby Art Gallery & Museum, Rugby Portland Cement Co. Ltd, Ruston & Hornsby Ltd, Ruston-Bucyrus Ltd, Sentinel (Shrewsbury) Ltd, Totternhoe Lime & Stone Co Ltd, William Twigg (Matlock) Ltd, VME Construction Equipment GB Ltd, Wareing & Co., Warwickshire County Record Office.

All manner of individuals have answered my questions over the years. They include managers and employees of the various works, farmers and other local residents, local historians, and fellow railway or canal enthusiasts. The names that I have recorded - and I apologise for any accidentally omitted - are:

S. Adams, S.R. Allen, G. Alliez, J. Arkell, P.R. Arnold, D.D. Bailey, A.C. Baker, W. Baird, H. Baker, Mrs C. Barratt, R.A. Bates, F. Bench, W. Biddle, N. Billingham, E. Booker, D.C. Bray, P. Briddon, A. Brookes, J.N. Cain, Irene Cardall, D. Clayton, R. Coles, Alf Cooksey, K. Cooper, R. 'Bob' Crick, C. Croft, Mrs C. Dale-Leech, C. Daniels, R.D. Darvill, W.J.K. Davies, K.C. Dickens, S. Elliot, A.H. Faulkner, C. Flavell, J.P.H. Frearson, L. Giles, S. Gough, Mr & Mrs P. Grace, Mrs P. Green, A. Griffin, K.E. Hartley, R. Hine, Mrs A. Hodge, F. Hodges, A.E. Holder, A. Hopkins, P. Ingham, M. Johnson, Mrs C. Jones, P.J. Kelley, C.H. & L.J. Lambe, K. Lane, P.O. Lane, J.B. Latham, M.J. Leah, R.V. Leleux, J. Lines, Sir Lister Lister-Kaye, N. Lutt, E. Manders, P. Manders, R..Mann, Mrs C. Matthews, Mr Monk, T. Morand, C.J. Morrison, G. Nichols, Mrs B.G. Otway, R.S. Palmer, J. Pemberton, K. Plant, I. Pope, H. Potter, R.N. Redman, R.C. Riley, M. Ryall, E. Sawford, J. Sharland, J. Sheasby, R. Spratt, G.M. Stephens, K. Stepney, M. Swift, B. Symonds, I.H. Thomas, E.S. Tonks, P.H. Trutch, K. Turton, Mrs M. Twigg, H.A. Vigar, P. Walpole, R. Waywell, R. Weaver, R.E. West, P.J. Wilde.

Lastly, but by no means least, my wife Zoe has lived with this project throughout the 50 years of our married life, and has actively encouraged me to finish it. I cannot thank her enough.

The main published sources consulted are listed below.

Brief History of Griffin's Blue Lias Lime & Cement Works, Simon J.Bartlett, edition 3.4 March 2010 (available on web)
Britain's Lost Waterways, M.E. Ware, Moorland Publishing, 1989
Canals of East Midlands, C. Hadfield, David & Charles, 2nd edition 1970
The Cement Industry 1796-1914: A History, A.J. Francis, David & Charles, 1977
The Cement Railways of Kent, B.D. Stoyel & R.W. Kidner, Oakwood Press, 2nd edition, 1990
The Dunstable Branch, Bill Simpson, Lamplight Publications, 1998
The Effects of Mergers, P. Lesley Cook & Ruth Cohen, Allen & Unwin, 1958 (section on the cement industry by P. Lesley Cook)
Geology of the Country around Warwick British Geological Survey, HMSO, 1987
A Hundred Years of Portland Cement, A.C. Davis, Concrete Publications, 1924
Illustrated History of Canal & River Navigations, Edward Paget-Tomlinson, Landmark Publishing, 2006

Industrial Archaeology - An Historical Survey, Arthur Raistrick, Methuen, 1972
Industrial Steam in the '50s & '60s, Eric Sawford, Sutton Publishing, 2004
Journeys from the Centre of the Earth, Iain Stewart, Century, 2005
LNWR Diagrams of Private Sidings: Rugby to London and Branches
The Midlands Canals - Memories of the Canal Carriers, Robert Davies, Tempus, 2006
Newcomen Society Transactions Vol. XXXIV 1961-62 & Vol. XXXV 1962-63
Portland Cement Industry: S. Midlands, E. Anglia & S. Wales
Portrait of a Parish, A. Payne, Roundwood Press, Kineton, 1968
Private Owners Wagons - a fifth collection, Keith Turton, Lightmoor Press, 2006
Railways & Preservation, J.B. Latham, 1975
Raw Materials in the Rugby Area, P.J. Wiles, May 1971 (Thesis for Lanchester Poly (Rugby))
Round about Napton (2nd edition), J.N. Cain compiled on behalf of the Napton School Association, 1985
Silent Highways, Ray Shill, History Press, 2011 – 'The forgotten heritage of the Midlands canals'
Stratford upon Avon & Midland Junction Railway, Arthur Jordan, Oxford Pub.Co., 1982
Tales from the Old Inland Waterways, Euan Corrie, David & Charles, 1998
Victoria County History of Warwickshire (VCH), late 1940s
The Warwick Canals, Alan Faulkner, Railway & Canal Historical Society, 1985
Various trade directories, but unfortunately there is often a gap of several years between the editions available in public record offices.

Much of the information about the locomotives used was obtained from publications produced by the Industrial Railway Society (formerly the Birmingham Locomotive Club - Industrial Locomotive Information Section):

Pocket Book A - West Midlands, 1957
Pocket Book D - East Midlands, 1960
Pocket Book F - North Wales, 1968
Industrial Locomotives of Central Southern England, 1981
Industrial Locomotives of Buckinghamshire Bedfordshire & Northamptonshire, 2001
Industrial Railway & Locomotives of Warwickshire, Preliminary Draft 2003

These periodicals were also consulted:

British Clay Worker - November 1903
Cement & Lime Manufacture - July 1963
The Engineer - 1st & 8th January 1909 'Cement Works at Southam'
Industrial Railway Record (journal of IRS): Nos. 11, 57, 135, 145, 151, 152, 165, 166, 174, 192
Model Railway News - various issues in 1946, 1963, 1964 & 1967
Narrow Boat - Spring 2007 Canal Boat Registers, Spring 2011 Famous Fleets - Charles Nelson
The Narrow Gauge (journal of NGRS): Nos. 37, 40, 89, 97
Narrow Gauge & Industrial Review No. 46 (April 2001)
Railway Bylines - April 2002
Railway Magazine – October 1993, May 2007
Waterways World - March 1998 - 'Cement Carriers - Part 1: The Stocktons'
Warwickshire Industrial Archaeology - issue 8, Summer 1998: 'Model Village, Long Itchington'

The source of an illustration is acknowledged in the caption. Despite enquiries, I regret that I have been unable to trace the owners of the copyright of some illustrations. Any such people should contact the publisher so that full acknowledgement can be made in subsequent editions of this work.

Sydney A. Leleux,
Stanton-by-Dale, Derbyshire
June 2014

Chapter One

Outline History of Cement Manufacture

Lime has been made on a small scale for very many years by farmers, both to put on their land and as a building material. Mortar is made from a mixture of lime, sand and water. Indeed, crude lime mortar was made 9,000 years ago by early Neolithic peoples (*Journeys from the Centre of the Earth*, p. 92). Later it was used by the Egyptians in the pyramids, and the Greeks used it to cover walls made of unburnt bricks.

The typical 18th or 19th century lime kiln was a vertical cylinder about 10 ft diameter and 8 ft long, tapering to a point at the lower end. It was constructed in a massive tower with walls 8 ft thick at the base. Coal and limestone (calcium carbonate) were fed alternately into the mouth of the kiln and lime (calcium oxide) mixed with ashes was drawn from the bottom. Often the kiln was built against a bank to make it easier to charge the raw materials (*Industrial Archaeology*, p. 71).

Later, towards the end of the 19th century, particularly when lime became a raw material for the chemical industry, special steel kilns were developed, but by then the industry was migrating to areas such as around Buxton where large quantities of pure limestone were available. The kilns in Warwickshire were the traditional stone or brick variety.

Lime manufacture was given a considerable boost by the construction of the canals, and later railways, which gave cheap access to both fuel and markets. The growing industrial towns needed lime for use in building construction or the manufacture of chemicals, and the agricultural areas served used it to improve the soil.

The Romans had discovered that compacted volcanic ash called tuff, when ground down into 'pozzolana' and mixed with lime formed cement which would set under water. This enabled them to construct concrete breakwaters for harbours. They also used pozzolana to make the first mass-produced precast concrete blocks (*Journeys from the Centre of the Earth*, pp 93 & 94).

Long after the Roman period, it was discovered that some raw materials produced so-called 'hydraulic lime', which made a mortar able to set under water. The first serious studies of the properties of limes, especially 'hydraulic setting', was made by John Smeaton in 1756 during the construction of the Eddystone lighthouse. 'Water limes' were all made from limestones containing clay, but the artificial addition of clay to pure lime had no effect. Research continued in the early 19th century. Medina Cement and the more popular Roman Cement were introduced in the late 18th century, but these seem to have been only improved hydraulic limes. Roman Cement, patented by James Parker in 1796, was made by burning certain natural nodules of clay containing veins of calcium carbonate found especially on the Isle of Sheppey and near Harwich. Unfortunately, the quality of 'natural' cement was unreliable due to variable composition of the raw material.

The principal discovery [for the satisfactory manufacture of cement] was made in 1824 by a Wakefield builder, Joseph Aspdin, who was burning chalk [another form of calcium carbonate] with some proportion of clay to produce a strong mortar. His material was fired at too high a temperature and produced a sinter or clinker. This, when ground up and mixed with water, was found to produce a very strong cement. Aspdin gave it the name Portland Cement, hoping that it might replace Portland stone. Instead it initiated the era of concrete. (*Industrial Archaeology*, p. 72)

9

Aspdin's patent is vaguely worded and he may have practised a better process than that described in his patent. By 1845 I.C. Johnson, the manager of J.B. White's works at Swanscombe, near Gravesend, Kent, knew, or had discovered, that for a true cement the materials had to be 'burnt until the mass nearly vitrified' and not merely calcined. The clinker so formed was then ground to give cement. Expansion of the use of true cement was hindered by a lack of understanding of the chemistry involved in its manufacture, and by competition from Roman Cement, but Portland Cement was increasingly used in public works from 1860 onwards.

There were only three manufacturers of 'artificial' cement in August 1847: J.B. White (Swanscombe), Evans & Nicholson (Manchester) and,

... thirdly, that of Mr Richard Greaves, of Stratford-upon-Avon, who makes a powerful water cement, which he calls blue lias cement, by mixing a proportion of indurated (hardened) clay or shale with the excellent blue lias lime of the neighbourhood, both of which are found in the same quarries; the former being previously broken and ground, and the latter burned and slaked, which is absolutely necessary in making an artificial cement from any of the hard limestones. (*A Hundred Years of Portland Cement*, pp. 45 & 46)

In fact Greaves was making cement by 1844, if not earlier.

Cement is made by burning together, to a clinker, a mixture in the proper proportions of any kind of calcium carbonate (limestone, chalk, or calcareous mud), with clay materials (clay, shale or clay mud). The use of correct proportions and a high temperature are vital. Before 1900 the industry was highly localized, particularly along the Thames and Medway, wherever raw materials were available. The early works mixed clay and chalk in roughly the correct proportions, but by 1924 a wide range of suitable raw materials were being used in accurately determined proportions.

In south Warwickshire,

... the blue lias subsoil had long been known as a valuable source for the manufacture of lime and [later] cement, and by 1850 the workings were described as 'very extensive' ... The quarries extend into the parishes of Long Itchington and Southam (though the best ones are said to be those north and east of Stockton village, the first to be worked), and, covering nearly all the north and west portions of Stockton parish, form the largest stretch of non-agricultural land in the rural half of Warwickshire. Stockton in fact has more of the character of an industrial village than any in Knightlow Hundred except Bedworth and its neighbours on the coalfield. The population trebled in the nineteenth century (1911 - 975, 1921 - 1006, 1931 - 935), at a rate comparable to Alcester, Bedworth or Kenilworth, and Stockton was one of the very few rural parishes where voluntary provision of school facilities was inadequate and a School Board formed (1878). (*VCH*, vol. 6 p. 226).

The strata quarried comprises alternate layers of,

... dark grey, blocky to fissile, shelly, commonly bioturbated mudstones, and paler grey, hard, argillaceous limestones (cementstones) which are mostly 0.1 to 0.2 m thick and contain organic debris and burrows. Cementstone also occurs as bands of nodules ... The proportion of limestone in the succession decreases northwards from about 35% at Harbury to around 30% at Long Itchington and Rugby ... The approximate thickness of the blue lias is 24m at Harbury, 25m at Long Itchington and 36 - 40m in the Rugby area ... Fossils are common at some levels ... (*Geology of the Country around Warwick*, page 39).

The well defined layers of different material made it easy to adjust the proportions of clay and limestone to the exact ones required to make cement. The stone is a good deal fissured and loosely packed so blasting is not usually required. The bedding planes are nearly level which assisted extraction, particularly by hand, as the quarries could be worked as a series of levels. In the early lime and cement works much of the clay was removed by hand sorting and then dumped, but from the mid-1930s all the material quarried was used. The correct proportions were then maintained by adding extra calcium carbonate obtained from another source, either additional limestone at Harbury or chalk at Rugby and Southam.

Initially the science of the process was little understood so production was by rule of thumb, but increasing knowledge of the chemistry and better grinding techniques enabled other materials, especially limestone, to be used. The wet grinding process was patented by Goreham in 1870. Cost was not very important in local markets, but the quality of the product became increasingly important. The first British Standard for cement was brought out in 1904, followed by improved British Standards in 1915 and 1920.

From 1850 to 1890 cement was an expanding market and very profitable. It was easy to set up a works, as little capital was needed and good managers were available. However, business competition became serious in the 1890s.

In the late 19th century cement works used either chamber kilns (patented 1872) or bottle kilns (patented 1878). The charge for a bottle kiln comprised layers of dry raw material and coke which were then fired. In a chamber kiln the heat from a bottle or other kiln was led through one or more chambers to the chimney. The wet raw materials, mixed as a slurry, were placed in these chambers and dried before being fired in the kiln itself. Chamber kilns were developed to a high efficiency and were installed up to 1903. They required about 8 to 9 cwt (400-450 kg) of coke to make 1 ton of cement.

Early production of both lime and cement used a batch process, in other words a kiln was loaded, fired and emptied before the cycle was repeated for the next batch. Production was necessarily intermittent, and fuel was wasted having to heat the kiln itself from cold each time. The first successful method of continuous cement production was the shaft kiln, installed from 1898. This type of kiln was fed from the top and the clinker was removed from the grate at the bottom. It needed dry materials and was labour intensive, but it was cheap to construct. A major failing was that the grate often contained imperfectly burnt material which had to be picked out by hand, otherwise an inferior product was made.

Rotary kiln patents were taken out in from 1877, and the first was installed in 1887. The kiln comprised a gently sloping rotating iron cylinder. Slurry was fed in at the higher end and fuel (gas or coal dust) was blown in at the lower end, from which a stream of clinker granules emerged. The first rotary kiln in Britain, 5 ft diameter and 26 ft long, was at Arlesey, near Hitchin, Hertfordshire. Early rotary kilns were failures as the process was not fully understood, but practical patents were taken out in 1896 in USA and successful rotary kilns were installed from 1900 onwards. Development was rapid, first to 60 ft long kilns, then 100 ft, 200 ft by 1914 and 300 ft was common by the 1920s. Rotary kilns could use coal as fuel whereas earlier kilns had used coke. There were increasing economies of scale, which coupled with improved plant layout and mechanical handling, enabled costs to be reduced by 40 per cent by 1929 (*Effects of Mergers*, p. 68).

The clinker was originally ground to a flour by millstones, but from about 1900 ball mills were introduced. These had heavy steel balls in a rotating cylinder which pounded the material into powder.

The period from 1895 to 1925 saw great changes, with all capital equipment changed at least once, as the industry developed from an empirical trade to one governed by chemists and engineers. Costs using pre-1900 methods were 18s. (about £55) per ton, and before World War I the output of rotary kilns cost 13s. (£36) per ton. Output from a single kiln before 1900 was 500 tons/week, which had risen by 1924 between 1,000 and 2,000 tons/week.

These changes naturally had their effects on the lime and cement works in Warwickshire, and the railways within those works. Alongside technical developments there were equally important changes in the business structure of the cement industry.

Financial Background

In 1900 H.O. O'Hagan was behind the formation of Associated Portland Cement Manufacturers (APCM), which brought together about 20 cement works in the Thames and Medway area having some 90 per cent of the UK output. Although APCM bought the rotary kiln patents it had no monopoly of their use, and there was plenty of incentive for others to enter the trade as the APCM price yielded good profits, even at the older works.

Many of the firms set up at this time [early 1900s] were away from the London area where competition tended to be fiercest. One fairly important one was Greaves Bull & Lakin at Harbury in Warwickshire; the output in 1907 was 600 tons/week. (*Effects of Mergers*, p. 43).

The remainder of the industry had a capacity of approximately 12,350 tons/week in about 1907. Half of this was produced by 10 substantial firms, four being in Warwickshire, presumably Greaves Bull & Lakin, Kaye, Nelson and Ruby Portland Cement (*ibid* page 58).

APCM created a subsidiary, British Portland Cement Manufacturers (BPCM), in 1911, buying up another 32 companies so having a capacity similar to the parent firm. APCM and BPCM each traded as Blue Circle Cement.

In April 1926 an investment company called British Cement Products and Finance Co. Ltd was incorporated to acquire interests in the cement industry ... Two other investment trusts also included, so [it is necessary] to speak of the Horne Group (H.S. Horne, financier). In 1926 the Ship Canal Portland Cement Manufacturers Ltd was acquired, having works at Ellesmere Port supplied with limestone from North Wales. In the next three years the Horne Group's cement interests were expanded by the acquisition of five more large companies and one small one.

In April 1927, Greaves Bull & Lakin was floated as a public company; this was an old established works at Harbury in Warwickshire. The authorized capital was £400,000 and the Ship Canal Portland Cement Manufacturers Co. Ltd took up 400,000 5s. shares and obtained an option on further shares at 6s. At the end of 1927 the Horne Group acquired the Dunstable Portland Cement Co. and the Holborough Cement Co. ...

The capacity of the Horne Group was 1,000,000 tons (one-third that of the Blue Circle group, one-sixth of the industry as a whole). Ship Canal Portland Cement changed its name to Allied Cement Manufacturers Ltd, formed on 2nd August, 1929, selling its products as Red Triangle cement, under the slogan 'Right across Britain'.

There was severe price competition, APCM versus Horne and independent manufacturers for five months to November 1928, when Horne and the major independents joined the Cement Manufacturers' Association. The Red Triangle group included building merchants etc. and in 1929 was within measurable distance of disposing of 90 per cent of its output. (*Effects of Mergers* pp. 74, 75).

At this time the potential annual output of the various cement producers was:

Producer	Potential Output (million tons)	
APCM	3.6	
Red Triangle	1.0	
5 major independents	0.8	
10 medium independents	0.5	
12 small independents	0.2	
Total	6.3	but in fact only 4.3 million tons.

In November 1929 Horne filed a petition of bankruptcy. Allied Cement Manufacturers earned 2.2 per cent on ordinary shares, and passed dividend for the year ending March 1930. Financial difficulties were apparent. Horne resigned and Board changes followed his resignation; an extraordinary general meeting on 23rd December, 1930 removed all the Directors except the Chairman and substituted four others, three of whom were Directors of Eastwoods Ltd. The *Financial Times* on 1st January, 1931 reported that the financial position had been investigated and no money was available to pay interest on First Mortgage Debenture Stock (£587,400 at 6½ per cent). A receiver was appointed on 13th January, 1931 as a result of an application by Barclays Bank and British Maritime Trust who were debenture holders.

The *Economist* of 17th January, 1931 felt that it was only the failure to find additional finance at short notice that deprived Eastwood of permanent control of the Red Triangle group, which would have affected the subsequent history of the industry. As it was, in April 1931 the receiver had an offer for the Red Triangle assets from the Blue Circle group. A report given at the AGM of APCM in April 1932 said that the 'outstanding event of the year was the acquisition of the manufacturing and marketing interests of the Red Triangle Group - liquidation was the only way of unlocking knots of interests'. In July 1931 a merger under one controlling company was proposed. The APCM offer had been accepted on 19th August, 1931, after the rejection of an earlier offer from APCM. By taking over the Red Triangle group APCM then had 70 per cent of the trade. Allied Cement Manufacturers Ltd ownership ceased from 7th December, 1931. The Red Triangle group failure was due in large part to poor management rather than an unsound structure (*Effects of Mergers*, p. 87-91).

The number of small cement manufacturing firms was decreasing rapidly by 1934. Although the Blue Circle and Red Triangle battle was over, one of the independent firms was about to make its presence felt. Halford Reddish became Chairman and Managing Director of the Rugby Portland Cement Co. (RPC) in 1933, positions he was to hold until the 1960s, and immediately embarked on expansion. Rugby works was reorganized and expanded and,

... in 1934 Kaye & Co. Ltd, a small firm near Rugby which was on the verge of liquidation, was acquired and a new works was erected. Although still small in 1934 this firm [RPC] had become active and was to become very much larger and more important. It was converted into a public limited company in 1935, the capital being increased from £120,000 to £250,000.

Besides acquiring Kaye & Co., an entirely new works was built beside the old one at Rugby, where the second kiln, previously regarded as standby, was brought into regular production. A new works was built at Halling, Kent, in 1936, with the pinnacle of RPC expansion coming in the late 1930s. In 1944 the company announced that its post-war expansion plans were ready.

After World War II demand for cement rose at both home and abroad, causing shortages in 1949, 1950 and 1951. Demand in the construction industry caused delays in getting new cement manufacturing plant operational, but even so proportional expansion of RPC was greater than for any other company. In the period 1938 to 1955 deliveries from all works in the UK rose by 64 per cent, but RPC output rose by 276 per cent, a vast increase in importance for a company of only medium size in 1938.

In these conditions of expansion and optimism ... smaller units in the industry were absorbed by large companies. In 1945 the RPC Co. acquired Charles Nelson & Co. Ltd, an old firm near their works at Stockton [*sic*]; this firm was in a weak state and the works in a poor condition ... (*Effects of Mergers*, pp. 92, 100, 114, 115).

The railways forming the subject of this book supported a very competitive and technically based industry.

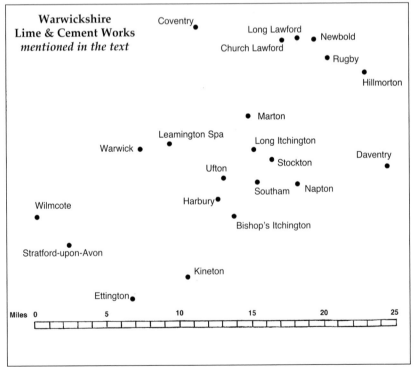

Southern Warwickshire, showing relative locations of the works mentioned in the text.

Chapter Two

Wilmcote Lime & Cement Works

1816	William James
1824	Richard Greaves
1840	Greaves & Kirshaw
1860s, by 1868	Greaves Kirshaw & Bull
1870s, by 1880	Greaves Bull & Lakin
Between 1900 & 1904	Greaves Bull & Lakin Ltd

Closed by 1908

Also 1845-1870s	Thomas Higgins & Co.

Wilmcote, famous as the home of Shakespeare's wife Mary Arden, is three miles north-west of Stratford-upon-Avon. The quarries and kilns were north and west of the village, one set of kilns being beside the Stratford-upon-Avon Canal, whose construction had started in 1793 and which was opened throughout in 1816.

Wilmcote stone had long been used for building purposes. Records show that Thomas Edkins, of Wilmcote, supplied stone to repair Clopton bridge in Stratford in 1541 & 1546. (Thomas married Katherine Arden, sister of Shakespeare's wife Mary, whose house in the village is open to visitors. Another Thomas Edkins is recorded living at Gipsy Hall Farm in 1850.) The local stone was used to repair St Mary's Church, Warwick, after a fire in 1694. In addition to its use for lime and cement making, some stone was quarried to make flagstones which were sawn to size by a beam engine. Wilmcote stone was used to pave the House of Commons and Royal Courts of Justice in 1904.

Although VCH (vol. 3, p. 243) states that 'Messrs Greaves, who were then developing stone quarries at Wilmcote, opened lime kilns here in 1824' and on an earlier page (vol. 3, p. 42) states that the cement works was 'opened in the [eighteen] thirties', the early trade directories are not very helpful. They contain no reference to lime burning until 1850, although in 1854 Wilmcote is 'Celebrated for its extensive lime works'. In 1860 Greaves & Kirshaw are listed as Lime Burners & Merchants at High Street, Warwick, and Stockton, Southam, and Wilmcote. The entry for 1868 for Greaves, Kirshaw & Bull omits Southam but adds Harbury. The office was at 14 Jury Street, Warwick, and they were 'manufacturers of Blue Lias, Portland, Bath and lias cements'. By 1880 the company had become Greaves Bull & Lakin whose 'extensive quarries and cement works ... employ a great number of men'. Between 1900 & 1904 the firm became a limited company, with a depot at Canal Wharf, Clapham Terrace, Leamington Spa. The absence of an entry in the 1908 and subsequent editions suggests that the operation at Wilmcote closed between 1904 and 1908.

'There were formerly extensive quarries of Lower Lias Stone at Wilmcote and Newnham [about a mile north of Wilmcote]. There were also limekilns in Newnham ..., but the industry was transformed by the completion of the Birmingham to Stratford Canal in 1816. In addition to the quarries two lime and cement works were opened at Wilmcote. By the 1870s these had been amalgamated, and they were worked until about 30 years ago [i.e. c.1915] by Messrs Greaves Bull & Lakin of Warwick, who also owned the limeworks (still in use) at Stockton and Harbury' (VCH, Vol. 3 p. 25).

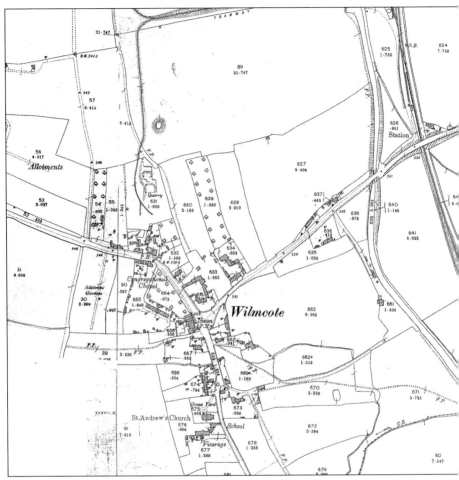

Wilmcote, composite using 1905 edition Ordnance Survey 25 in. sheets 37:11 and 12 and 38:15 and 16, with the Stratford-upon-Avon Canal and GWR (then single track) running close together along the right hand edge, past the eastern end of Greaves' tramway. The original lime works site is on the west bank of the canal, the later works is beside the railway. The main tramway runs west, then heads north-west to two works, and a branch runs south to serve a small quarry on the edge of the village. Note the original site of the station, north of Featherbed Lane. In the lower half of the map is the embankment for the tramway linking the canal with either a quarry near the church or a possible coal yard near the Swan PH, probably following the line of the footpath.

Crown Copyright

While there were earlier limestone quarries in the area, the first person to capitalize on their potential once the proposed Stratford-upon-Avon Canal was completed was William James, one-time agent for the Earl of Warwick. He had been keen to improve the navigation to Stratford and he leased the Upper Avon Navigation as part of a grander scheme. He also promoted railways and was at the heart of an early project that would have linked London with the North-West. A short section of this railway was made between Stratford and Moreton-in-Marsh. He owned collieries at Wyken (just north-east of Coventry), Pelsall (near Walsall) and Wednesbury (near Wolverhampton) and an ironworks at Birchills (near Walsall).

On 17th May, 1815 he bought Spring Hill and nearby land for limestone, which was beside the route of the proposed canal. Spring Hill was the field beside the canal later traversed by the quarry tramway leading to the canal bridge. Once the line of the canal was fixed, James intended to use the remainder of the land to supply limestone to industries in the Black Country, including his furnaces at Birchills. He became very wealthy, but unfortunately became bankrupt in 1823.

One member of a syndicate which bought the Upper Avon Navigation from James, possibly as a result of his bankruptcy, was John Greaves, a merchant and carrier of Stratford-on-Avon. He was a Director of the Stratford & Moreton Railway, which used Wilmcote stone for its sleeper blocks when it was constructed in 1820-26. He had three sons. The eldest son, Richard (1801-1870), took over his father's business at Stratford. The second son, Edward, became a solicitor at Warwick and later an MP. The third son, John Whitehead Greaves, established a slate manufacturing business at Blaenau Festiniog; his slate mine became one of the largest in the world, and is now a tourist attraction.

Richard Greaves became the principal carrier of goods on the River Avon and between Stratford and Birmingham, and greatly expanded his fleet of canal boats. He began to quarry limestone at Gipsy Hall Farm, Wilmcote in 1824, possibly having purchased the land from the bankrupt William James. Soon he had other quarries at Stockton near Southam (about 15 miles north-east of Wilmcote and 10 miles east of Warwick). Limekilns were built beside the canal at Wilmcote in 1830 for the manufacture of Blue Lias Lime, and later more kilns were erected at Stockton. Greaves' Blue Lias Lime was on the London market by the 1830s, carried there in his own boats. He went into partnership with John Kirshaw in 1840 and, trading as Greaves & Kirshaw, soon began to manufacture his own brand of cement.

Although the cement may have been of variable quality as the processes, in particular the need to form clinker, were not then understood, the works at Wilmcote was one of only three making 'artificial' cement in 1847. Annual output was about 16,000 tons. Workers cottages were built in the village, for example 48 to 56 Aston Clinton Road, and the firm employed 150 people, bringing prosperity to Wilmcote.

In 1845 Messrs Thomas Higgins & Co. also had kilns in Wilmcote, but this firm had amalgamated with Greaves by the 1870s. This works may have been at the southern end of the village, and could explain why the 1886 25 in. OS map marked the lime kiln on the canal bank south of Featherbed Lane bridge as 'Old'. More likely (in my opinion), Higgins' works may have been the small one south-east of Gipsy Hall Farm, using the quarry behind the Masons Arms.

The Oxford Worcester & Wolverhampton Railway attempted to buy the Stratford Canal for use as the route for its proposed new railway. Richard Greaves vigorously opposed this proposal, as its construction would greatly interfere with the transport of his lime. Instead, in conjunction with the Great Western Railway (GWR), he promoted the Stratford-upon-Avon Railway in the 1850s, and became its first

Underframe of a tramroad wagon (approximately 2 ft gauge) standing on a point using L-section cast-iron rails at Coalbrookdale Museum, Shropshire. The railway used to construct the canal may well have been a tramroad, with rails and wagons similar to this, although possibly of wider gauge, the wagon bodies probably being a shallow wooden box, 17th April, 1973.   *Author*

Quarrymen at Wilmcote. Note the flat bodies on the wheelbarrows, which seem to have been used for both stone and clay.   *P. Manders*

Lime kiln at Wilmcote.   *P. Manders*

Lime kiln north of Gipsy Hall Farm, *c.*2000.   *Aston Clinton & District History Society Archives*

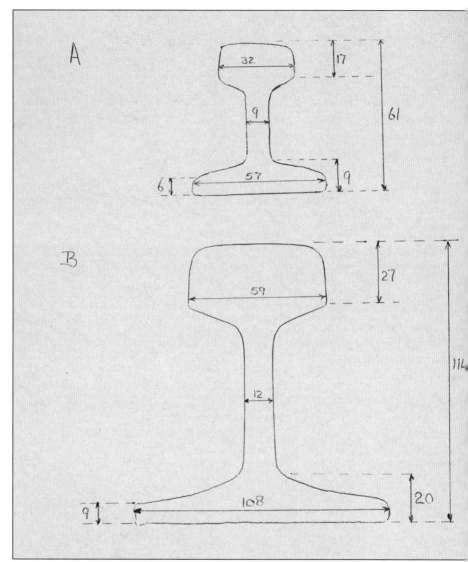

Rail sections for weight calculation (all measurements mm): Treat the rail as three rectangles: the head, the web and the two halves of the foot put together. Calculate the area of cross-section, and so the volume of metal in one yard of rail. Multiplying this by the weight of a unit volume of water, and the specific gravity of steel (7.86), gives the weight per yard. Alternatively, assuming the rail has been measured in millimetres, multiplying the area by 0.0158379, which combines all the constants involved, gives the weight in pounds per yard. As a matter of interest, multiplying this weight by 0.4974 (i.e. effectively halve it) gives the weight in kilograms per metre. For the rail A, the area of head is 32x17, web 9 x (61-17), foot (9+6) x half (57-9), respectively 544, 396 and 360 mm^2, total 1300mm^2. Multiplied by 0.0158379 gives 20.59 lb/yard or 10.24 kg/m. Rail B calculated weight is 63.8 lb/yard.

Chairman. This mixed gauge (broad - 7 ft - and narrow gauge (in GWR terms, standard gauge to everyone else!)) line opened on 10th October, 1860. The new railway was worked by the GWR, which absorbed it in 1883. The broad gauge facility had disappeared in 1869, but had probably been hardly used since the line opened. Wilmcote station was situated on the north side of Featherbed Lane. Soon after the new railway opened, Greaves extended his tramway across the canal to a new works built beside the railway immediately north of the station.

Another promoter of the local railway was John Coulson Bull, a son of the Rector of St Thomas, Birmingham. John Bull had worked for many years with the Oxford & Birmingham Railway (later part of the GWR), and became a partner in Greaves & Kirshaw in the 1860s, the company then trading as Greaves, Kirshaw & Bull. In the late 1860s, by 1868, they opened a works at Harbury (about 14 miles east of Wilmcote).

Richard Greaves became Mayor of Warwick in 1857, High Sheriff of Warwickshire in 1861, and a JP. He had married Catherine, a daughter of Samuel Holland, one of the pioneers of the Welsh slate industry, but they had no children, so on his death in 1870 he was succeeded in business by his sister's son, Michael Henry Lakin (1843-1931). Kirshaw retired in the 1870s, and the firm became Greaves Bull & Lakin. When Bull retired in the 1880s Michael Lakin took charge, being joined in the business by his brother. Michael Lakin was very public spirited, was involved with local politics, and became an Alderman in Warwick. He was elected to the county council in 1889, and was Deputy Chairman 1919-1931. In 1909 he was made baronet (Sir Michael) for his services to Warwickshire. The Wilmcote operation had closed by 1908, the quarries having become uneconomic to work due to increasing depth of overburden, and Harbury became the main centre of production. The rails were probably lifted for scrap in World War I, if not before. It is possible that some track and rolling stock was transferred to the firm's works at Ettington, about five miles south-east of Stratford, which opened sometime after 1909 (*see Chapter Three*).

The quarry and lime works had been a major employer in Wilmcote. Employment figures for 1883 show farming 26 per cent, the quarry 55 per cent, and services 14 per cent. Many local women used to repair lime sacks. Some 130 to 150 men were employed at that time, about 60 from Wilmcote and the remainder from nearby villages.

The stone was dug by hand. While stone could have been loaded directly into wagons on the narrow gauge railway, the only photographs I have seen of quarries at Wilmcote were devoid of railways, the men having shallow wooden wheelbarrows. Maybe the stone was tipped from a wheeling plank into wagons beneath, as at Kaye (*see photograph on page 99*) and Rugby (*see photograph on page 195*).

Following the opening of the Stratford-upon-Avon Canal on 26th June, 1816, William James bought the railway used for its construction from the contractor, William Whitmore of Newhall Street, Birmingham and laid it to serve his quarries. This early contractor's railway, probably introduced around 1812, had been used to carry bricks, lime and spoil, and comprised about two miles of track. It may well have been a tramroad or plateway, with L-section cast-iron plates as rails. When Richard Greaves took over quarrying in 1824 he replaced the existing railway with a new 3ft gauge tramway. Latterly it was laid with light flat bottom rails having a calculated weight of 20 lb./yard, but it may have had fish-belly rails originally. Two surviving rails in a barn at Gipsy Hall Farm are quite squat, with a foot 2⅜ in. wide but they are only 1¾ in. high overall. The head is 1½ in. wide x ½ in./ thick. Their calculated weight is about 14 lb./yard.

The following description is taken mainly from the 1905 25 in. OS map, when the railway was probably at its greatest extent. The 3 ft gauge quarry tramway terminated

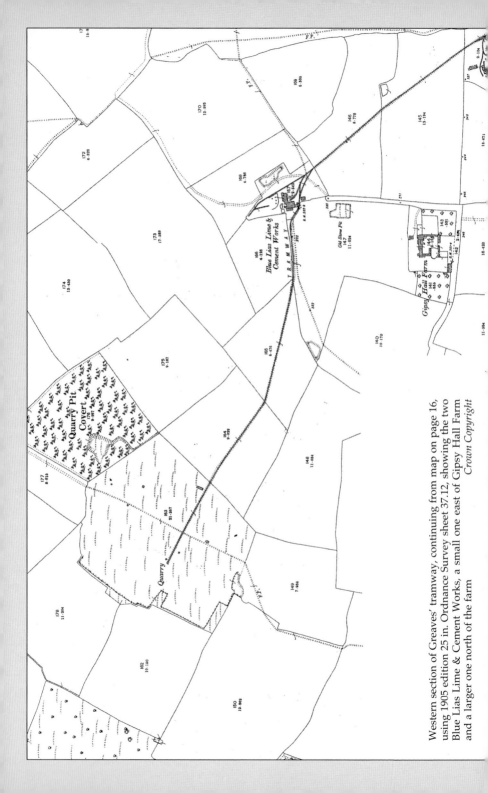

Western section of Greaves' tramway, continuing from map on page 16, using 1905 edition 25 in. Ordnance Survey sheet 37.12, showing the two Blue Lias Lime & Cement Works, a small one east of Gipsy Hall Farm and a larger one north of the farm

Crown Copyright

beside a standard gauge siding about 240 yards north of Featherbed Lane. A row of four kilns was close by, on the side nearer the canal. After about 50 yards the line turned west, with a loop the length of the curve. A siding which entered one of the works buildings, presumably the tip for stone, joined and the line crossed the canal on an iron bridge with stone abutments. The abutments remain although the bridge itself has long since been removed. The tramway ran west across Spring Hill through a cutting some 15 ft deep for about 380 yards, being joined after 160 yards by the original line to the canal wharf. There were about 55 yards of track on the wharf and a short loop. Three lime kilns were set into the embankment later used to carry the line to the bridge.

At the end of the cutting the tracks divided. One branch ran due south for 340 yards to a quarry close to the Masons Arms public house on Aston Cantlow Road. The 1886 map marks this as 'Old Stone Pit' and there was no rail connection. The other track ran north-west. After 170 yards it threw off a short branch to the west to a small 'Blue Lias Lime & Cement Works' about 350 yards east of Gipsy Hall Farm. This works was marked in 1885 but then it had no rail access. It is possible that this was Higgins' works, originally served by the quarry near the Masons Arms. This quarry could have been closed following Greaves' takeover but was later reopened, its tramway being shown on the 1905 map. The cottages beside the Masons Arms were converted from former quarry stables and barn in 1934.

The main line continued 450 yards to another 'Blue Lias Lime & Cement Works' about 280 yards north of Gipsy Hall Farm. Here was a loop and a couple of sidings. Between the works and the farm was an old stone pit, marked disused in 1886. Leaving the works, the railway ran west-north-west to reach the stone pits in Quarry Pit Covert. In 1885 the face was 560 yards from the farm, with a length of 520 yards. By 1905 the face had receded by 300 yards and had contracted to a length of 350 yards. The total length from quarry to canal in 1905 was thus just over ¾ mile.

The 1926 25 in. OS map showed the tramway cutting near the canal, but no there was no sign of any works or the railway.

The 3 ft gauge wagons were hauled by horses, although gravity operation downhill also seems to have occurred. Traffic must have been quite heavy, carrying stone to all three works, lime and cement from the two works at Gipsy Hall Farm to the canal or railway, and coal in the reverse direction.

Although Richard Greaves enthusiastically supported railways, he also had an extensive fleet of canal boats. He, and Greaves Bull & Lakin (GBL) between them, had registered at least 17 boats in the period 1866-77, mainly at Stratford-upon-Avon or on the Grand Junction Canal. Just south of the cement works wharf was (and still is) a winding hole (a short canal cul-de-sac) for turning boats. Cement was dispatched in barrels and lime in bags. Return cargoes were coal, and night soil from Birmingham, which was sometimes unloaded over Bearley aqueduct, two miles north of Wilmcote, into carts on the road below. This iron aqueduct is the longest in England, 475 ft long and 28 ft high, crossing a road, a stream, and formerly two railways. The towing path is alongside the trough carrying the water. When the GWR branch to Alcester was in use, steam locomotives could take water by drawing up beneath the aqueduct where a suitable pipe and valve had been fitted to the trough. There was even the standard coal burning stove to prevent the pipe freezing in winter.

The main line railway through Wilmcote was opened in 1860. Originally single track, it was doubled in 1907 from Stratford to Bearley as part of the GWR's development of the Honeybourne to Cheltenham line. This is probably when the station was moved from the north side of Featherbed Lane to its present position on the south side of the road.

Site of bridge over Stratford-upon-Avon Canal, Wilmcote, looking south, when the canal had been drained for maintenance. The wharf was on the right, and the mound beside the embankment once held several kilns. The GWR is behind the trees to the left. The branch to the winding pool (for turning boats) is just visible immediately beyond the embankment, 6th December, 1972. *Author*

Cutting west of the canal, Wilmcote, looking west, 19th July, 1996. *Author*

The works' standard gauge sidings were north of the original Wilmcote station, west of the GWR. A loop served the narrow gauge transhipment point, and a couple of other sidings served the works site. Shunting was probably done by main line locomotives. However, most output went by canal.

Several groups of remains survive. Potential visitors are reminded that most of them are on land belonging to Gipsy Hall Farm, although some public footpaths pass nearby. North of the farm is a kiln, now covered with soil (SP 159591), and a small brick 'foreman's hut' beside the course of the railway. There are now no remains of the similar plant east of the farm. There is a high quarry face on the western boundary of Gipsy Hall Farm (SP 155592), as well as two smaller stone pits. On both sides of the canal, about 350 yards north of Featherbed Lane, are more remains (SP 167585).

Quarry face near Gipsy Hall Farm, 6th December, 1972.   *Author*

Embankment behind Pear Tree Cottage, Wilmcote looking towards the canal on 6th December, 1972. It may have been used for a limestone tramway, but a line serving the yard of a coal merchant seems more likely, using equipment as in the photograph on page 18.   *Author*

Small Early Works and Coal Tramway

The 1886 6 in. OS map shows an 'Old Lime Kiln' on the west bank of the canal about 170 yards south of Featherbed Lane (SP 167581). No quarry or stone pit is marked, although there is a possible small quarry immediately north of St Andrew's Church (SP 162579). However, when the houses of Swansfold were being built in the 1960s, in the field called Swans Close, rails were found during excavations for foundations. The next field had been called Stone Pits Meadow, now the name of the road serving the houses built there. This could well have been the site of a shallow quarry serving the kiln by the canal.

The wharf area is now served by a private road called The Wharf, along which there are several houses. No obvious remains of any kiln survive. In the village, behind Pear Tree Cottage, is a low embankment running east along the hedge towards the canal which is about 280 yards away. The 1905 25 in. OS map clearly marks the embankment, which curved northwards and then finished at a field boundary about 90 yards west of the canal. The embankment still exists, with a public footpath beside it, which crosses the embankment close to where it finishes. The embankment is then about 4 ft 6 in. high and 6 ft wide. There is no sign of an embankment onwards to the canal. If there had once been a quarry near the church or in Stone Pits Meadow it would have been about 240 yards west of Pear Tree Cottage, with a level crossing over Church Road, but there is nothing marked on the 1905 map. The route would have been level, or gently falling, all the way to the canal.

This embankment may not have been for a limestone tramway at all. When Richard Greaves began to work the quarries in 1824 he bought a new tramway, and the old one was sold to the Manders family, coal merchants at the wharf, to carry coal to the village. The present remains would be entirely consistent with such a line, which probably continued another 150 yards to terminate in the coal yard opposite the Masons Arms in the centre of the village. It would have been useful for this purpose at least until the GWR was opened in 1860. This tramway is also reputed to have brought limestone from Temple Grafton, about 3½ miles to the south-west, until about 1910, being laid on the road as required!

The narrow width of the embankment, a bare 6 ft, suggests that the gauge was quite narrow, possibly 2 ft 6 in. or even less. It could have been a tramroad, in which case the wheels of the wagons would not have had flanges, but would have been guided by the vertical flange on the L-section cast-iron plates forming the rails.

Chapter Three

Ettington Lime Works

c.1912 Greaves Bull & Lakin Ltd

Closed c.1920, by 1921

Ettington (formerly Eatington) is a village about five miles south-east of Stratford-upon-Avon. The East & West Junction Railway opened its section from Stratford-upon-Avon through Ettington eastwards to Kineton on 1st July, 1873. In 1908 it amalgamated with neighbouring lines to become part of the Stratford-on-Avon & Midland Junction Railway (SMJ) line from Towcester (near Northampton) to Broom (near Alcester). The limeworks and quarry were situated north of the railway at the eastern end of the 60 ft deep Goldicote cutting, west of Ettington station, about a mile north-west of the village (SP 255505), and were served by a main line siding.

Although trade directories in the 1880s state that the blue lias stone here was good for lime, there were few references to any limeworks. In 1872 under 'Eatington' it stated that a 'quarry had recently been opened by Mr William Thompson of Stratford on Avon', and in 1876 there was reference to the Kineton & Ettington Blue Lias Lime Works. The 1886 6 in. OS map showed some lime kilns east of Kineton station (SP 331502) but modern houses in Little Pittern now occupy this site. The 1906 25 in. map showed an old lime kiln in the goods yard at Kineton station, itself now used by Alchemie. Maybe these were the Kineton & Blue Lias Lime Works.

The GBL entry for Harbury works in the 1912 trade directory included a reference to Ettington. After some years with no reference to any limeworks in Ettington, in 1916 there was an entry for Greaves Bull & Lakin Ltd, cement manufacturers, but it was missing from the 1921 edition. The Industrial Railway Society records state that the small quarry opened 'after 1909' and closed around 1920, which is borne out by these references.

The site of Ettington works is marked on the 1923 25 in. OS, which shows two lime kilns at the east end of the site, but there is only the formation of the main line siding and no track within the site, so it had probably closed by then. It was difficult to locate on the map, being a very small site right on the edge of two sheets.

A visit was made in February 2008 from a bridleway which passed very close. The whole area was a thicket with no trace of any buildings or masonry, but there were vague indications of possible main line sidings. At the eastern end of the site, beside one possible siding, was a concrete block, approximately 29 ft x 15 ft x 2 ft 3 in. which might have been a loading bank. The quarry face was about 12 ft high. The quarry area seems to have been an area about 30 yards wide and 70 yards north of the railway, before narrowing and petering out altogether after a further 100 yards, making the whole site an L-shape. The small extent of the workings confirms its short life. The soil in the corner of the adjoining field within the L was grey with clay, suggesting it was the site of a spoil heap, since ploughed out.

On the edge of the thicket, probably used once as a fence post, was a 5 ft 6 in. length of flat-bottomed rail with a calculated weight of 18 lb. per yard. Photographs in Jordan's book on the SMJ suggest the internal tramway was 2 ft 6 in. to 3 ft gauge. The wagons were wooden side tippers, with inside frames extended to form dumb buffers and a very short wheelbase - the wheels were almost touching. As couplings

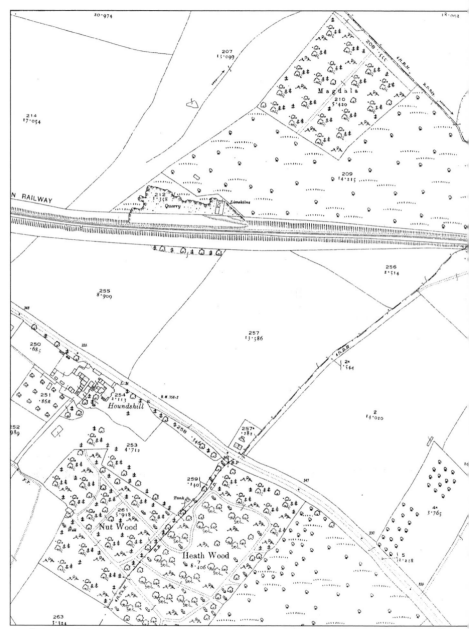

Ettington Quarries, 1923 edition 25 in. Ordnance Survey, sheet 50.4. The quarry appears to have closed as all the railways have been lifted, although the cutting for the main line siding is shown. The main road is now A422, with Ettington village about a mile south-east of Houndshill.

Crown Copyright

were fitted horse haulage may have been used, although it is possible they were vehicles transferred from the much larger system at Wilmcote. One photograph shows a pile of broken stone on the loading bank so raw stone may have been dispatched as well as lime.

Ettington Works. Illustrations from *Stratford upon Avon & Midland Junction Railway* (Arthur Jordan, Oxford Publishing Co, 1982), photographs originally credited to George Freeston. The wagons may have been second-hand from Wilmcote. Note their very short wheelbase, inside frames and simple but robust body tipping to one side only. The photograph shows that the loading bank was at the eastern end of the site, with a headshunt curving away beside a nearby brook. The single track SMJ is in the foreground, with Stratford to the left.

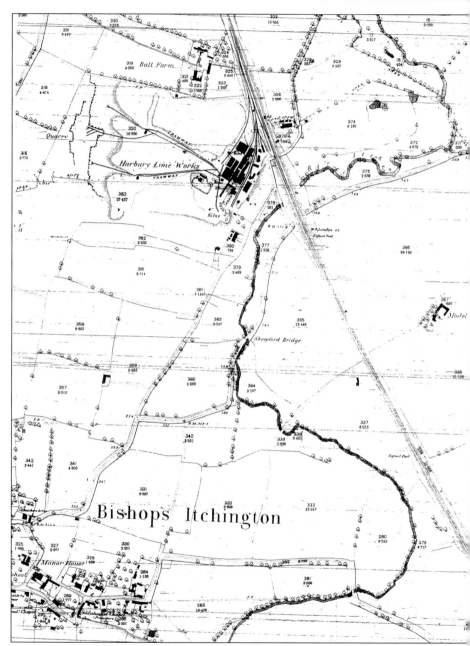

Harbury Works, 1887 edition Ordnance Survey 25 in. sheet 40.14, showing two separate double track tramways to the quarry which is still a field width away from the road, shown crossing the top left corner.

Crown Copyright

Chapter Four

Harbury/Bishop's Itchington Cement Works

1855	Greaves & Kirshaw
1860s, by 1868	Greaves Kirshaw & Bull
1870s, by 1880	Greaves Bull & Lakin
1900-1904	Greaves Bull & Lakin Ltd
1927	Greaves Bull & Lakin (Harbury Works) Ltd
1927	Red Triangle Group
1931	Associated Portland Cement Manufacturers Ltd
1978	Blue Circle Industries Ltd

Ceased production 1970, closed as distribution depot early 1990s.

The Harbury works of Greaves, Bull & Lakin, later Associated Portland Cement Manufacturers, were located about seven miles south-east of Leamington Spa, 1½ miles south-east of Harbury and ½ mile north of Bishop's Itchington (SP 396585). The works were on the west side of the GWR main line from Banbury to Leamington (opened 30th September, 1852), about ¾ mile south of Southam Road & Harbury, one of the original stations, near the southern entrance to Harbury cutting. In 1860 Harbury cutting was the deepest in the UK, being 100 to 110 ft deep, 600 ft wide, and ½ mile long, and included a tunnel 73 yards long under a road. Some 3,000,000 cubic yards were excavated in its construction. It is said that local landowners prevented the use of an easier route through Southam. Had this been possible then Harbury works might not have been built at all, or maybe it would have been a near neighbour of Kaye's works. The GWR was laid with mixed gauge track from the outset, although as the standard gauge did not then link to any other standard gauge line it was, effectively, broad gauge only at first. Standard gauge traffic developed from around 1856, and broad gauge was abolished north of Oxford from 1st April, 1869.

Although trade directories show no entry until 1868, when Greaves, Kirshaw & Bull had a 'very extensive lime and cement works' at Harbury, the official history of APCM states that the firm began production 'at its eventual site [i.e. Harbury] having left Wilmcote in 1855 [sic]'. If correct, this would have been soon after the GWR line had opened, which provided ready access to markets.

Greaves Kirshaw & Bull, established by Richard Greaves in 1828, had operated a pioneer cement works at Wilmcote near Stratford-upon-Avon (see Chapter Two). The company's offices were at Northgate Street, Warwick. The Harbury site was called 'Greaves Ground Lias Lime Works' in 1872. The firm had become Greaves, Bull & Lakin by 1880. Output was 600 tons per week in 1907. By the 1912 edition trade directory, Greaves, Bull & Lakin Ltd were listed as cement manufacturers and lime burners, head office Harbury, works at Bishops Itchington (which had just been modernized) and Ettington, Wilmcote having closed a few years earlier.

The telephone was connected during the 1920s, being Southam 31, possibly when new offices were built in 1926. A second line, Southam 32, was in use by 1940. From time to time excavations in the quarry uncovered fossils, which Lakin used to put on display for a time, giving the proceeds to charity. Two fossils found at Harbury are illustrated in *Newnes Pictorial Knowledge*, (vol. 1 pp. 26 and 27), published 1930, an

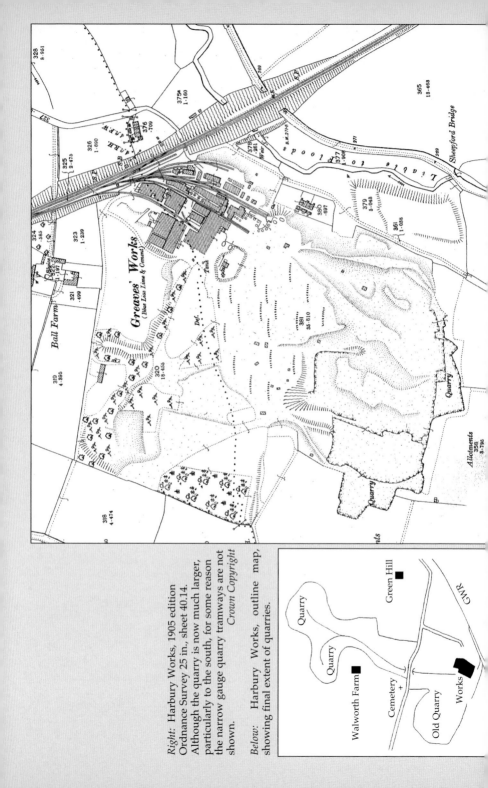

Right: Harbury Works, 1905 edition Ordnance Survey 25 in., sheet 40.14. Although the quarry is now much larger, particularly to the south, for some reason the narrow gauge quarry tramways are not shown.
Crown Copyright

Below: Harbury Works, outline map, showing final extent of quarries.

ichthyosaurus now at the Natural History Museum, and a plesiosaurus, 100-200m years old.

On the formation of Greaves Bull & Lakin (Harbury Works) Ltd in 1927 the works was valued at £416,479, and had sufficient raw material for 100 years. Almost immediately the business was sold to the Red Triangle Group but unfortunately Red Triangle failed in November 1929 following severe price competition. Eastwoods Ltd expressed a strong interest in buying the Red Triangle Group but were unable to find the necessary finance quickly and so the Associated Portland Cement Manufacturers group (trading as Blue Circle) bought the works from the receiver in August 1931 (*see Chapter One*). APCM became Blue Circle Industries Ltd from 1st June, 1978, which was itself purchased by Larfarge in 2001. The Greaves, Bull and Lakin families are described under Wilmcote works in *Chapter Two*.

A pamphlet produced in 1927 showed views of works in 1840 and 1927, and included testimonials from Corporation of Coventry Gas Department and Birmingham Corporation Tramways which stated that, 'Greaves Bull & Lakin rapid hardening cement saves three to four days on the job compared with others used for floating tracks and others'. One of the first concrete roads in the UK was laid from Harbury station to the works, to demonstrate the advantages of concrete for road making. Greaves Bull & Lakin Blue Lias lime was used for important tunnel work on a number of railways: Great Central, City & South London and extensions (later London Transport 'Northern Line'), Great Northern, Central London ('Central Line'), Baker Street & Waterloo ('Bakerloo Line'), GWR, London & North Western Railway (LNWR), Great Eastern, London Brighton & South Coast, and the Pennsylvania Railroad. At that time coal for the works was brought from the Warwickshire coalfield, 30 miles away. Annual cement output was then 125,000 tons.

The old works had three large chimneys. One was blown down in a terrific gale in 1925, breaking some overhead electricity cables. When rebuilt under Red Triangle, the works had three smaller chimneys. Later APCM built one new chimney for all three kilns. Lime production appears to have ceased in the late 1930s. Cement production in 1953 was 231,000 tons of clinker.

As at other works, before excavators were introduced the nearby blue lias quarries were worked by hand, the men being paid piecework. The quarry had 30-40 ft of stone in layers separated by thin bands of clay. As the quarry moved westwards the overburden became steadily thicker, and by the 1960s it was 20-30 ft thick, made up of sand, gravel, shale, and thin bands of limestone. There was in fact another 25 ft of limestone lower down, but as it was covered by a bed of clay about 5 ft thick it was normally not used, although once it had been worked at the eastern end of the quarry. It became the practice to leave the last bed of limestone above the thick clay untouched, to form a firm foundation for the excavators and quarry railway. By 1973 much of the old working area was flooded.

Although the limestone had a carbonate content of over 80 per cent, the overall carbonate content of the quarried material was only about 60 per cent, and cement manufacture requires about 77 per cent carbonate. Thus either clay had to be removed by hand picking, as in the early days, and then dumped in old workings (latterly transported by ropeway), or additional carbonate had to be obtained from elsewhere. The first source was at Ufton (*see Chapter Five*), about two miles away with a 9 ft seam, later at Lighthorne, three miles south-west of the works, and finally Ardley (four miles north-west of Bicester) with a 9 ft seam but 24 miles away (*see Appendix One*).

Cement production at Harbury stopped on 2nd December, 1970 as the quality of the raw stone was variable, making costs too high. The works were subsequently

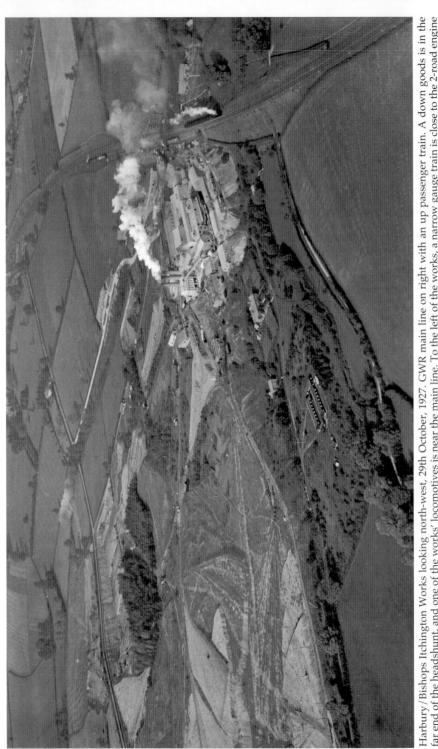

Harbury/Bishops Itchington Works looking north-west, 29th October, 1927. GWR main line on right with an up passenger train. A down goods is in the far end of the headshunt, and one of the works' locomotives is near the main line. To the left of the works, a narrow gauge train is close to the 2-road engine shed. A second narrow gauge locomotive is in the quarry, close to the tunnel under the road from Bishops Itchington to Harbury. In the new quarry workings beyond the road there is a third locomotive and two excavators. A horse appears to be pulling a short train away from the overburden tip opposite demolished except for the silos, which were retained for storage of cement for local distribution, brought in by the trainload from a new works at Northfleet, near Gravesend, Kent. Typically 780 tons/day were received, six days a week, until the early 1990s. Once cement manufacture finished the roses in the works' garden were very poor in comparison to former times, probably due to the lack of continuous lime dusting!

(For many years legislation about industrial smoke and dust emission was not very stringent. Pollution was then more accepted, and as the technology to reduce it was less advanced the surroundings of a typical cement works were covered with pale grey dust. Items like chimney pots on nearby houses often had accretions of solidified cement all over them.)

The site was for sale in July 1994, and by February 2008 it was being offered as up to 15 acres of open storage land, with potential for rail connection, and near M40 junction 12. On the same date the old quarry west of the road was used for coarse fishing. As Bishop Bowl Lakes it had received an award for restoration as a commercial fishery.

The first quarries were immediately west of the works, and were worked steadily towards the fields bordering the road from Bishop's Itchington to Harbury, until the face was 350 yards from the works. By 1905 the workings had spread a similar distance south-west, until terminated by a fault. The quarry was then worked right up to the road, and finally workings were opened west of the road, probably in the mid-1920s. These were worked southerly until the fault, then northwards. Eventually the face was a mile away from the works.

The 1887 25 in. OS map shows two railway lines from the works to the quarry, each with a loop from their junction by the works to the quarry entrance, about 200 yards in each case, presumably to allow full and empty trains to pass easily. Later editions of maps show railways serving the various working faces.

In 1961 the 3 ft gauge quarry railway was pretty basic. The track terminated a train length beyond the tip which supplied the stone crusher. The tip itself had a simple corrugated iron shelter for weather protection. Going towards the quarry there was a loop, and beside it the site of the former engine shed.

The wooden engine shed here had capacity for four locomotives on two tracks. It became unsafe and was demolished around 1959 to make way for some slurry tanks. The shed had contained a pit, extending outside the rails, which were carried on longitudinal girders, so there was easy access both between the frames of locomotives and outside them. The roof had a ventilator for smoke almost the whole length of the ridge above each track. A replacement shed was constructed in the early 1960s, on the other side of the main line.

A couple of sidings trailed in beyond the shed as the line headed west, entering a cutting before tunnelling under the road. An old tunnel, a few yards south of the one then in use, had been used to store records from the London offices during World War II. The track crossed old workings, and then went under a stream flowing in a wooden trough to serve the long face at the southern end of the quarry. By 1966 excavation had moved northwards, and the face was served by a balloon loop. Trains ran anticlockwise round the loop, the points at the entrance being operated by a weighted lever. One electric excavator was used to dig the stone, and another excavator removed the overburden.

Flat bottom rail weighing 45 lb./yd was used, laid on sleepers 5 ft x 7½ in. x 3½ in., although full size British Railways (BR) sleepers were used in soft patches to spread the load. The tunnel was 11 ft 6 in. high, 10 ft 6 in. wide, and 55 ft long, with a refuge each side at the midpoint. Some track materials came from Ufton when it closed in 1952.

Tip at works, with Fowler 2-4-0DM No. 1 and train on 6th July, 1960. Note the shelter.

Author

No. 1 with train being loaded in quarry, 12th July, 1961.

Author

No. 2 with loaded train approaching the tunnel under the road, 19th March, 1966. *R.E. West*

Excavator loading train, with above and behind a conveyor used to dump overburden in worked-out areas, 19th March, 1966. *R.E. West*

Horses were originally used for haulage. In those days the stone was dug by hand in a series of steps and overburden was carried in barrows along elevated planks for tipping in old workings. At one time wagons went down an incline into the pit, but following the introduction of iron wagons they were craned in. At first wagons were pushed by hand in the pit, but eventualy a pony was used, hauling two or three wagons at a time. There used to be eight horses on the 'main line', four used in mornings and four in the afternoons. The stables were opposite the clock house by the garage, near the later ropeway (which ceased operating around 1960), and also near the standard gauge locomotive shed. This ropeway had been used to carry shale and clay, separated from the stone by hand, to dumps in old workings.

Steam locomotives were introduced into the quarry in 1901, becoming steadily larger over the years. A pair of diesel locomotives was supplied in 1935, initially working trains with stone for the cement works while a steam locomotive brought stone for the lime works. There were usually three or four locomotives in daily use, each serving a different pit. Five steam shovels were used in the quarry at one time.

In the last years two trains were in regular operation. While one was being filled at the quarry the other was being emptied at the tip, which was protected by a steel grid covering the hole in the ground. The wagon nearest the locomotive was emptied first. The empty train then drew steadily forward into the nearby loop and waited for the return of the other train. In 1961 each train comprised 11 wagons which were pulled to the quarry and the loaded wagons were pushed back. The then quarry inspector suggested that the last wagon should carry a bell on a flexible mounting, so that it would give audible warning of an approaching train, particularly when it was being pushed. One and a half buckets of the electric shovel used filled a wagon. If one diesel locomotive was unavailable due to breakdown then a Sentinel steam locomotive was used instead, and after the last Sentinel was scrapped in 1953 a dumper was used to haul a shortened rake of five wagons. The railway was in daily use Mondays to Fridays, and sometimes on Saturdays as well, handling about 600 tons/day in 1963.

When additional stone to increase the carbonate content was brought in by eight-wheel lorry from Lighthorne Quarry, near Gaydon, an empty wagon was placed over the hopper grid, with its body tipped towards the lorry, to deflect the stone into the grid and prevent it spreading around the hopper. This could well have been done when stone had been brought by lorry from Ufton. However, stone from Ardley was brought in by the trainload and emptied by tippler.

In 1966 the quarry railway was ¾ mile long, and was a good mile by January 1968, when a new branch was noted by a visiting enthusiast, although it was not yet ballasted. However, the 3 ft gauge closed around January 1970, having been replaced by Euclid dumpers carrying stone from the quarry to the works over public roads. All of the narrow gauge track had been lifted by mid-1971.

The 3 ft gauge railway at Harbury had five distinct phases of locomotives, with some overlap of course. The initial fleet in the early 1900s was five small Bagnall 0-4-0ST. These were replaced after 1914 by four assorted locomotives, mainly second-hand. In turn, from 1921 these were replaced by three new Peckett 0-4-0ST, which were themselves replaced by three second-hand Sentinel locomotives in 1932. Finally, John Fowler & Co. supplied a pair of diesel locomotives in 1935 which lasted until the end of the railway in 1970, longer than the time the line had been steam operated!

The first steam locomotive at Harbury was *Mercedes*, ordered from W.G. Bagnall of Stafford in May 1903 and delivered in June 1904, Works No. 1730. This firm often laid down batches of standard narrow gauge locomotives for stock, and so could complete one quickly once a firm order was received. *Mercedes* was an 0-4-0ST of typical Bagnall design, and cost £375. A sparse cab was fitted, comprising a curved roof supported on an iron pillar in each corner, but there was neither weatherboard nor back sheet, and the sides were open above the bunker. This locomotive was one of the first to have Bagnall-Price valve gear (*see below*). It was scrapped in 1922.

Mercedes was followed by two similar but smaller (and slightly cheaper) Bagnall locomotives, *Maudie* (1782) ordered in July 1905 and delivered in September, and *Mildred* (1844) ordered January 1907 and delivered the following September. They were cabless and Bagnall-Price valve gear was fitted. Unfortunately they were found to be too small for the work. *Maudie* was sold in March 1915 to T. Mitchell & Sons, Bolton, later going to a contract in Scotland. *Mildred* is believed to have been requisitioned during the World War I, and around 1925 went to H. & J. Martin, Roundwood Reservoir contract, Ireland.

Around 1912 Greaves Bull & Lakin bought two second-hand Bagnalls, *Robinson* (1632) and *Walton* (1633) which were very similar to *Mercedes* except they had Baguley valve gear (*see below*). They had both been ordered originally in July 1900 by the contractor Enoch Tempest for the Walshaw Dean reservoir contract in Lancashire. *Robinson* had arrived by September 1912, and *Walton* sometime after 1914. They disappeared, scrapped or sold, in the 1920s. Some 40 years after the Bagnalls had gone they were still remembered as being 'good'.

All these five engines had the same type of launch or bull-head boiler, favoured by Bagnall for its small locomotives. The inner firebox of a typical British industrial locomotive was a cuboid made of copper, with the grate forming the bottom face, well below the level of the underneath of the boiler barrel. Specially shaped steel wrapper plates surrounded the inner firebox, leaving a water space, and fastened it to the boiler barrel. The basis of the firebox of Bagnall's launch-type boilers was a horizontal steel cylinder about the same diameter as the boiler barrel. It was surrounded by a cylindrical wrapper plate, diameter about half as much again as the barrel, and co-axial with the boiler barrel. The bottom of the cylindrical firebox was close to the bottom of the wrapper plate. The plane of the grate was a chord about one quarter the way up the firebox cylinder, with the boiler fire tubes fastened into the further end of the cylinder. The bull-head boiler was cheaper to construct than the conventional design, but more difficult to fire. Two other disadvantages were the restricted space for ash under the grate, and it took longer to raise steam than conventional types, but that did not deter customers from buying these small locomotives. Bagnall also fitted steel boiler tubes instead of brass.

Another distinctive feature of many small Bagnall locomotives was their valve gear. A typical industrial locomotive used either Stephenson's valve gear, fitted between the frames and driven by eccentrics on the crank axle, or outside Walschaert's valve gear, driven by a small return crank bolted to the main crank pin and also having a link to the crosshead. Inside valve gear was well protected but more difficult to access, even for routine lubrication. Outside gear was easily accessible but more liable to accidental damage from trackside obstructions. Bagnall's chief draughtsman, E.E. Baguley, designed a valve gear similar to Walschaert's but all the motion was obtained from the crank pin itself. The rod driving the valve gear was protected, being mounted between the connecting rod and the face of the wheel. This was known as Baguley valve gear, patented in 1893. It was used while Baguley was with the firm and for a few years after he left in 1901.

In 1903 Bagnall and his works manager, S.T. Price, patented the Bagnall-Price valve gear, probably to avoid having to pay royalties to Baguley. This gear again dispensed with the vulnerable return crank. An eccentric on the crank axle between the frames drove an oscillating link. A slide in the oscillating link was pivoted to the combining lever attached to the connecting rod near the crosshead, to the valve rod,

Bagnall official photograph of *Mercedes*, 1730 of 1904, a standard 7 in. locomotive with Bagnall-Price valve gear. Note the link, almost hidden by the connecting rod, from the vertical slide to a pivot on the connecting rod close to the crosshead.   *A.C. Baker Collection*

Maudie, Bagnall 1782 of 1905 (*left*) in Thomas Mitchell's yard, Bolton, after sale in 1915. Note lack of a cab.   *F.D. Smith Collection*

and to the lifting arm of the reversing gear. (These valve gears were fully described by Alan Baker in *Industrial Railway Record* No. 11.)

GB&L ordered a new locomotive, *Hawk*, an 0-4-2T of Kerr, Stuart's 'Tattoo' class (1213), which was delivered to nearby Southam Road station on 8th August, 1914. It was not quite the standard design as built, since the tank was shorter, stopping behind the rocking shafts of the valve gear. The rods forming the motion were circular in section instead of the more common rectangular section. In 1925 it was sold to APCM's new Holborough works in Kent, but it saw little use and was scrapped in 1938. *Cement Railways of Kent* (Stoyel & Kidner, Oakwood Press, 1990) has an illustration (p. 101) of *Hawk* out of use.

In 1919 a much larger locomotive was bought from the dealers J.F. Wake of Darlington. *West Baldwin* was an 0-6-0ST by Hunslet of Leeds (758), originally built for Douglas Corporation, Isle of Man, in 1901 for the construction of the West Baldwin reservoir. It then had several other owners before coming to Harbury, where the first spares were sent in June 1920. It had about double the tractive effort of the Bagnalls, but had a tendency to spread the track and was scrapped in 1926.

Another Kerr, Stuart locomotive was a second-hand 'Skylark' class 0-4-2T, *Eagle* (756), originally ordered in February 1901 by Holme & King Ltd, for a contract at St Helens. It came around the time of World War I and was scrapped in 1924.

The last of the assorted second-hand locomotives was *Lark*, an 0-4-0ST built by Hudswell, Clarke, Leeds, (708), leaving the works on 29th January, 1901. Costing £590, it went new to Sir Robert McAlpine, Glasgow (named *Biggar* in the official Hudswell photograph, but No. 10 in practice) for the Culter Reservoir contract near Biggar for Motherwell Town Council. It came to Harbury in 1922 as No. 2 *Lark*, and lasted until about 1938. It was fitted with rail washers to assist adhesion on dirty track - clean wet rails give almost as much adhesion as clean dry ones.

By the early 1920s Greaves Bull & Lakin were looking for new locomotives. The Bagnalls had been too small, and *West Baldwin* was unsuitable as it spread the track. Peckett of Bristol prepared a specification in 1923 for a 3 ft gauge inside-framed version of their 'Jurassic' class 0-6-0ST (as used by Kaye and Nelson - *see Chapters Seven and Ten*) for Harbury, but in the event supplied three 'Cranmore' class 0-4-0ST. These were very similar in size and power, being basically a four-wheeled version of the 'Jurassic' class, but they required heavier track as there were only two axles. Maybe experience with *West Baldwin* prevented adoption of an 0-6-0ST. Cylinders were only 7 x 10 in. The boilers had little water space, and the very small fireboxes were soon burnt due to scale formation. Delivered on 6th January, 1924 (1663), 29th January, 1924 (1654), and 22nd June, 1926 (1720), they were fitted with name and number plates taken from Nos. 3, 4 and 6 *Eagle*. Despite their small size they lasted until about 1938 when all three were scrapped (G. Alliez did not see any of them - or *Lark* - when he visited the works in April 1938).

The final three steam locomotives were built by Sentinel, Shrewsbury, and were totally unlike any of their predecessors. Instead of the normal horizontal boiler, supplying saturated steam at relatively low pressure to horizontal cylinders which drove the wheels directly, Sentinel locomotives had a vertical boiler in the cab which produced high pressure superheated steam, supplied to relatively small vertical cylinders which drove the wheels through reduction gears, with the final drive to one axle being by chain. A second chain coupled the axles together.

The three locomotives (6255, 6256, 6257) had been built in 1926 for Little Orme Limestone Quarry, on the north-east side of the Orme headland near Llandudno, Caernarvonshire. Originally owned by the Ship Canal Cement Co., the quarry passed to Allied Cement Manufacturers Ltd, part of the Red Triangle group formed on 2nd August, 1929, and so had been taken over by APCM in August 1931. This

Hawk, Kerr, Stuart 1213 of 1914. The smaller 'dome' on the boiler is the sand box.

Celia Barratt Collection

Eagle, Kerr, Stuart 765 of 1901, with engine shed behind.   *F. Jones*

Hudswell, Clarke official photograph of *Lark*, 708 of 1904.   *Ron Redman Collection*

Lark. Apart from fitting dumb buffers, struts to support the front of the cab, and having a new coat of paint including the name in mixed upper and lower case (unusual) with full lining, *Lark* does not seem to have altered much over the years. Again an iron skip is just visible.

Celia Barratt Collection

Above: West Baldwin, Hunslet 758 of 1901, taken at Preston Corporation Spade Mill Reservoir contract *c*.1907.   *F.D. Smith Collection*

Top right: Illustration and specification of 'Cranmore' class 0-4-0ST in Peckett's 1938 *Abridged illustrated list of Tank Engines*. Note the outside frames on the 2 ft gauge example shown, unlike No. 4 (*see photograph below*).   *Author's Collection*

Bottom right: No. 4, Peckett 1663 of 1924.   *E.S. Tonks Collection*

Below: West Baldwin at Harbury. An iron skip is just visible.   *F. Jones*

Saddle Tank
Locomotive

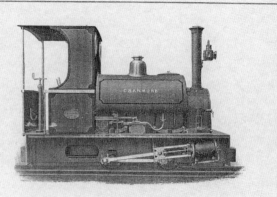

Class " Cranmore "

Cylinders	.. ..	7″ diameter
,,	.. ..	10″ stroke
Diameter of Wheels	..	1′ 8″
Wheel Base	.. ..	3′ 6″
Weight, empty	..	6 tons
,, loaded	..	7½ ,,
Gauge of Railway	.. ..	2′ 0″
Capacity of Tank	..	125 gallons

Radius of sharpest curve will traverse easily, 22 feet

Weight per yard of lightest rail recommended, 24 lbs.

Extreme height, 8′ 9½″

,, width, 5′ 6″

,, length over Buffer Beams, 12′ 0″

DUTY OF ENGINE

Working Pressure, per sq. in.	..	..	..	160	lbs.
Tractive Force	..	..	..	3332	,,
Indicated Horse Power at 10 miles per hour		88	
Will haul up an incline of 1 in 30	..	28	tons
,, ,, ,, 1 in 40	..	37	,,
,, ,, ,, 1 in 50	..	46	,,
,, ,, ,, 1 in 60	..	54	,,
,, ,, ,, 1 in 80	..	68	,,
,, ,, ,, 1 in 100	..	82	,,
,, ,, ,, 1 in 200	..	123	,,
,, on a level	..	..	160	,,

The cover of a Sentinel calendar, showing 'A 'Sentinel' Locomotive which has HALVED running costs. (Little Orme Quarries, Llandudno).' 'This locomotive and its two sisters, all built in 1926, came to Harbury in 1931/32.   *Author's Collection*

No. 12, Sentinel 6255 of 1926 with a train of small skips (compare with the skips in the photographs on pages 36 and 37), 15th April, 1938. Note the chain drive coupling the axles.
                                                                                               G. Alliez

quarry had closed on 18th December, 1931, and these three locomotives were sent to Harbury, probably following the closure.

These Sentinels were Type 951L, box-like but neat. The bonnet housed the water tank, and, at the front, the vertical cylinders which protruded slightly above the bonnet casing. The full cab contained the vertical boiler, and had rear waist-high sliding doors to give access to the boiler back. Wooden dumb buffers were fitted at each end, like all the other locomotives at Harbury. The gearbox was below the cylinders, with the chain drive to the leading axle on the left side, the axles being coupled by a chain on the right side.

The spirally corrugated Sentinel vertical boiler raised steam at 275 psi (about 100 psi more than 'conventional' industrial locomotive boilers), which was superheated to 650° F (about 340° C). Saturated locomotives used steam taken direct from the boiler to the cylinders. In a superheated locomotive, before leaving the boiler the steam pipe was exposed to hot gases from the fire, which heated and dried the steam. This enabled the engine to make better use of the steam, saving both fuel and water and increasing efficiency. The Sentinel boiler evaporated about 1,800 lb. (180 gallons) of water each hour. The two-cylinder Sentinel vertical engine had poppet valves operated by a camshaft (like in a car - most steam locomotives had valves that slid across the valve openings, covering or uncovering the ports). The valve gear gave two cut-offs, 33.33 per cent and 89 per cent of the piston stoke in each direction.

These locomotives had featured on a Sentinel calendar when they were at Little Orme Quarries. The caption read 'A "Sentinel" Locomotive which has HALVED running costs'. On the reverse was written 'Save 50% in Fuel, 50% in Repairs, 50% in Stores, and haul 25% more load weight for weight. A mass of first hand testimony as to these facts on request'. Latterly the Sentinels were kept as spares to the diesels, and were scrapped in the early 1950s when boiler repairs became due.

The final 3 ft gauge locomotives were a pair of unusual 2-4-0 diesel-mechanical locomotives designed and built by John Fowler & Co. (Leeds) Ltd (20684, 20685) in 1935. Despite the use of water softeners, the steam locomotives had all suffered from the hard water and the diesels were intended to overcome this problem.

The locomotives, No. 1 and No. 2, had a cab slightly off-centre, with a bonnet either side. The larger bonnet housed the engine, a Ruston 6VQ, developing 106 hp at 1,000 rpm, and a small petrol engine for starting it. The other bonnet housed the transmission and fuel tank. The unusual wheel arrangement was adopted to keep within the specified maximum axle load and yet not suffer from a long rigid wheelbase (*West Baldwin* again!). A 2 ft gauge 85 hp 2-4-0 version, built in 1934 for service in Natal, is described and illustrated in *The British Internal Combustion Locomotive* by Brian Webb (David & Charles, 1973, p. 91), while an 0-6-0 version was built for use in Queensland in 1935. The engine drove a three-speed gearbox, with nominal speeds of 4½, 7 and 11 mph. The final drive was to a jackshaft at the rear of the locomotive, which drove the leading coupled axle by a connecting rod. This drive to the leading wheels was in line with Fowler's standard practice at the time, and was intended to reduce relative angular movement of the connecting rod due to the rise and fall of the wheels as the springs flexed. Both locomotives were in daily use. After the 3 ft gauge closed in January 1970, the Fowler locomotives remained on site for some months, being observed at the end of March. By mid-November 1970 they had been transferred to APCM Kilvington works, east of Nottingham, where they worked alongside the two big Rustons from Ufton quarries (*see Chapter Five*) which had also gone there. However, the two Fowlers did not stay there long, No. 2 going for preservation in 1974 at Butterley, Derbyshire, with No. 1 as a source of spares. No. 2 eventually returned to Leeds for display at the Armly Mills Industrial

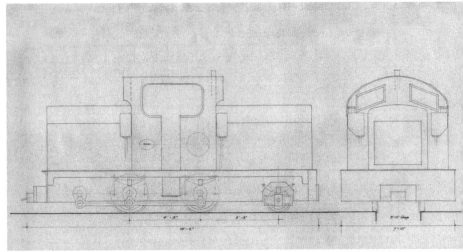

Outline drawing of 3 ft gauge 2-4-0DM No. 1, John Fowler 20684 of 1935 by R.E. West.

A John Fowler official photograph of one the 2-4-0DM supplied in 1935. Note the jackshaft at the rear, driving the leading axle by a long connecting rod, behind which the coupling rod drives the rear axle under the cab.   *Author's Collection*

Museum, alongside other examples of Leeds-built locomotives, but unfortunately it has not yet been restored.

The locomotive livery varied. The Bagnalls were green with yellow/black/yellow lining. *West Baldwin* was chocolate or maroon. The Kerr, Stuart *Eagle* was black with white lining and *Hawk* was green with yellow/black/yellow lining. The Pecketts seem to have been in this firm's standard green, lined black and yellow. The Sentinel locomotives were yellow with blue lining (APCM colours). On the cab side was a large white disc with a blue border. Within the circle, in blue letters, was 'Blue Circle' (APCM's trade mark), and in white above and below it was 'Portland Cement'. The Fowlers were originally green with white lining and lettering, but this was soon changed to yellow, again with a disc on the cab side. In their final years they were again green, unlined, with red rods. By 1966 No. 2, but not No. 1, had 'Keep clear' painted on the radiator at each end, possibly at the instigation of a quarry inspector.

Gauge 3 ft

*Mercedes**	0-4-0ST	OC	WB	1730	1904	New	Scr 1922
*Maudie**	0-4-0ST	OC	WB	1782	1905	New	(1)
Mildred	0-4-0ST	OC	WB	1844	1907	New	(2)
Robinson	0-4-0ST	OC	WB	1632	1901	(a)	s/s
Walton	0-4-0ST	OC	WB	1633	1901	(b)	s/s
*Eagle**	0-4-2T	OC	KS	756	1901	(c)	Scr 1924
*West Baldwin**	0-6-0ST	OC	HE	758	1901	(d)	Scr 1926
1 *Hawk*	0-4-2T	OC	KS	1213	1914	New	(3)
2 *Lark*	0-4-0ST	OC	HC	708	1904	(e)	Scr 1938
3 *Eagle**	0-4-0ST	OC	P	1654	1924	New	(4)
4	0-4-0ST	OC	P	1663	1924	New	(4)
6	0-4-0ST	OC	P	1720	1926	New	(4)
12 formerly 2	4wVBT	VCG	S	6255	1926	(f)	(5)
13 formerly 1	4wVBT	VCG	S	6256	1926	(f)	(5)
3	4wVBT	VCG	S	6257	1926	(f)	(6)
	4wPM		MR	2127	1922	(g)	(7)
	4wPM		MR	2261	1923	(g)	(7)
No. 1	2-4-0DM		JF	20684	1935	New	(8)
No. 2	2-4-0DM		JF	20685	1935	New	(8)

* Known to have had cast nameplates

(a) Ordered in July 1900 by the contractor Enoch Tempest, being delivered to the Walshaw Dean Reservoir (Halifax Corporation) contract in Yorkshire in August 1901. Tempest sold them in 1910 to the contractor Holme & King, who sold them to Harbury works by 9.1912.

(b) Ex-John Kinniburgh, after 1914. Earlier Enoch Tempest, Walshaw Dean Reservoir (Halifax Corporation) contract, Yorkshire.

(c) Originally Holme & King, St Helens contract, Lancashire.

(d) Ex-J.F. Wake, dealer, Darlington, 1919, previously Preston Corporation Spade Mill No. 1 Reservoir Contract via W. Underwood & Bros, Dunkinfield ordered 2.5.1901, steamed 16.9.1901, sent away 17.9.1901. Original owner Douglas Corporation, West Baldwin Reservoir construction, IoM, subsequent owners (dates given are when spares were sent, not transfer of the locomotive) Preston Corporation 9.1909 presumably Spade Mill No. 1 Reservoir construction, Wm Underwood & Bros (12.1911, 5.1912, 3.1914, 7.1914: 1914 dates and possibly earlier ones in use on construction of Mountain Ash Waterworks at Hirwain), J.F. Wake, Darlington 5.1918 (note in HE records), GBL Harbury 6.1920.

(e) Ex-Sir Robert McAlpine Ltd, Glasgow, by 1922, originally used at Culter Reservoir contract, Peebleshire.
(f) Ex-APCM Little Orme Quarries, Carnarvonshire 1931, or more probably 1932 after the quarry had closed on 18.12.1931.
(g) Ex-George Cohen Sons & Co Ltd by 20.4.1934, earlier Preston Corporation Water Department, Longridge Reservoir, Lancashire. While they may have been actually delivered here, no-one ever mentioned them to me in conversation so it is probable that they merely passed through, en route to Ufton Quarries.

(1) To Thos Mitchell, Bolton, Lancashire, 3.1915, resold to Taylor & Co, Forres, Morayshire 3.1917.
(2) Believed requisitioned c.1914-1918, later H. & J. Martin, Vartry Upper Reservoir contract (Dublin Corporation) 1919-25.
(3) To Holborough Works, Kent 1925. Scrapped there c.1938.
(4) Scrapped c.1935, by 1937.
(5) Derelict 1943, frame only left 9.1950, scrapped soon after.
(6) Derelict 1937. Scrapped after 6.1953.
(7) Probably to Ufton Quarries 1934, else s/s.
(8) To Kilvington Works, Nottinghamshire 11.1970.

From the mid-1920s a 2 ft gauge line had been used to remove the increasingly thick overburden from the quarry west of the road. This line ran north from a shed near the road by the cemetery, crossing over the 3 ft gauge shortly after the stream. Initially horse haulage was used, but from the mid-1930s three locomotives were in daily use. They were stored sheeted when not in use, and the shed was provided for repairs. There were about 36 iron V-skips, which operated in trains of six. The track was removed in 1946 and dumpers were used instead.

This overburden line was operated from 1933/34 by a fleet of Motor Rail petrol locomotives, similar to the ones at Kaye's and Nelson's works. The early design, supplied to both the War Department Light Railways (WDLR) and some industrial users, had 'bent' channel steel frames, wider in the centre than at the ends. This was to reduce overhang on sharp curves. The locomotive from Kent Construction was probably constructed largely using Motor Rail spares bought from army surplus sales after World War I.

Gauge 1 ft 11½ in

No. 2 former 8	4wPM	MR	984	(a)	(1)
No. 2 former 8	4wPM	MR	2154	(b)	(1)
No. 4	4wPM	KC	c/1926	(c)	(1)
14	4wPM	MR		(c)	(1)
	4wPM	MR		(d)	(1)
	4wPM	MR		(e)	s/s

(a) Ex-BPCM, Martin Earle's works, Kent, originally WDLR 2705 delivered 8.1918.
(b) Ordered by APCM 7.11.21, 20 hp petrol 2½T bent frame, 24 in. gauge, ratios in gearbox altered to give low speed of 4¼ mph (3.4 mph standard), cost £612 15s. 0d. (£645 less 5 per cent) delivered to BPCM Saxon Branch, Fulbournes. At BPCM Norman works, Cambridge 6.1924, spares to Harbury 18.6.1935.
(c) Identities and origins not known.
(d) Ex-WDLR.
(e) Ex-Edmund Nuttall Ltd, contractors, by 1935.

(1) Scrapped c.1950 (after 11.1948, by 1.1953).

The original 3 ft gauge wagon fleet appears to have been about 100 wooden tippers made at Harbury works. They held about 2 to 3 tons and were replaced around 1920 by about 100 iron V-skips made by Bagnall (Stafford) and Howard (Bedford). These iron wagons held 3 tons. Most of the wooden wagons were side tippers but a few, used on the spoil tip, were end tippers. When APCM took over in 1931 there were some old iron wagons with dumb side buffers which held 5 tons. They had been made by a Scottish firm. They were coupled by a chain which went over a pin on the wagon, and were emptied using a tippler where the later shale conveyor was sited. There had once been some long shallow wagons which went as scrap to Simms, Leamington. In addition, there were 8 to 10 small V-skips which were used on the tip.

In the last years the railway used steel V-skips wagons made by Allen & Co., Tipton. These came from Ufton Quarries in 1951. The wagons had a frame 9 ft long with a wheelbase of 4 ft and 18 in. wheels. Springing was by blocks of rubber. The body was 3 ft deep x 6 ft 8 in. wide and 7 ft 11 in. long, holding 3 cubic yards (5 tons). The ends were slightly raised. Most had disc wheels, but a few had wheels with four holes by Henry Brown & Co. (Irvine) Ltd, Scotland. Link and pin couplings were fitted. They were painted pale yellow livery, with numbers in blue.

It is likely that the original main line sidings were mixed gauge, but the broad gauge rails would soon have been unnecessary. The loop and sidings serving the works were on the down (west) side of the GWR main line, and were controlled by Greaves Siding signal box. In 1970 the loop had three connections to the main line. Going north along the down line, the first connection was a trailing crossover with the up line direct to the loop, with a trailing single slip where it crossed the down line. Just north of the signal box a facing crossover gave access to the loop from the down line, and nearer Southam Road & Harbury station the loop made a trailing connection with the down line. This last connection was removed in the early 1970s, and the far end of the loop then became a headshunt, terminating a train length north of the intermediate crossover. Trailing sidings from the loop entered the works yard opposite the signal box. The layout obviously varied over the years, but the layouts in 1887 and 1970 were remarkably similar, with three sets of lines going right through the works. The early map showed several additional short sidings near the main line. In 1970 a sharply curved siding served the coal tippler, wagons running back to the tippler from the bufferstops by gravity. About 2,000 tons of slack coal were required each week, brought from the Coventry area mainly by rail. Gypsum came from East Leake, a few miles north of Loughborough in Leicestershire. Another siding served the tip for incoming limestone from Ardley, and probably gypsum as well. A pair of sidings ran either side of the silos for loading cement, and one of these terminated in the corrugated iron locomotive shed. This was approximately 40 ft by 22 ft, with sliding doors and a full length pit, and was painted white. By 1966 a generator house had been built on the site of this shed, and the former wagon repair shop was used as the shed instead.

For many years standard gauge rail traffic was incoming coal and outgoing cement. However, from around 1957 when limestone began to be brought from Ardley by the trainload, rail traffic increased. In 1966 this comprised two trains daily, Monday to Friday, using 24 ton hopper wagons. The works diesel shunted them over the crusher bunker's elevator. At that time coal came from Williamthorpe Colliery near Chesterfield.

Once cement was no longer made at Harbury there was no longer incoming coal or limestone so the layout was simplified. The main line loop was cut back as already

Above: Train of empty 24T hopper wagons leaving Harbury to return to Ardley Quarry, hauled by a '9F' 2-10-0. The white roof and grey walls of the signal box is due to years of fallout of cement dust from the works, 19th March, 1966.
R.E. West

Right: Class '47' Co-Co No. 1599 backing a train of cement tanks from Northfleet into the silo sidings for emptying, 30th July, 1973. Note the 'bent' tanks.
Author

described. Two sidings were laid into the works either side of the silos. Either siding was used to discharge the tank wagons bringing incoming cement, but Presflo wagons carrying sulphacrete could only be handled on the southern siding. A plate attached to a buffer stop showed that T.W. Ward had the contract for maintenance at this time.

Shunting was originally done by horses, six being used altogether, locomotives only being introduced around 1925.

Originally the main line goods trains drew (or reversed) into the loop and wagons were exchanged. The main line locomotives were not allowed to enter the private sidings, certainly not for any distance, until after December 1970, when Harbury had become a distribution depot. Then the APCM locomotive assembled the empties in the southern part of the loop before 3 pm, when the daily cement train from Kent was due. On arrival, the loaded train drew into the headshunt (the northern end of the former loop) and then reversed into the works sidings, the BR locomotive being allowed to go almost as far as the silos. Once the BR locomotive was clear of the loop, the APCM locomotive pulled the empties into headshunt. The BR locomotive then backed down and was coupled to the empties, the APCM driver put the tail lamp on the last wagon, and the empties left about 20 minutes after the full wagons had arrived. The APCM locomotive then split the full train in two for discharge. The typical train in the early 1970s comprised ten 100 ton (gross laden weight) tankers, each wagon having two cement tanks (*see later*).

The first locomotive appears to have been a GWR 0-4-0ST borrowed for six to eight weeks in 1925. Possibly this was to test the feasibility of replacing the horses, because two locomotives were bought soon after from the dealer Adams of Newport (Mon). Little is known about them; No. 5 *Hawk* was an 0-4-0ST, probably built by Hudswell, Clarke, and No. 7 was another 0-4-0ST, said to have been built by Kerr, Stuart. It was known as 'The Canadian', possibly because it had a spark arresting chimney, and may have carried the name *Irwell*. It was 'not much good' and was scrapped around 1931, probably following the arrival of *The Blue Circle*. The arrival of *Whitby* in 1933 was probably the reason for *Hawk* to be scrapped in 1934.

The locomotive purchased in 1929, named for some years *The Blue Circle*, was unique. It was the first steam locomotive built by Baguley Cars Ltd at Burton-on-Trent, and it was the only standard gauge steam locomotive constructed by this firm. The works number given was 621, although it should have been 2001, as steam locomotives had been allocated numbers 2001 to 2032. No. 621 was originally designed as a 150 hp petrol-hydraulic locomotive for the Lachine Railway, near Montreal, Canada. Construction commenced in 1914 but was abandoned due to World War I. The chassis lay around the works and in 1917 a steam locomotive was designed around it. The conversion was finished in 1920 and was sold to Sir Thomas Salt, a Burton brewer. Records show that it was rebuilt by Hudswell, Clarke, Leeds, in 1925, possibly to remove defects in the original design, and in 1928 it was sold to Greaves Bull & Lakin. Despite this chequered start the locomotive survived, latterly as spare, until April 1958 when it was scrapped. It was the only standard gauge locomotive fitted with the patent Baguley valve gear.

Whitby, a Peckett 0-4-0ST (1505), built in 1918, came from APCM's Ellesmere Works in 1933. (The Little Orme Limestone Quarry, source of the 3 ft gauge Sentinels at Harbury, had supplied Ellesmere works.) *Whitby* was fitted with rail washers. Around January 1962 it was surplus to requirements and was sent, dismantled, to the nearby Southam works of Rugby Portland Cement as spare to its diesel, but was not required and was scrapped in 1963 without being reassembled.

Above: No. 8 *Blue Circle*, Baguley 621 of 1919. *Celia Barratt Collection*

Above right: No. 9 *Whitby*, Peckett 1505 of 1918 beside the main line on 30th September, 1950. *K. Lane, IRS Collection*

Right: Cunarder, Hunslet 1690 of 1931 on 13th September, 1958. *J. Faithfull Collection, RCTS*

The final steam locomotive, arriving in March 1957, was *Cunarder*, a Hunslet 0-6-0ST (1690), with outside cylinders and Walschaert's valve gear. It had been dispatched from the works in Leeds on 27th July, 1931, the last of eight ordered by J. Mowlem & Co. Ltd for their Southampton Graving Dock contract, hence the name. One of them featured in the background of publicity photographs taken when Prince George (Duke of Kent) visited Hunslet's works in May 1931. Later *Cunarder* passed to Samuel Williams' wharf at Dagenham and then to the contractor Nuttall, who sold it to APCM. When it first arrived at Harbury it carried a spark arresting chimney but this was soon replaced. *Cunarder* went to Hunslet for repair early in 1961, which may have been when the large dumb buffers carried on arrival at Harbury were replaced by conventional spring buffers with large heads (to prevent buffer locking), as fitted to the other locomotives. By 1966 *Cunarder* was spare to the diesel, and was only normally used on Mondays when the diesel was busy on main line traffic. This periodic steaming was required for insurance purposes, but later this seems to have lapsed, as an enthusiast reported in January 1968 that *Cunarder* had not worked for a very long time, and on 2nd March, 1968 *Cunarder* was noted dumped outside the shed. However, this was not the end as it went to what is now the Buckinghamshire Railway Centre at Quainton Road station near Aylesbury on 24th April, 1969. Eventually, in August 2010, it passed to the restored Somerset & Dorset Railway station at Shillingstone, near Blandford, Dorset.

A 4-wheel Fowler diesel-hydraulic locomotive, 4220008, had been purchased new in 1959. It carried a plate showing that it had been registered in 1960 as suitable for use on BR track, registered number 2925. A Leyland EN900 engine developing 185 bhp was fitted, which drove a Schneider single-stage torque converter and then an air-operated epicyclic multi-speed gearbox made by Self-changing Gears Ltd. There was an air-operated reversing and final drive gearbox under the cab to a jackshaft at the rear of the locomotive. Side rods transmitted the power to the rear wheels, which were coupled to the front ones by side rods.

Presumably because the Fowler required overhaul and *Cunarder* was by then out of use, another Fowler locomotive, 4110008 of 1950, was hired from the dealers L. Sanderson Ltd, Birtley, Durham from about February to May 1968.

The final locomotive at Harbury was No. 4, a 4-wheel Sentinel diesel-hydraulic, No. 10007 of 1959, transferred from APCM's Swanscombe works, Kent, in February 1982. It was powered by a 200 hp Rolls Royce C6SFL engine and weighed 34 tons. When not in use it was parked in the sidings against the empty cement tank wagons.

The locomotives had a variety of liveries, with green predominating. No. 5 *Hawk* (Hudswell, Clarke) was green but the Kerr, Stuart No. 7 *Irwell* was black or red. Baguley No. 8 *The Blue Circle* was originally green but was later yellow. *Whitby* was green lined black. *Cunarder* arrived painted dark green, was then dark red, then yellow lined blue and by 1966 it was mid-green. The Fowler diesel No. 4220008 was originally green but had been repainted yellow and blue with red wheels by August 1971. The Sentinel diesel was yellow all over - even the faces of the buffers and coupling chain - with blue handrails and 'Blue Circle Cement' in large blue letters on the side of the cab.

Fowler 422008 of 1960 with a train of bogie cement tanks on 30th July, 1973.   *Author*

Sentinel 10007 of 1959, parked by the silos in 1988.   *M. Holmes*

Standard gauge

5 *Hawk*	0-4-0ST	OC	HC			(a)		Scr /1934
7 *Irwell?*	0-4-0ST	OC	KS			(a)	(1)	
8 (*The Blue Circle*)	0-4-0ST	OC	Bg	621	1919			
			REbHC	1925		(b)		Scr 4/1934
No. 9 *Whitby**	0-4-0ST	OC	P	1505	1918	(c)	(2)	
*Cunarder**	0-6-0ST	OC	HE	1690	1931	(d)	(3)	
	0-4-0DM		JF	4110008	1950	(e)	(4)	
	0-4-0DH		JF	4220008	1959	New	(5)	
No. 4	4wDH		S	10007	1959	(f)	(6)	

* Known to have carried cast nameplates.

(a) Ex-A.R.Adams & Son, dealers, Newport (Mon).
(b) Ex-Thomas Salt & Co., Burton-on-Trent 1928.
(c) Ex-Ellesmere Port works, Cheshire 1933.
(d) Ex-Edmund Nuttall, contractors 3.1957. Previously S.Williams, Dagenham.
(e) Hired from L. Sanderson Ltd, dealers, Birtley, Co Durham, *c*.2.1968.
(f) Ex-Swanscombe works, Kent 11.2.1982.

(1) Scrapped *c*.1931, by 9.1932.
(2) To RPC, Southam in dismantled condition, c1962.
(3) To London Railway Preservation Society Ltd (Quainton Railway Society Ltd since 24.4.1971), Buckinghamshire Railway Centre, Quainton Road station near Aylesbury, Buckinghamshire 24.4.1969. It was later owned by the Swanage Railway Society who transferred it to the North Dorset Railway Trust at Shillingstone Station in August 2010.
(4) Returned to L. Sanderson Ltd, Birtley, 5.1968.
(5) To North Downs Steam Railway, c/o Chatham Dockyard, Kent 10.1982.
(6) To Spa Valley Railway, Groombridge, East Sussex, after 8.10.1993, by 23.10.1994.

Examination of the locomotive lists above suggests that for the decade from the mid-1920s the 3 ft and standard gauge locomotives were numbered in a single series, and the petrol locomotives on overburden removal may have been included. The suggested combined list is given below. Numbers appear to have been reused once a locomotive had been scrapped.

1	*Hawk*	KS	1213	N
No. 1		JF	20684	N
2	*Lark*	HC	708	N
No. 2		JF	20685	N
3	*Eagle*	P	1654	N
3		S	6257	N
4		P	1663	N
5	*Hawk*	HC?		S
6		P	1720	N
7		KS?		S
8	*The Blue Circle*	Bg	621	S
No. 9	*Whitby*	P	1505	S
10				O?
11				O?
12		S	6255	N
13		S	6256	N
14		MR		O

Key: N – quarry 3 ft gauge, O – overburden 2 ft gauge, S – standard gauge

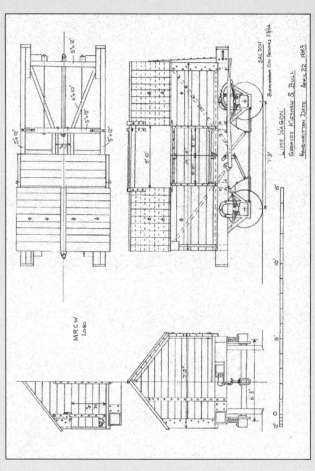

Lime Wagon built for Greaves Kirshaw & Bull (GKB) by 'Metropolitan Railway Carriage & Wagon Co Ltd, late J. Wright & Sons, Saltley Works, Birmingham'. The original drawing has the handwritten date 22nd April, 1869. J. Wright was one of earliest builders of railway carriages, starting in Clerkenwell, London in 1835. He constructed the carriage for the first royal journey by train, from London to Rugby, made by Queen Adelaide on 15-10-1839. The works moved to Saltley in 1845 and the name changed to Metropolitan Railway Carriage & Wagon Co. in 1862. Note the wooden construction, ridged roof and dumb buffers, bound with iron at the ends. The roof is made of two layers of planks laid at right angles. There is a pair of cupboard-type doors on each side, with above them a door hinged on the ridge of the roof. There is also a 2 ft 9 in. high top-hung door at one end. The two stanchions at the other end are about 4 in. wide, and taper from 4 in. at the bottom to 2 in. at the top. They are faced with a strip of metal. Brake blocks are wooden, apparently on one side only, and a ratchet mechanism (not very clear on the original drawing) could hold the brake lever at any desired position. The shaft carrying the brake lever also carried a short T-piece, the arms of which were connected to the brake blocks. The drawbar was apparently unsprung.

Redrawn from original Metro-Cammell drawing 23/64 held in Birmingham City Archives

Birmingham City Archives have two drawings of wagons built by Metropolitan Railway Carriage & Wagon Co. Ltd (later Metro-Cammell), Saltley works, Birmingham. One depicts a wooden lime wagon with ridged roof and dumb buffers for Greaves Kirshaw & Bull. The drawing is dated 22nd April, 1869. Basically it was a six-plank open wagon, with sides 3 ft high, and a pair of cupboard (i.e. vertically hinged) doors covering an opening 4 ft wide central on each side. One end was fitted with a top hinged door, five planks (2 ft 9 in.) deep. The wagon's ends were raised by five planks to support the ridged roof, which was made from horizontal planks suitably covered to make it watertight. Apart from a longitudinal timber forming the ridge, the roof stopped either side of the doors. This gap was covered on each side by a flap 5 ft wide hinged along its upper edge, the six inch overlap either side preventing the ingress of water. Ridged roof vans were once common for lime and cement traffic, no doubt because the flat surface made it easier to obtain a watertight seal round the roof door. The side and roof doors gave reasonable access for men loading and unloading the wagon. The wagon had dumb (solid wood) buffers and there did not appear to be any springs in the drawbar either. It had wooden brake shoes acting on both wheels on one side only.

The other drawing, dated 14th January, 1892, shows a 9 ton covered lime van for Greaves Bull & Lakin. It was almost entirely constructed from metal and had a normal curved roof. Again, it had a pair of vertically hinged doors, consisting of oak frames with sheet steel screwed on. The floor was also wood. The buffers at each end were sprung by a horizontal leaf spring bearing on the buffer shanks. The drawbar also was sprung. Metal brake shoes applied by a lever acted on the wheels of one side only.

Unfortunately no details of order size, running numbers, or livery survive for either drawing. These wagons could, of course, have been used at Wilmcote as well as Harbury.

While there may have been a few internal wagons, most if not all of the standard gauge rolling stock owned worked over the main line. Edwards Bros, Cardiff, formerly produced drawings for railway modellers. Among these was an iron van for lime and cement, with a curved roof, No. 235, belonging to Greaves at Harbury works. It was 'lead colour all over, black wheels etc, white lettering and Venetian Red Triangle' occupying the full width of the doors. This suggests that it dates from 1927-29. On several occasions the *Model Railway News* illustrated APCM wagons. In the issue for October 1946 there was a drawing of a six-plank open wagon, 247, with side and end doors, presumably for incoming coal as it was labelled 'Return Loaded. Southam Rd. GWR' in place of the usual 'return empty to'. Livery was middle grey, and the lettering white with black shading. The tops of the letters of 'Harbury' painted centrally on the bottom of the door formed an arc i.e. H & Y were the same height, sloping up to or away from BU. The August 1963 issue illustrated a seven-plank open wagon No. 173, with side doors only, but it could have been based at any APCM works. It was lemon yellow, including the solebars, sky blue circular logo, all lettering white and ironwork black. The same issue also shows iron van No. 177 with curved roof, lemon yellow body and solebars, blue circular logo and lettering, black ironwork below the solebars. As it was built in 1921 it would not have been seen at Harbury, if at all, until after 1932. The August 1964 issue, and also one of Edwards' drawings, shows another similar iron van (Nos. 167 and 158 respectively), again yellow body and blue lettering but white roof. There is no logo but instead it is lettered '"Ferrocrete" The Rapid Hardening Portland Cement' but again it could have been based at any APCM works. By 1964 APCM had some modern vans with

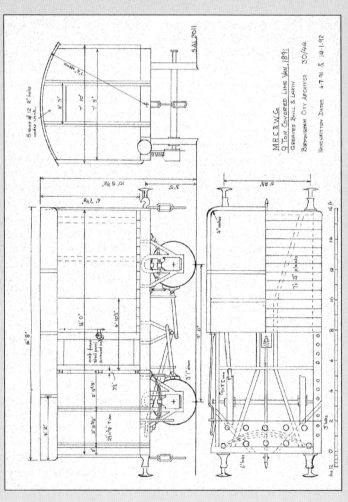

A 9 ton covered lime van for Greaves Bull & Lakin. The original drawing has the handwritten date 14.1.92. Note all metal construction except for the floor, made of 7 x 2½ in. planks secured by ½ in. bolts. The frame is well braced, and has a 2 ft wide gusset plate ³⁄₁₆ in. thick at each end, lightened by ten 6 in. diameter holes. There are also lightening holes in the top flange of the 9 x 3 in. steel channel frames. The body sides are strengthened by T-irons. There is a pair of cupboard-type doors on each side, comprising a rectangular oak frame to which the 'No 11 BWG' steel plate is attached by 'No 14 wood screws'. All the body rivets are countersunk on the inside. The axles run in 'Ellis's patent axle-box'.

Redrawn from original Metro-Cammell drawing 30/44 held in Birmingham City Archives

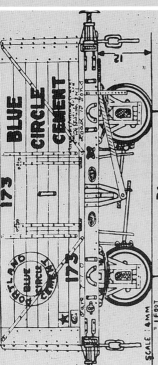

APCM 7-plank open wagon 173 (standard RCH design). Livery: Lemon yellow including solebars, black ironwork. Sky blue circle with white lettering, other lettering unshaded white. Some examples had a black centre in the blue circle. The small lettering reads: Associated Portland Cement/Manufacturers Ltd/Westminster S.W.1/Load 12 Tons. The example shown had the hatched portion of the brake lever painted white, 'probably a war-time "blackout" aid'.

Model Railway News, August 1963, Author's Collection

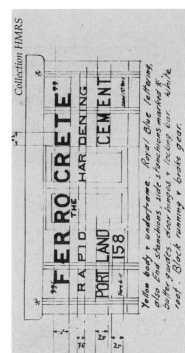

Collection HMRS

APCM 6-plank open wagon 247 with side and end doors. Livery: Middle grey, lettering white, some with black shading. Small letters on left-hand side read: Return Loaded/Southam Rd. G.W.R. Note that HARBURY has a level base but the top of the letters form an arc.

Model Railway News, October 1946, Author's Collection

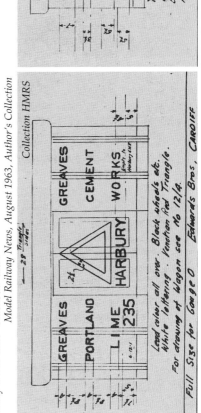

Collection HMRS

Above left: APCM iron van 167 'FERROCRETE'. Livery: Lemon yellow body and solebars, white roof, lettering unshaded blue, running gear black. Italics reads: Tare 6.12.0/Load 10 Tons/Associated Portland Cement/Manufacturers Ltd/Portland House, Tothill St./Westminster S.W.1. Note the wooden frames for the cupboard-type doors. This van carried a LNWR registration plate.

Above right: APCM iron van 177, built 1921. Livery: Lemon yellow body, black ironwork below the solebars. Blue unshaded lettering, except NON POOL is white on a red background. The small lettering reads: Associated Portland Cement/Manufacturers Ltd/Portland House, Tothill St./Westminster S.W.1.

(Both) Model Railway News, August 1963, Author's Collection

long wheelbase, painted light grey with black underframes with lettering white or red on a yellow background. The Blue Circle logo was prominent on the wide double doors. They were intended to carry cement bags on pallets. Again, they could have been based at any APCM works.

In 1973 main line wagons were tanks, having either four or eight wheels. The smaller tanks had a tare weight of 12 tons and a capacity of 32 tons (45 ton total weight), while the bogie wagons had a tare 22 tons 13 cwt and carried a load of 77 tons 7cwt in two tanks. All the tanks were 'bent', with a slope towards the centre, to assist discharge. The wagons were built by Metro-Cammell. Some, numbered in the 202xx series, were owned by Lloyds & Scottish Leasing Ltd. The tanks were fitted with Hermann's Aeration system, so a bogie wagon could be unloaded in 40 to 45 minutes, or by gravity if necessary (*see also Appendix Six*).

APCM modern long wheelbase 22 ton van passing through Northampton Castle station on 21st April, 1964. Livery: Light grey body, black underframe, lettering white or red on yellow. *Author*

Chapter Five

Ufton Quarries

APCM   1934   Closed 1954

Ufton is a village about two miles west of Southam and one mile north of Harbury. The quarries were about a mile south-east of Ufton, and they were worked steadily westwards and northwards, eventually crossing the Harbury to Ufton road (B4452). Access to the site was via a private road ¾ mile long from near Southam Road & Harbury station (GWR). The lorry loading point (SP 395610) was about 1¾ miles by road from Harbury works.

The 1889 6 in. OS map shows a lime kiln and small quarry about ½ mile south-south-west of Ufton church but this seems to have been a very small operation as nothing appeared on the 1906 map. The APCM quarries around Ufton Hill Farm were opened in 1934 as a source of extra limestone for Harbury, with an intended life of about 12 years. A 3 ft gauge railway was installed from the outset, but in 1952 it was replaced by conveyor belts and lorries. Stone was always taken to Harbury works by road; there was never a standard gauge siding here. The quarries were closed and abandoned in May 1954, although APCM kept them for emergencies. It is believed that a little stone was taken from Ufton in the very hard winter of 1962/63. Following the closure of Ufton, APCM opened a new quarry of 100 acres at Lighthorne (SP 345565), about 3½ miles south-west of Harbury works. This quarry also was always served by road. Later still, stone was obtained from Ardley, near Bicester (*see Appendix One*). Both Ufton and Lighthorne produced white lias stone, whereas Harbury was blue lias.

APCM used to own Ufton Hill Farm, but in the mid-1980s the farm was sold to Peter Mann whose son Richard now works it. Peter Mann started the landfill operation in the old quarries to help pay for the farm, but he sold this enterprise to Biffa Waste Services Ltd in September 1992, due to the imposition of stricter regulations regarding landfill.

As Ufton Quarries were so short lived, they came and went between editions of the OS map, so details of the track layout are hard to come by. Furthermore, few railway enthusiasts appear to have visited the site. OS 1:2500 map sheets SP 3861-3961 and 3860-3960 show the extent of the quarry but no railway. Fortunately, RAF vertical (i.e. looking straight down) aerial photographs taken in 1946 and 1948 show the quarry when it was in operation.

A private concrete road, single track with passing places, runs from the east end of the bridge over the main line to Birmingham, from close to the former station, northwards for about ¾ mile to terminate near the quarry locomotive sheds and loading dock (SP 395609). Near the end of the road, still standing in 2007, were a small brick generator shed, the foundations for the washing plant, and a concrete loading platform for machinery. Fifty yards away, the two-road corrugated iron locomotive shed with brick workshop extension remained in use as a shelter for cattle, particularly calves. This shed was 23 ft 3 in. long x 16 ft 2 in. wide, with an extension on the west side 6 ft wide. At the rear was a brick extension 9 ft 10 in. long x 15 ft 11 in. wide, with 4 in. steel joists at the corners. These two extensions may have been a workshop, stores and/or a messroom. The main doors were 9 ft 9 in. high. The girder frame for the shed was 6 in. x 3 in. steel channel, and the doors had a frame of 2¼ in. steel angle. An unusual feature was the curved roof, with its axis across the tracks instead of along them. This shed would have held four large Simplex locomotives easily. There was once a second smaller shed with a pit, which had been demolished by July 1961.

Ufton Quarries, looking north, taken by RAF on 13th May, 1948. The main road from Southam to Leamington runs across the top of the photograph - Ufton village is just off the top left-hand side. The concrete access road runs from the centre foreground to the locomotive shed and depot area, approximately level with Ufton Hill Farm (*centre left*). The areas east and north of the depot are old workings (note the ridges of overburden). Workings either side of the farm's approach road have largely been returned to agriculture. The Harbury to Ufton road runs diagonally upwards from the left-hand edge, and quarrying has recently started west of it (this area is now a nature reserve). A train (the locomotive is a black dot on the original print) is on the main line north-east of the farm.   *English Heritage (NMR) RAF Photography*

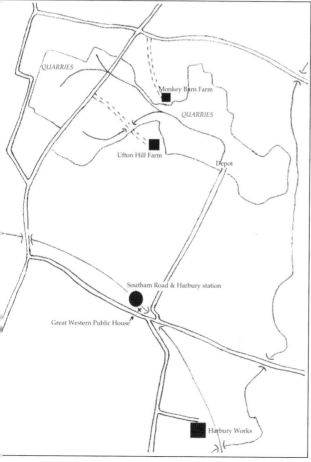

Above: Locomotive shed and depot area. The access road entered near the furthest brick building. Note the transverse curved roof of the engine shed, 25th February, 2008. *Author*

Left: Ufton Quarries, based on 2008 edition Ordnance Survey Explorer sheet 221, aerial photographs and field observation.

The track layout around the sheds and unloading point is uncertain. Close study of aerial photographs and my own notes made in 1961, suggest that the large shed was at the end of the line. The two tracks from it joined, running north-east, and then diverged to make a loop curving to the west. At the beginning of the loop were trailing connections for the line serving the small shed and for a track running in front of the washing plant. Two photographs of stationary trains suggest that the actual tipping point for the wagons was on the inner track of the loop, a conveyor then taking the stone into the washing plant. There was no sign of any sunken hopper in 1961, but as a hazard to livestock it had probably been filled in soon after the quarry closed. The waste clay from the washer was pumped to lagoons beside the nearby River Itchen, where it was allowed to settle. Clean stone was loaded into lorries for transport to Harbury.

The first quarries appear to have been immediately east of the shed area, and could account for the remains of a line past the washer. Later stone was worked north and west of the sheds. From the shed area the railway immediately curved about 90 degrees to the west, finally running west-north-west for ¾ mile, passing between Ufton Hill and Monkey Barn Farms, to a level crossing over the Harbury to Ufton road. In places it ran on low stone embankments. Old shallow quarries extended on both sides of the line, those to the north being much more extensive than those to the south. The level crossing was about 100 yards north of the road to Ufton Hill Farm. In 1961 the only sign of the crossing was a fenced gap in the hedge and tarmac over the concrete crossing. The track bed east of the road is still clearly visible, running on the south side of the field hedge. A tunnel under the farm access road served a quarry in the adjoining field which had been worked in the 1940s. The tunnel was close to the junction with the road to Biffa's site, but the entrances were later filled in to exclude livestock. Nearby was a small magazine.

The line divided immediately west of the level crossing, with lines turning north and south to serve the quarries west of the road, which appear to have been started in 1947. This area is now Ufton Fields Nature Reserve (SP 378613). A notice at the entrance states that this quarry had been excavated for limestone in the 1950s. When quarrying had finished the place had been left with ridges of clay, and pools of water had formed between them. In 1972 APCM gave 78 acres of the former quarry to Warwickshire County Council and the Warwickshire Wildlife Trust as a nature reserve. It is a Site of Special Scientific Interest (SSSI), being the home of five species of orchid, six of dragonfly, and 26 of butterfly. A path 1¼ miles-long encircles the site.

Sleepers were wood, 54 in. x 8 in. x 4 in., laid at 3 ft 3 in. centres. Measurements of old flat bottom rails used for fence posts and stakes around Ufton Hill Farm give a calculated weight of 45 lb./yard. Measurements of lighter rails found on site in 1961 give a calculated weight of 40 lb./yard or, in one case, only 25 lb./yard.

Operating conditions apparently were appalling, with very rough track, no ballast, and 'seas of mud' (*Ruston & Hornsby Locomotives*, E.S. Tonks, IRS 1974, p. 33). For some time during World War II, the locomotives worked 24 hours a day, seven days per week, having a headlight for night work, and the quarry was illuminated by arc lights over its lip. In the late 1940s two locomotives appear to have been in daily use. An aerial photograph taken in May 1948 shows a train of eight or nine wagons. All the photographs I have seen of trains show the locomotive at the shed end of the train, suggesting that empties were pushed to the quarry and the loaded wagons pulled back.

A walking dragline had been used to remove overburden. It had been taken away by road from a concrete layby at the south end of the nature reserve. This is probably where lorries had been loaded from the quarry conveyors once the rail system had been abandoned.

The first locomotives were 40 hp Motor Rail 'Simplex' design, built for main line haulage on the 60 cm ('2 ft') gauge War Department Light Railways serving the front in

World War I, and subsequently converted to 3 ft gauge. They were totally enclosed for protection from small arms fire, with massive curved ends, and slots for vision under the roof. Originally fitted with petrol engines, they had been rebuilt with Fowler Saunders diesel engines. Towards the end of World War II they were getting too old for the work, and two 48 hp Ruston & Hornsby diesel locomotives were obtained as replacements in 1946 and 1947. As the known Simplex locomotives were numbered 3 to 6, it is probable that two other locomotives worked here when the quarry was first opened, and are discussed below.

Ardley Quarry had closed around 1933-34 and had three 3 ft gauge petrol locomotives (*see Appendix One*). It seems probable that two of these locomotives were sent to Ufton, where they would have become the missing 1 and 2. However, for some reason they did not last long. Perhaps they had not been well maintained at Ardley, or maybe they had been stored in the open once the quarry closed and so had deteriorated beyond economic repair, being discarded once replacement locomotives were obtained from elsewhere. This would also explain why only two of the three came here, if the third one was in even worse condition, or had been used as a source of spares.

The two second-hand Rustons, 48 hp locomotives of type 48DL, were not equal to the task either, so they were replaced in late 1949 by two new 100 hp Ruston & Hornsby locomotives, type 100DL, the biggest narrow gauge diesels in the UK. Even so, they were unable to cope with the factors piled against them. It has been suggested that the whole rail system had only minimal maintenance, which cannot have helped. The decision was taken in 1952 to replace the rail system by lorries and conveyor belts. Most of the locomotives were sent to other works, and the two big Rustons eventually joined up again at Kilvington gypsum works, about 15 miles east of Nottingham, where the Fowler diesels from Harbury had also been transferred. No locomotives from Harbury ever worked at Ufton.

The 100DL locomotives were impressive. There was a long bonnet over the 100 hp Ruston 6VRH engine, and an angular fully enclosed cab with rectangular windows. The six driving wheels were connected by side rods, which extended backwards to a jackshaft under the cab. Cast balance weights replaced about half of the spokes in the driving wheels. Thick, deep, buffer beams at each end had a set six slots for coupling links. It is likely they were delivered in the standard Ruston dark green livery. Out of 32 built altogether, these were the only two locomotives of this type to work in the UK.

One of these large locomotives was preserved in 1984 (the other was scrapped on site at Kilvington). It came into the hands of the Irchester Narrow Gauge Railway Trust at Irchester, just south of Wellingborough, most of whose stock is metre gauge. Years later, in 2006-7, RMS Locotec obtained the contract to renew approximately three miles of the Manx Electric Railway for the Manx Department of Tourism & Leisure, and needed a suitable 3 ft gauge locomotive. With only a limited choice of 3 ft gauge locomotives in the UK, the Ruston at Irchester was identified as suitable and RMS Locotec negotiated successfully for its hire. It was given a thorough overhaul costing £20,000 at the firm's depot at Dewsbury and, as locomotive H048, was shipped to the Isle of Man. Following completion of the contract it was left on the island in the care of the Department of Transport as the firm hoped to win further contracts. In the spring of 2010 it had been out of use for some 18 months with gearbox trouble. Later it was shipped back to the mainland, arriving at Glasson Dock, Liverpool in early October, en route to Irchester.

The records of the Stephenson Locomotive Society state that the tiny 2 ft gauge Kerr, Stuart 0-4-0ST from APCM Stockton works (*see Chapter Eight*) came here before it was scrapped in 1936. In my opinion, the most likely use for such a locomotive would have been to assist with the construction of the concrete approach road. Narrow gauge railways

No. 3, a former WDLR 40 hp Motor Rail locomotive which once worked at Ufton, seen derelict at Sundon (Bedfordshire) cement works, 25th August, 1973.   *I. Thomas*

The 40 hp ex-WDLR Motor Rail petrol locomotives at Ufton originally looked like LR3090. The armour plate not only provided some protection for the driver but also gave useful weight for adhesion. Beside it is a 20 hp Motor Rail, similar to those used on overburden disposal at Harbury. Photographed at the Apedale Heritage Centre (Moseley Railway Trust), Newcastle-under-Lyme, Staffordshire on 9th May, 2009.   *Author*

Official Ruston Hornsby photograph of 100DL 0-6-0 locomotive. *Collection Andrew Neale*

No. 20, 100 hp Ruston Hornsby 281290 of 1949 with train, 5th November, 1950.
Ken Cooper, IRS Collection

A train hauled by a Ruston Hornsby 0-6-0DM at the depot.   *Author's Collection*

Now numbered H048, Ruston Hornsby 281290, with other engineers' locomotives at Dhoon Quarry, Isle of Man, during repairs to the Manx Electric Railway, 24th September, 2009.
T. Heavyside

were a common feature of road construction projects in the 1920s and 1930s. It could then have been used to bring in materials for the buildings, washer etc. A short-lived 2 ft gauge line at Ufton could also account for the light 25 lb./yard rail that I found in 1961.

Gauge 2 ft 0 in.

0-4-0ST	OC	KS	4266	1922	(a)

(a)   Ex-Stockton works, loan, *circa* 1934, and returned. Possibly assisted in the construction of the concrete road and development of the site.

Gauge 3 ft 0 in.

1	4wPM	MR?			(a)	Scrapped
2	4wPM	MR?			(a)	Scrapped
3	4wDM	MR			(b)	(1)
4	4wDM	MR			(b)	(2)
5	4wDM	MR			(b)	(2)
6	4wDM	MR			(b)	Scrapped *circa* 1951
	4wDM	RH	221618	1943	(c)	(3)
	4wDM	RH	281619	1943	(d)	(3)
No. 20	0-6-0DM	RH	281290	1949	New	(4)
No. 21	0-6-0DM	RH	281291	1949	New	(5)

(a)   Probably from Ardley Lime Pits, Bicester, Oxfordshire *circa* 1933-34.
(b)   Converted from petrol locomotives. One is MR 2127, ex-George Cohen, Sons & Co. Ltd, 1934, one is ex-Preston Waterworks, 1934, possibly MR 2262 of 1923 sold for £888 2.10.33. Delivered to Harbury works, probably for temporary storage.
(c)   Ex-Admiralty, Broughton Moor, Cumberland, 1946.
(d)   Ex-Admiralty, 1946.

(1)   To BPCM, Sundon works, Bedfordshire.
(2)   One to BPCM, Sundon works, Bedfordshire, the other scrapped, 1948.
(3)   To Holborough works, Kent, 1950.
(4)   To G. & T. Earle Ltd, Humber works, Yorkshire (ER), 6.1952, to Kilvington 1959, to Northampton Locomotive Group, Irchester 15.12.1984. Loaned to IoM 2006, returned 2010.
(5)   To Notts Gypsum Products Ltd, Kilvington, Notts, 1952 (by 17.3.1953), scr on site 17.2.1984.

The original wagons appear to have been wooden side tippers. An underframe, 7 ft 6 in. long made of 5½ in. square timbers 20½ in. apart, having 2 ft 6 in. wheelbase, lay beside the course of the line in 1961. Other wagons had large steel V-skip bodies, some about 4 ft 2 in. wide by 5 ft 6 in. long and 2 ft 6 in. deep and others 4 ft 10 in. wide, 4 ft 5 in. long, and 2 ft 6 in. deep. (Both of these had a nominal capacity of one cubic yard.). Eventually Allen & Co., Tipton supplied some three cubic yard capacity steel side tipping V-skips. The wagons had a frame 9 ft long with a wheelbase of 4 ft and 18 in. wheels. Springing was by blocks of rubber. The body was 3 ft deep x 6 ft 8 in. wide and 7 ft 11 in. long, holding three cubic yards (5 tons). The ends were slightly raised. Most had disc wheels, but a few had wheels with four holes by Henry Brown & Co. (Irvine) Ltd, Scotland. Link and pin couplings were fitted. The Allen wagons were sent to Harbury in 1951 when the line closed. One discarded skip body still lay in the north-east corner of the nature reserve near 'post 10' in 2007.

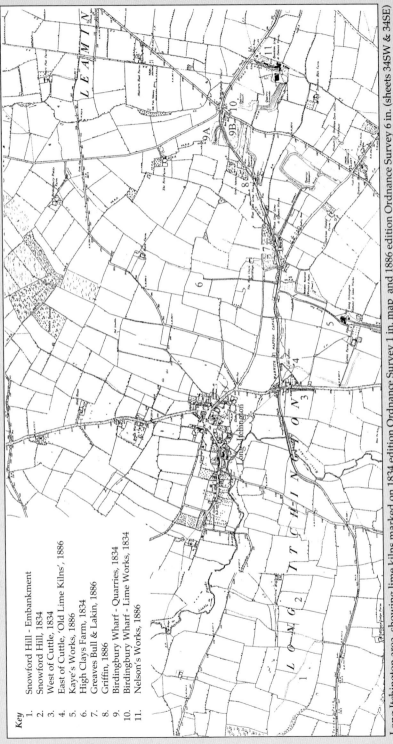

Key

1. Snowford Hill - Embankment
2. Snowford Hill, 1834
3. West of Cuttle, 1834
4. East of Cuttle, 'Old Lime Kilns', 1886
5. Kaye's Works, 1886
6. High Clays Farm, 1834
7. Greaves Bull & Lakin, 1886
8. Griffin, 1886
9. Birdingbury Wharf - Quarries, 1834
10. Birdingbury Wharf - Lime Works, 1834
11. Nelson's Works, 1886

Long Itchington area, showing lime kilns marked on 1834 edition Ordnance Survey 1 in. map and 1886 edition Ordnance Survey 6 in. (sheets 34SW & 34SE) along route of Warwick & Napton Canal.

Crown Copyright

Chapter Six

Small Works in the Long Itchington, Southam and Stockton Areas

The Warwick & Braunston Canal Act received the Royal Assent on 28th March, 1794. Just over a year later, in August 1795, it proposed an alteration to its route east from Leamington Spa, to pass near Offchurch, Ufton, and Stockton to meet the Oxford Canal at Napton. This would shorten the canal by seven miles, obviate the need for a tunnel 800 yds long, and save £50,000. Parliamentary approval, including changing its name to the Warwick & Napton Canal, was obtained in May 1796. The canal was constructed by direct labour and it was opened in 1800. Opening this canal enabled the lime industry to develop along its banks between Long Itchington and Stockton. The First Edition 1 in. OS map of 1834 showed five limeworks along this three mile stretch of canal, and that was before works were built for Messrs Greaves, Griffin, Kaye and Nelson. No wonder the Victoria County History of Warwickshire said:

The Blue Lias subsoil has long been known as a valuable source for the manufacture of lime and cement, and by 1850 the workings were described as 'very extensive'. Stockton cement has been used in many large contracting works, including the Victoria Embankment. The quarries extend into the parishes of Long Itchington and Southam (though the best ones are said to be those north and east of Stockton village, the first to be worked), and, covering nearly all of the north and west portions of Stockton parish, form the largest stretch of non-agricultural land in the rural half of Warwickshire. Stockton in fact has more of the character of an industrial village than any in Knightlow Hundred except Bedworth and its neighbours on the coalfield. (*VCH* Vol. 6 p. 226)

From west to east the following works are shown on 19th century OS maps (the scale and date of the map, and the grid reference, being given in brackets):

1. South of Snowford Hill Farm, south-west of Long Itchington (1834 1 in., 1862 1 in., SP 401643) 1 mile west of the main road (Southam to Coventry), north of Bascote Lodge.
2. 150 yards west of the main road and 350 yards south of the canal, later the site of Long Itchington station (1834 1 in., 1862 1 in., SP 414643) but there was no sign of any works or quarry on 1886 6 in. OS.
3. 250 yards east of the Cuttle inn, Long Itchington ('Old lime kilns' shown on 1886 6 in., SP 419645).
4. High Clays Farm half-mile east of the main road, 530 yards north of the canal (close to the Blue Lias inn on Long Itchington to Stockton road, at the end of a canal arm running north from almost opposite the junction with the arm serving the reservoir and, later, Kaye's works) (1834 1 in., 1862 1 in., SP 425652). The canal arm was shown on 1886 6 in. OS, but with no sign of any quarry or works.
5. Long Itchington Cement & Lime works, later Kaye's, on a southward arm of the canal serving the reservoir, south of High Clays Farm, (1886 6 in., SP 423643). Situated ¼ mile south of the canal and ¼ mile east of the main road.
6. Blue Lias Lime & Cement works, later Greaves Bull & Lakin, where the Long Itchington to Stockton road crossed the canal at the Blue Lias inn (1886 6 in., SP 429647).
7. Blue Lias Lime works, later Griffin, (1886 6 in., SP 435650) beside the canal quarter-mile east of Greaves' works and about the same distance west of Birdingbury Wharf.

73

Route of proposed Marton Tramway. The route from Marton station (off the top of the map) is south along the main road through Long Itchington to the junction of the roads to Southam and Stockton. The route then left the road, probably to avoid a hump back bridge over the canal, and went over a field, to cross the canal near the Old Limekilns by the Cuttle inn. Here it branched, one line bearing west to rejoin the main road which it followed to Southam. The other line followed a long curve, crossing Kaye's canal arm, where there was a branch along the eastern boundary of the works, and then skirting the southern edge of Stockton Reservoir it continued north-east to the GBL works. The route from here was similar to, but just to the south of, the later LNWR branch line, to terminate at on the west bank at the southern end of Nelson's canal arm. Note what appears to be the remains of a canal arm running beside the road, from the 264 ft spot height northwards to opposite the Cuttle.

The Waterways Archive - Gloucester

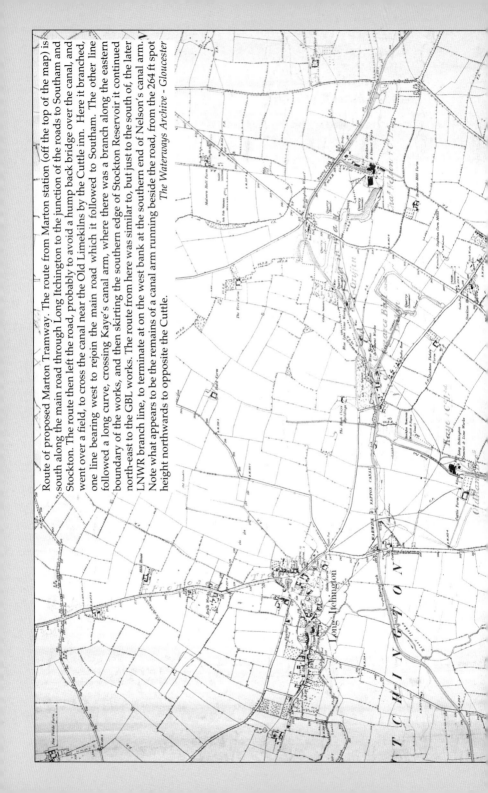

8. Stockton Lime & Cement(?), north of Stockton, on south side of the canal close to Birdingbury Wharf (1834 1 in., 1862 1 in., 25 in. 1888 (disused), SP 440649).
9. South-west angle of the crossroads at Birdingbury Wharf, where the map appears to show quarries (or maybe branch canals) west of the main road (Southam to Dunchurch and Rugby) on both the north and south sides of the main canal. (1834 1 in., SP 437651). These are Tomes & Handley's workings.
10. Stockton Lime & Cement, later Nelson's works, on a short southward arm of the canal north-east of Stockton and ¼ mile east of Birdingbury Wharf (1889 6 in., SP 442647).

Summarized, in 1834 there were five works, in 1862 six, and 1888 seven on a three mile stretch of canal. By 1860 lime 'was extensively manufactured in the neighbourhood and was considered "the best in England"'.

Once railways became common the larger works naturally wanted ready access to a railhead, to avoid carting at least two miles to the nearest station at Marton, on the LNWR Rugby to Leamington branch (opened in 1851), or alternatively using the canal (about 16 miles and as many locks from Stockton top lock) to Weedon to reach an interchange with the LNWR main line. Accordingly, a Bill was proposed in 1889 for the construction of a tramway to connect Marton station with the various lime works around Stockton, and with Southam itself. Its deposited plans are listed on Portcullis, the Parliamentary Archives on-line catalogue, under the reference HL/PO/PB/3/plan1889/M4.

According to the *Gazette Notice*, the proposed tramway was to be standard gauge, with haulage of both 'carriages and trucks' by 'steam or other mechanical power as well as animal power'. The reference to carriages suggests that passenger transport was envisaged, probably restricted to those employed in the lime and cement works, although with GWR Southam Road station being 2½ miles from Southam, and Marton station the same distance from Long Itchington, maybe a public service was proposed. The names of Greaves, Bull & Lakin, John Griffin, William Griffin, Charles Nelson, Thomas Oldham, John Oldham and Henry Oldham all feature in the application as owners, whilst Messrs Kaye & Cox appear on the List of Lessees. All these were either assents or had not given an answer in respect to the application. The set of deposited plans show the proposed line in its entirety. The *Gazette Notice* has the following description of the proposed tramroad:

Tramroad No. 1, commencing by a junction with the sidings on the north side of the Rugby and Leamington Branch of the London and North Western Railway at Marton Station, passing in a south-westerly direction to and under the bridge carrying that branch over the Coventry and Southam road, and thence in a southerly direction through the village of Long Itchington over the Warwick and Napton Canal, and terminating in Coventry-street, Southam at a point 3 chains [66 yards] or thereabouts north of Wood-street. Tramroad No. 2, commencing in the Parish of Long Itchington by a junction with Tramroad No. 1, at or near the corner of the field numbered 616 [SP 420644] on the 25 inch ordnance map, thence passing in an easterly direction over the canal leading to Long Itchington Lime Works, and terminating in the Parish of Birdingbury in the property adjoining the Stockton Lime and Cement Works, and numbered 185 on the said ordnance map.

The deposited plans give some idea as to how the tramroad would have entered the goods yard at Marton and a run-round loop was to be constructed in Coventry Street, Southam. A map in the British Waterways Archive (BW92/4/1/6) shows most of the proposed tramway. From its terminus at Nelson's works the line ran westwards, past Griffin and GBL for about a mile and quarter to Kaye's works, on a very similar route to the later LNWR branch. Just before it crossed Kaye's canal arm, as the route curved north-west, a trailing connection was made with a branch into Kaye's works. The main line crossed the canal close to Oldham's old lime kilns and headed for the fork between the main Southam to Coventry road and the lane to Stockton. Having reached the main road it then ran along it, through the village of Long Itchington, for almost two miles to Marton station. Here it went under the bridge carrying the LNWR Leamington line over the road and then up into the goods yard. By the canal crossing there was another trailing junction. This branch ran south across the field to the main road, which it used for about a mile and quarter to Southam itself, where a run-round loop was to be constructed in Coventry Street. The contours on the 1 in. OS map show that the average gradient from the canal up to Southam would have been 1 in 36 for three-quarters of a mile, while the climb towards Marton beyond Long Itchington would have averaged about 1 in 100. The distances and gradients suggest locomotives would have been used, presumably with skirts hiding the wheels and motion to prevent frightening any horses on the roads.

The Bill passed the House of Lords but was withdrawn from the Common, no reason being given in the Journal of the House of Commons. According to the Journal of the House of Lords, there were two Petitioners against the Bill, lodged by the Warwick and Napton Canal Navigation on 7th March, 1889 and by the LNWR on the following day. The objection from the canal company is easy to understand. Maybe the LNWR objected because it already had plans to extend its Weedon to Daventry branch (opened 1888) through the limeworks area to join the Rugby to Leamington branch. The LNWR obtained the necessary act in 1890 and the line opened in 1895. It is hard to say whether the Marton Tramway proposals were really serious, or were just intended to galvanize the LNWR into action (so that rail access would be obtained at someone else's expense).

It is interesting to consider what might have happened had the Marton Tramway been built. I think that the Daventry branch would not have been extended to Leamington, as the prime sources of traffic, the various lime and cement works, would have already obtained rail access. In addition, as there was no potential loss of traffic from the LNWR to a rival company, there was nothing to encourage extension of its existing branch. The local lime and cement works would no doubt have continued as they did, and Kaye's works would probably still have been taken over by Rugby Portland Cement. The residents of Long Itchington and local road users would have protested once incoming trains of chalk were added to incoming trains of coal and outgoing trains of cement, together with increased numbers of outgoing empty wagons. The County Council could well have insisted that the 1930s modernization of Southam works included improved rail access. RPC would then have been forced to build a railway from Southam works to Marton Junction, on or close to the alignment of the actual LNWR branch, but probably (bearing in mind the chalk trains) with the junction facing Rugby instead of Leamington. When the Rugby to Leamington line closed, RPC might have been willing to take over the eight mile section from Rugby to Marton because it already owned the further two miles to Southam. It would have then been able to carry stone from Southam to Rugby by train instead of lorry. However, this is all just speculation.

The individual works are now described in more detail, from west to east.

Snowford Hill

1831	Oldham & Witheringtons	
By 1854	George & Charles Witherington	Closed c.1870

An early works was at Snowford Hill (SP 401643), about ¾ mile south-west of Long Itchington. The works were shown on the 1834 and 1862 OS maps but then it disappears. Bartlett mentions a 'Lease for Lime Rock at Long Itchington' by J.H. Anthony to Messrs Oldham & Witheringtons, dated 21st April, 1831, which probably refers to this location. George and Charles Witherington were described in trade directories 1854-66 as 'Farmer, brickmakers & limeburners, Long Itchington' (there was a brickworks quarter-mile north of the village on Coventry Road). However, in the 1872 directory they had separate entries and both were described simply as farmers. Oldham had left this works by 1854, possibly well before, obviously thinking that he could do better.

An unmade road runs north from the canal at Toll House bridge, near Bascote Lodge Farm, towards Long Itchington. The 1834 map shows a track leading east from this road for 350 yards to the works, which were almost due south of the farm. The works and access track had totally disappeared by 1886, as the 6 in. OS map shows nothing at all in this area, only empty fields. All that was marked was a low embankment to former quarries west of the road. Nothing is now visible in the works field, although it is covered with flat pieces of limestone up to 4 in. square.

The small embankment, presumably for a narrow gauge railway, can still be seen crossing a field west of the road from the canal. In 1996 the farmer, Mr B. Symonds, said that about 2 ft of stone had been quarried, down to the underlying clay, and then carted to the canal at Bascote Wharf by the top lock and toll house (which is now a private residence). The stone was taken to Kaye's works at Long Itchington for burning. The farmer called this field (SP 392646) 'Stonefield'.

Possibly the western quarries outlasted the limeworks, but both seem to have ceased before 1880, when the trade directory made no mention of either quarrying or lime burning in Long Itchington.

West of Cuttle Inn

The 1834 1 in. OS map marks a lime works about 350 yards south of the canal and 150 yards west of the main Coventry road (SP 414643). However, the 1886 6 in. OS map shows absolutely nothing here, only empty fields. There is a possible pointer to a works in this area, as the 1834 map shows a canal arm about 300 yards long running south to the works, while the 1886 map shows a canal arm about 200 yards long running immediately alongside the road. There is also an unfenced track marked for about 290 yards running west from the road and about 350 yards from the canal. This could have been the works access, all trace of the works itself having disappeared by then. Alternatively, maybe the works were confused with those on the other side of the road (see below).

Bridge under a farm track on the Cuttle tramway, looking north from Southam & Long Itchington

Embankment south of the Cuttle inn, Long Itchington, 11th July, 1961. The canal wharf and site of lime kilns are by the nearer buildings on the left hand edge. The route of the canal is marked by the diagonal hedge from the buildings towards the top right corner.

Author

Cutting south of the Cuttle inn, Long Itchington, looking north, 11th July, 1961.

Author

East of Cuttle Inn

After 1834   William Oldham?   Closed after 1860 but well before 1886

The 1886 6 in. OS map shows 'Old Limekilns' beside the canal immediately west of Long Itchington lock, 250 yards east of Coventry Road (SP 418647). Possibly this was the works marked on the 1834 map west of the road, otherwise this works must have operated for quite a short time, starting after 1834 yet being 'old' by 1886. Studying trade directories suggests that these kilns were probably operated by William Oldham, a major local landowner, possibly after leaving the Witherington brothers at nearby Snowford Hill (*see above*). His entry in 1860 states he was a farmer and manufacturer of hydraulic Blue Lias lime and patent cement, of Coventry Road. In 1868 there was no reference to lime manufacture, only cement. William Oldham retired in 1868 and died around 1870.

The lime works was in the field beside the canal and the kilns were still visible in the 1970s, although filled with earth to prevent cattle falling in. The site was later (*c.*1980) occupied by Warwick Buildings. The kilns had obviously been connected to their quarry by a tramway. An embankment, 5 or 6 ft high at the canal end, ran south-south-west straight across the field towards the bridge carrying the main road over the LNWR at Southam & Long Itchington station. Close to the road and railway the embankment gave way to a cutting which was spanned by a brick bridge carrying a farm track.

This bridge was 6 ft 9 in. high in the centre and 10 ft wide, ample for a horse. By 1960 it was blocked by a transverse brick wall erected halfway along the arch. The arch was partly filled in on the north side and the bridge parapet was also missing, but on the south side the space formed a coal store for the stove used to protect the railway water tower immediately beside the bridge from frost damage.

The map shows that after the bridge the tramway turned through a right angle and ran almost as far as Cuttle Farm, which stood close to the later site of the offices of Kaye's cement works. However, no sign of the quarry could be seen in 1960, part of the site being occupied by the LNWR goods yard and the remainder covered with spoil when Kaye's works was extended by Rugby Portland Cement in the late 1930s.

Long Itchington Cement & Lime Works

Kaye's, later Rugby Portland Cement Co. Southam Works.

This works was situated about 600 yards south of the canal and 600 yards east of Coventry Road (SP 423643) (*see Chapter Seven*).

High Clays Farm

1819   Charles Handley & John Tomes
1844   George Nelson?
By 1860   Charles Nelson?   Closed by 1886

The limeworks at High Clays Farm (SP 425652), north of the Long Itchington to Stockton road was shown on the 1834 map. It was served by a private canal arm about 600 yds long, constructed in 1819 by Charles Handley and John Tomes, probably

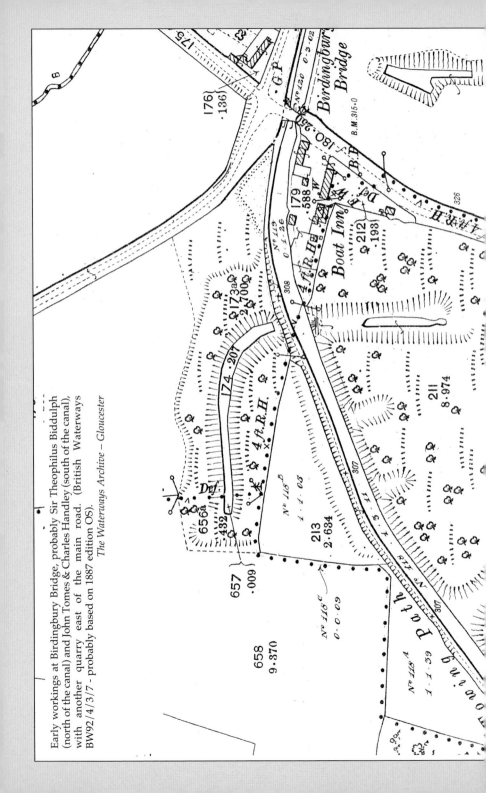

Early workings at Birdingbury Bridge, probably Sir Theophilus Biddulph (north of the canal) and John Tomes & Charles Handley (south of the canal), with another quarry east of the main road. (British Waterways BW92/4/3/7 - probably based on 1887 edition OS).

The Waterways Archive – Gloucester

following exhaustion of their quarries at Birdingbury Wharf (*see below*). The canal historian Charles Hadfield says this could refer to Kaye's arm, but as Kaye's arm originally served only the Stockton reservoir it can hardly have been considered to have been a 'private cut'. A map of the Stockton area in Faulkner's book labels it as Sitwell's Arm. The two arms joined the main canal almost opposite each other. *Portrait of a Parish* says that this works 'once had its own smaller boats and allowed the transport of stone and lime from the pits on High Clays' (pages 112-117). According to the 1860 trade directory, Charles Nelson had a lime works at Southam as well as at Stockton, and this could have been his. There are no entries for him here in either 1854 or 1863, but his father George may have operated here from 1844.

The 1886 6 in. OS map clearly shows the High Clays branch but no buildings or quarry workings are indicated. A site visit in 1970 found the canal arm little more than a ditch, with the overgrown remains of a wharf at the end. A derelict office stood by the road and the quarry workings could be seen as shallow ridges in the field north of the wharf. The works area itself was a thicket. The entrance to the branch canal was sealed by piling in the 1930s and the towpath reinstated. The bridge carrying the road over the branch was later demolished.

Blue Lias Lime & Cement Works

Greaves Bull & Lakin, later APCM

This works was situated immediately east of the bridge carrying the Long Itchington to Stockton Road over the canal by the Blue Lias inn (SP 429647) (*see Chapter Eight*).

Blue Lias Lime Works

Griffin

This works was situated beside the canal approximately midway between the Blue Lias inn and Birdingbury Wharf (SP 435650) (*see Chapter Nine*).

Birdingbury Wharf (1)

c.1793   John Tomes & Charles Handley   Closed by 1820

About 2½ miles north-east of Southam, the main Southam to Rugby road, running approximately south-west to north-east, crosses the canal at Birdingbury Wharf. Here it is immediately crossed by a lane from alongside the north bank of the canal which continues to northwards Birdingbury, about two miles away. The canal bridge is half-way round the bend which turns the canal from going north-east to south-east.

The development of limeworks around Stockton really began following the Enclosure of Stockton Lands in 1792. Stockton church was awarded a plot of approximately 13½ acres (13a-2r-4p) in 'Long Highlands', in lieu of the scattered plots it had held previously. This plot was found to contain 'a rock of limestone' which the church soon sold for £937 10s. 0d. About 4.6 acres (4a-2r-24p) was bought by the proposed Warwick & Napton Canal and the remainder was sold to Messrs Tomes & Handley of Warwick. John Tomes, of Warwick, was a solicitor and the Chairman of the Warwick & Napton, and Charles Handley, of Barford near Warwick, was its Chief Engineer. By 1807 the church had spent almost half of the proceeds on repairs to the church building, and the remainder was invested in land at Napton whose rent supported a schoolmaster in Stockton. *White's Directory* in 1850 noted that the present schools had been built in 1844 (boys) and 1841 (girls), and the pupils comprised 33 boys and 19 girls. The *VCH* states that quarries 'north and east of the village [Stockton] were the first to be worked', which fits the area of Birdingbury Wharf.

The 25 in. OS map marks an area on the south bank of the canal, west of the road, as being 'old quarries' with an area of 8.9 acres. This is presumably the quarry operated by Tomes & Handley. It became exhausted by 1820, which was probably the reason for them opening quarries at High Clays (*see above*) in 1819. Faulkner's map of the Stockton area shows two 'sites of arms to old quarry'. One of these was in this area, running along the southern boundary as far as the road. The 1834 map showed an L-shaped feature, possibly a disused canal, in the area between the Boat Inn (at the cross roads), the canal, and the later route of the LNWR. A short branch canal could easily have served these workings, especially bearing in mind the official positions of the proprietors. In 1850 *White's Directory* noted that 'about nine acres [of the former quarry] has been left in so bad a state that it is let at the yearly rent of £2-10s. [£150]'.

Birdingbury Wharf (2)

1802	Sir Theophilus Biddulph
1844	George Nelson?
By 1860	Charles Nelson?

In the western quadrant of the crossroads on the north bank of the canal, the 1834 map shows what appears to be a small quarry with a possible canal stretching 150 yards due west, although it has is no label. Later large scale maps show this as 2.7 acres of rough ground. Sir Theophilus Biddulph is recorded as building branch canals into quarries at Birdingbury in 1802 and 1819, and this small quarry is probably the earlier one.

The 1834 OS map shows a large limeworks in the southern quadrant of the crossroads, just south of the canal (SP 439651). Faulker's map marks the course of an old canal arm here, which could have served this works and its quarry as well. The 1886 6 in. OS map has no indication of a limeworks here but marks a narrow disused quarry extending south for about 300 yards from the canal which presumably had once served these works. When the LNWR branch line from Weedon to Leamington was constructed in the 1890s a bridge was built to carry the new railway over this old quarry.

This works may have been operated by George Nelson from 1844, and later by his son Charles before his new works was built several hundred yards to the east.

Stockton Lime & Cement Works

Charles Nelson, later RPC

This works was situated beside the canal about 500 yards east of Birdingbury Wharf, ½ north of Stockton village (SP 442648) (*see Chapter Ten*).

Chapter Seven

Southam Works

1854	Thomas Oldham, later William Oldham
1870	Kaye & Tatham
c.1875	Kaye
1880	Kaye & Co. Ltd
1934	Rugby Portland Cement Co. Ltd
1999	Readymixed Concrete (RMC) Group
2005	Cemex UK

Kiln closed 2000 but quarry still active

The Southam works of Rugby Portland Cement, operational until 2000, was situated about ¼ mile east of the main Banbury to Coventry road (A423), ½ mile south of Long Itchington and over a mile north of Southam (SP 422640). The canal is about quarter-mile north of the works, whose northern boundary was skirted by the LNWR Daventry to Marton Junction and Leamington line, opened 1st August, 1895. Both canal and railway were used to bring in the extra raw materials required, namely coal and later chalk, and to dispatch the cement and lime manufactured. *Portrait of a Parish* (pp. 112-117) describes the location in terms of travelling eastwards along the Warwick & Napton Canal:

> The next lock encountered is the 'Shop' lock, so named because ... of the workshop. Past this is an offshoot of the canal. Once simply a feeder to the canal (from the nearby reservoir), it was widened and lengthened to reach into the heart of the cement works - Kaye's Arm. On the opposite side [slightly east of Kaye's arm junction] is a blocked off arm which once had its own smaller boats and allowed the transport of stone and lime from the pits on High Clays [*see Chapter Six*].

The workshop was marked as 'Canal Works' on the 1905 25 in. OS map, and was disused on the 1939 edition.

According to *The Engineer* (1st & 8th January, 1909 'Cement Works at Southam') the 'Works were first started there in the year 1854 by the late Mr Oldham, of Southam, who realised that the deposit of limestone in the district was exactly the material with which to make cement'. Thomas Oldham included free use of the canal arm by the lime works in his will, this free use being incorporated in a number of subsequent deeds. The trade directory for 1854 lists William Oldham, farmer and railway contractor of Coventry Road, Southam, and also having lime and brick kilns. Unfortunately there is a gap of 13 years in the Warwickshire Record Office's collection of trade directories, and the previous one is 1841 which has no entry for him. However, Bartlett mentions a 'Lease for Lime Rock at Long Itchington' by J.H. Anthony to Messrs Oldhams & Witheringtons, dated 21st April, 1831. This was probably the kiln at Snowford Hill. Oldham, a major land owner in the area, probably began lime burning himself in the mid-1830s.

While the 1830s first edition OS map shows a canal arm serving the reservoir and extending beyond it, supporting Faulkner's statement that the branch was built in 1819, the works is not marked until the 1886 edition, which shows the kilns of Long Itchington Cement & Lime works east of the canal arm, with a tramway south to the

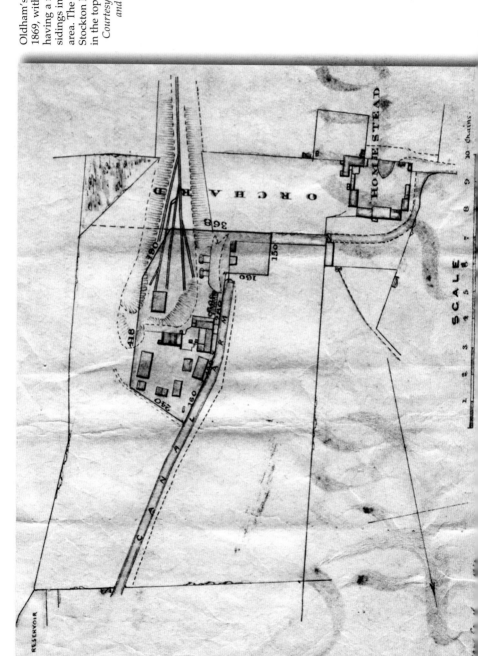

Oldham's Works in 1869, with a tramway having a number of sidings in the works area. The tip of Stockton Reservoir is in the top right corner. *Courtesy John Frearson and CEMEX/RPC Archives*

quarry. This reinforces the possibility that Oldham's original works was the one by the canal behind the Cuttle inn, supplied by a quarry close to Cuttle Farm, and that he subsequently built a new works 700 yards to the south.

Accompanying the lease dated 1st January, 1870, granted by William Oldham to Messrs Tatham Kaye & Tatham, was a map dated 1869 of the 'Long Itchington Warwickshire Estate the Property of Henry Oldham Esq RE'. It showed the works close to Cuttle Farm, a tramway south to the quarry, the canal arm, and the tip of Stockton reservoir. Maybe the extension to the branch canal, noted on the 1830 map and later known as Kaye's Arm, had been dug originally to serve the nearby quarry, and the works had been sited to take advantage of it.

The 1860 *Trade Directory* states that, 'The blue lias lime and cement are extensively manufactured in the neighbourhood [of Southam], and are considered to be the best in England. There are both lime and brick kilns'. From 1860 until 1868 the directories describe William Oldham as a farmer and hydraulic blue lias lime and patent cement manufacturer, although by 1868 he seems only to have made a small amount of Roman cement.

Oldham had been joined in his business by Lawrence Malcolm Tatham, a London lime merchant, although Tatham's name does not appear with Oldham in the local trade directories. After Oldham retired in 1868 the works and quarries were leased to Tatham Kaye & Company. Tatham and Arthur Lister Kaye had previously worked together at the Newbold and New Bilton lime and cement works on the outskirts of Rugby (*see Chapters Eleven and Twelve*). However, there appears to have been a disagreement between these two and the other partner Walker, and the Rugby partnership was dissolved in 1868, hence perhaps the new enterprise at Southam where Tatham was already involved. Captain Arthur Lister-Kaye RA (1834-1893), the second son of the second baronet, had been in the Army in Australia and had retired for health reasons. Kaye had, '... perceived that the raw materials were capable of yielding a much stronger article, and it was not long after he started operations that a cement was made that was found to possess all the properties of first-class Portland cement'.

Kaye & Co. began in 1870, with Kaye holding the works and quarry under a lease dated 1st January, 1870. There were various supplemental leases and agreements dated 30th May, 1891, 3rd May, 1900 and 30th July, 1901. The lease was for 49 years and could be terminated at the end of every seven years. The original rent was £515 per annum (about £23,000) plus a royalty of 4d. (about 80p) per ton of lime and cement made.

Around 1875 Tatham retired, but Kaye continued the business. He formed the limited company Kaye & Co. Ltd, registered 14th February, 1880, for the 'purchase and acquisition of manufacturing and trading business as Lime and Cement Manufacturers of Messrs Kaye & Co., and together with the cement kilns, lime kilns, ... tramways', ... and the works known as "Oldham's Patent Cement & Blue Lias Lime Works" and the trucks, waggons and boats used ...' with a capital of 2,500 £10 shares. Arthur Kaye lived at Stretton-on-Dunsmore (five miles north of the works). Edmund John Tremlett (Lt-Col RA) was joint partner with Kaye, the men having 140 shares each. The company's registered office was 10 South Wharf, Paddington, probably Tatham's offices, but it was moved to Southam on 28th January, 1882. Arthur Lister Kaye died in 1893 and was succeeded by his son Lister, later Sir Lister Lister-Kaye, who became the sixth baronet in 1955 following the deaths of relatives having either no children or no male heirs. Arthur's widow, Eugenia, assisted her son to manage the works.

A map of the works dated 1890 showed 11 circular kilns, increased to 14 soon after the LNWR branch opened, and a considerable area occupied by buildings. The route of the LNWR Marton Junction to Daventry line, opened on 1st August, 1895, bordered the works and so the provision of sidings was straightforward. The new railway removed the necessity of carting to Marton or Daventry stations, and also reduced reliance on the canal. A bridge was built east of the new station for the footpath from the Cuttle inn to the works, presumably provided for workers from Long Itchington.

The firm's profits increased slightly following construction of the LNWR and the associated private sidings, not least due to savings in the cost of fuel brought in by rail. During the seven years prior to 1906 the company paid an average dividend of 21 per cent. However, the company's works was haphazardly arranged due to the additions over the years, and so D.B. Butler AMInst CE, a cement expert of Messrs Henry Haigor & Co., 41 Old Queen Street, Westminster, was commissioned to investigate and produce a report.

Butler's report, dated 23rd March, 1906, advised the construction of an entirely new plant, saying that it would be a false economy to convert the old one. The report was accepted and a new works containing two of the new rotary kilns was planned for the meadow west of the canal wharf, close to the company's offices and stables. The new kilns would permit an annual output of 25,000 tons, with provision for expansion, compared to the output of 10,000 tons from the existing plant. The cost would be reduced from 24s. 3d to 14s. 3d. per ton (from approximately £68 to £40), and a minimum profit of 8s. (£22.60) per ton could be expected, so that it would be easy to repay any debenture stock. The cost was estimated at £30,000 (£1.7m) and Mr Butler was to supervise the work. Debentures were issued and in 1912 the capital was increased. A chimney dated 1913 still stood in 1960. New offices (still in use) were constructed in 1913.

Most British cement works were then situated on the Thames and Medway, and their cement was taken by lighter to Poplar Dock for transport inland. Attached to Butler's report was a list of freight charges to the Midlands from Poplar Dock and from Rugby. This showed that there was an average saving of 5s. 6d. (approximately £16) per ton on the Southam product, so there was little cause to fear competition from the south.

The new 'Cement Works at Southam' was described in detail in *The Engineer* of 1st and 8th January, 1909. The works was designed by William Gilbert, MInst CE, in conjunction with D.B.Butler, erection being superintended by A.H.Bristow, AMInstCE.

The cement manufacturing process at the old works began with crushing the stone to fine powder, which was then mixed with water to give a stiff slurry. The slurry was dried by spreading it on floors heated by exhaust steam. After drying, the dessicated slurry 'compo' was placed in alternate layers with coke in pot kilns and burnt. When calcination was complete the clinker formed was ground in two stages, first using French burr millstones then in two horizontal tube mills. The cement so made was of 'excellent quality'. The old process ceased once the new works came into operation. However, lime production continued, burning limestone in kilns with coke. Some of these old kilns still existed in the undergrowth near the narrow gauge engine shed in 1994.

The strata in the quarry had well defined alternating layers of limestone and clay, and so it was easy to adjust the proportions of clay and limestone to the exact ones required to make cement. The stone was fissured and loosely packed so blasting was not required. (In more recent years small blasts were made if the usual method of loosening the stone, namely drilling a hole and filling it with water, failed.) The limestone and clay beds were over 40 ft thick, resting on a thick bed of clay. The bedding planes were nearly level so water was not a problem, a sump dug through the lowest bed of clay enabling water to drain away. Stone was worked at several levels in the quarry, and conveyed to the works by narrow gauge railway. The railway had been improved by the introduction of the first locomotive in 1903, with others quickly following in 1906, 1909 (after the opening of the new works), 1911 and 1913.

The trucks of stone and clay were weighed on arrival at the works then hauled up an incline to be tipped at the feeding platform for a Hadfield type stone crusher. A certain amount of storage space for stone was necessary, since although the works were in operation continuously, the stone and clay were only quarried in the daytime. By 1909 'chemical analyses were continuously carried out, and subsequent operations were all performed in accordance with instructions from the chemical department'.

The two new rotary kilns were made by Fellner & Ziegler of Frankfort, Germany. They were 100 ft long and 7 ft diameter, with a ferro-concrete firing platform. Each kiln had three sets of bearings, near each end and in the middle, where a toothed ring was driven by gearing powered by ropes from the main driving shaft. They were the first rotary kilns in this area. Although the new plant became operational in 1908 it still had not been paid for by the outbreak of World War I, so payment had to be deferred until the cessation of hostilities.

Incoming coal was tipped into a hopper and taken by a conveyor to the drier, which used hot air from the clinker cooler. The coal was then ground to powder on site, ready to be blown into the kilns as fuel. Exhaust gases from the kilns could be led to one of two riveted iron chimneys, but usually they were diverted through a rotating drum to remove dust, and were then used to dry incoming raw materials before being discharged through a third riveted chimney. The dry materials were then ground and put into concrete bins of 350 tons capacity, sufficient to keep the plant in operation over weekends and holidays when the crusher and grinder were not working.

The clinker from the kilns was led to coolers, where it fell into tip wagons which were pushed by hand to an elevator feeding a steel hopper (280 ton capacity). This hopper was used to store the output at weekends and other times when the grinding plant was not in operation. The clinker was ground in two Krupp tube mills and the cement produced was then taken to one of three 1,500 ton 40 ft diameter concrete silos. A conveyor at the base of the silos fed the sack filling machine. Other conveyors linked the various processes within the plant.

Three Babcock & Wilcox boilers with Bennis stokers, each evaporating 5,500 lb (550 gallons) of water per hour, raised steam at 150 psi for the two Pollit & Wigzell horizontal tandem compound steam engines, one 540 hp, one 125 hp, which powered the works. (Compound engines expand the steam in two or more cylinders of increasing diameter before it is exhausted. It improves the engine's efficiency at the expense of increased complexity. Tandem compounds have the two different diameter cylinders in line, sharing the same piston rod.) Jet condensers, using cooling water from the canal, enabled the boiler water to be constantly reused. The cooling water 'is not returned directly into the canal but is led away some distance … and discharged into the canal at a point where the level is lower … [thus] keeping the condensing water much cooler than it would otherwise be'. Presumably it was drawn from the level of Kaye's arm and returned below the 'Shop' lock.

Supplementary boiler feed water also came from the canal, but was exceptionally hard so that it had to be softened by apparatus beside the boiler house.

The smaller engine could work in parallel with the larger by means of a clutch on a countershaft. Electricity was generated by two dynamos in the engine house. One dynamo, driven by shafting, had an output of 410 amp at 220 volts (90 kw), and was used for driving sundry motors in the plant. The other dynamo, which was coupled direct to a separate vertical steam engine, had an output of 80 amps at 220 volts (17.6 kw). It was used for lighting, and also for power when the main engines were not running.

The Engineer noted that, 'The works, as a whole, are exceedingly well arranged. Every advantage has been taken both of the configuration of the ground and of the railway and canal'. The works was served by three sidings from the LNWR. One served the sack-filling area, one went over the coal hoppers for both the kilns and boiler house, while the last led to a coal storage area behind the boilers. This one was carried on a series of concrete piers, erected by Kaye's staff, and terminated near the end of the canal arm. Cost analysis had shown that for structures of equal strength the reinforced concrete was cheaper than steel. The article finished by publishing analysis and test results which showed that Kaye's cement was better than the requirements of the BSI specification.

Trade directories record other developments. In 1900 Kaye & Co. had the telegraphic address 'Kaye, Southam' and by 1912 the firm had a telephone (Southam 2), with two lines by 1932. The capital was increased by £20,000 (approximately £1.1m) on 29th October, 1912, to fund the recent extensions. Also in October 1912 construction began of the Model Village for employees, on a site opposite the works entrance. The village eventually passed to the Rugby Portland Cement company, and by 1996 houses were being sold as they became vacant.

The firm's trademark was an equilateral triangle standing on one vertex, with several cutouts making a K. The Kaye symbol on mortar, concrete, and ferroconcrete was a square standing on one corner, with a second horizontal square inside the first. The company had branches at King Edward Road, Birmingham, at 5 New Brown Street, Manchester, and at 81 Cauldon Road, Stoke-on-Trent.

During World War I some women were employed in the quarry. By 1916, and possibly a few years earlier, Kaye bought the Stockton works of J. Griffin, mainly for its stone reserves and for the quarry to be a reservoir (*see Chapter Nine*). It was potentially a most useful asset, despite the water being 40 degrees harder than Southam, although the 1920s recession probably prevented this potential from being realised.

The 1928 *Concrete Year Book* stated that Kaye had had a good reputation for over 70 years and the cement 'has always been accounted the strongest it is possible to obtain'. The cement industry was very competitive in the late 1920s, with a trade war between the Blue Circle and Red Triangle groups. Kaye suffered a lack of orders, and a quarrymen's strike in 1929/30 due to muck (surplus clay) being sent in with the stone probably aggravated the situation. As a result, Kaye succumbed, going into receivership and selling out to the Rugby Portland Cement Co. in early 1934, becoming the first of its acquisitions.

The new owners extended the works in 1936, which then had only two chimneys. The new plant took all the material quarried, both clay and stone, and in order to increase the calcium carbonate content of the kiln feed to the level required for cement manufacture it used chalk from the company's quarries at Totternhoe, near Dunstable, Bedfordshire (*see Appendix Two*). In 1957 the plant was again modernized, with a kiln 110 m-long (361 ft), which was then the largest in Europe. Now it had only a single chimney. The large increases in fuel prices in the 1970s resulted in the 'semi-wet' process being introduced about 1980, to economize on fuel. A press house was constructed to reduce the moisture content of the input to the kiln to 17 per cent. By 1996 it was realised there were also environmental reasons for reducing the amount of fuel used. Dust emission from the chimney was prevented by electrostatic precipitators.

In the 1960s the works had an annual production of about 500,000 tons of cement, 3 per cent of British production. Each day it used 2,000 tons chalk, and 350 tons of coal from the Midlands, particularly Derbyshire. In addition, 500 tons of gypsum were used each week. The gypsum was ground with the clinker to control the setting time. The daily output of cement was 2,000 tons, dispatched either in paper sacks or in bulk. By now most of the output went by road, although still some cement was sent by rail and a little by canal, both of these methods having been much more important in earlier years. The firm was a major employer in Southam and Long Itchington, employing 210 people in the works and another 80 as drivers.

The quarry has a 10 m (34 ft) thick bed of clay beneath 24 m (80 ft) of stone. Once chalk began to be brought in from Tottenhoe the old quarry workings were reworked for clay, although the clay banks of discarded material were ignored because it was oxidized and contaminated. From around 1982, Southam clay was exported by road to Rugby works, following the closure of Rugby's quarry. By 1996 the quarry output was shared between the two works, with three days' production, stone and clay, for Southam and two days' production, clay only, for Rugby. The 2006 edition of the OS Explorer 2½ in. map shows that the quarry occupies most of the triangular area south of the works between the main roads to Coventry (A423) and Rugby (A426).

For 30 years chalk was brought in by train from Tottenhoe, but in 1964 a private pipeline was opened (see Appendix Four), and henceforth chalk arrived suspended in water as slurry, which was stored in two large tanks constructed north of the railway.

Southam ceased production early in 2000, following the commissioning of a new kiln at Rugby. However, except for the period 2003-6, the quarry remained in operation, supplying Rugby works with stone and clay ground to 50 mm (2 in.), with some 2,500 tons per week in 2010. Sub-contractors driving either 8-wheel rigid or articulated lorries convey it to Rugby. Beginning in the 1960s, cement kiln dust from Rugby was dumped in the quarry as landfill.

Ready Mixed Concrete (RMC) acquired RPC in 2000, and was itself taken over by Cemex in 2005. The 1913 office building now houses laboratories for the whole Cemex Group. There was a proposal to construct a plant at Southam to manufacture Climafuel for Rugby's kiln from a mixture of household, commercial and industrial waste, but planning consent was refused in November 2009.

The 1869 map accompanying Kaye's lease showed kilns on the east bank of the canal arm served by a number of tracks, with a single track running south to the quarry. According to a letter Kaye wrote some 34 years later, the works and quarry then contained '4,781 yards … of Railway Metals' i.e. sufficient for about 1⅓ miles of track. Allowing for numerous branches to different parts of the face this is comparable to the amount of track shown on the 1888 25 in. OS map. At that date there were only two tracks in the works area, which joined, and then after 500 yards the single track divided into two branches at the entrance of the quarry. Each quarry branch turned west then south and had a loop before reaching the working face. Each face was about 400 yards long, one working eastwards and the other westwards.

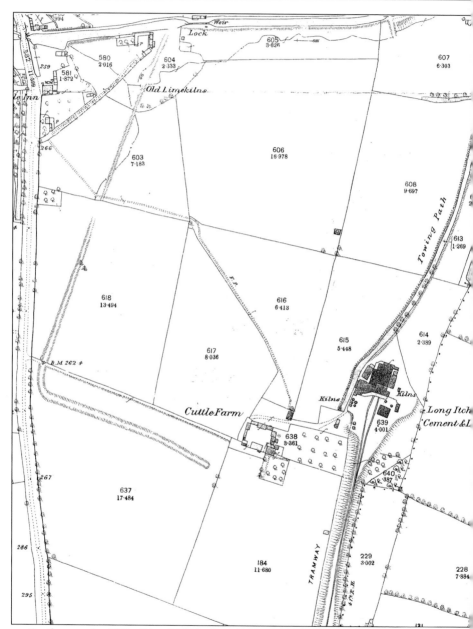

Southam works, 1887 edition OS 25 in. sheet 34.15. Kaye's works is enlarged but is still entirely on the east bank of the canal branch. If the map is correct, the tramway in the works area has been simplified but still heads south to the quarry. The tip of Stockton Reservoir is on the right hand edge, and the Warwick & Napton Canal is across the top. Note the embankment then cutting from the Old Limekilns east of the Cuttle inn to Cuttle Farm.   *Crown Copyright*

The 1905 edition 25 in. OS map shows the tramway from the quarry dividing into three parallel tracks as it approached the works. The eastern and central tracks each split into two and entered a large building, probably a store for stone, while the western track probably served a tip to feed the kilns. A siding from the easternmost track served a building, probably the original engine shed. There was also an isolated section of track about 70 yards long running along the canal bank in front of the kilns. It began at an isolated pair of kilns about 20 yards beyond the end of the canal, ran along the canal bank past other kilns, and finally climbed up to the loading bank beside the LNWR, being joined there by a line serving the eastern side of the works. This was presumably a hand- or possibly horse-operated system to carry lime from the kilns either to the boats or the railway, and maybe it also served a packing area within the main building.

Years later, this map was used by the Grand Union Canal as the basis of a plan showing the route of pipes taking cooling water from the canal to the works (British Waterways' Archives BW58/11/7/30, dated 26th March, 1930). At least the main line railway had been relabelled 'London Midland & Scottish Railway'!

Following the opening of the LNWR branch line from Daventry to Leamington in 1895, an agreement dated 2nd June, 1896 permitted Kaye to construct a loading bank 670 yards east of Southam & Long Itchington station having '105¼ yards of tramway on LNWR land maintained by trader at own cost'. The loading bay was served by a single standard gauge siding, apparently an extension of the headshunt of the nearby goods yard. Towards the western end of this extension a narrow gauge line curved away from the main line, ran along the bank of the branch canal past the west side of the works and six kilns, to terminate near two isolated kilns beyond the end of the branch. A second line left the loading bank to run past the east side of the works, terminating close to another group of six kilns. By the time the narrow gauge railway closed in 1956, and probably since about 1910 (bearing in mind the construction of the 1908 works), the loading bank was the storage area for locomotive and excavator coal. In 1897 Kaye noted that the new LNWR connection had 'improved facilities to the supply and storage of coal and coke, therefore effecting a saving of 1s. to 1s. 3d. (£3 to £3.70) per ton in the carriage of such goods brought by rail'.

Kaye's Private Letter Books in Cemex Archives show that in July 1903, Lister-Kaye was '... rather busy, planning out the alterations in the quarry for the Loco. ... I have ordered a Loco. Price £520 delivered here from Peckett & Sons, of Bristol, who are the best people & where Nelsons got their 3 from. We shall not get it for 7 weeks, but when it gets to Work, I think it should make a considerable reduction. I have enquiries out for suitable wagons, but have not decided on anything yet.' This suggests the steel V-skips were introduced at the same time as the locomotives. The cement storage shed was also being extended. On Wednesday 23rd September Lister-Kaye wrote, 'On Tuesday next I am going down to Bristol for the day, to see the new Loco put through her pacings & if satisfactory, hope to get her to work the following week'. On Thursday 1st October he wrote again: 'I was very pleased with the Loco on Tuesday, & am now very busy making the necessary alterations in Quarry to rails etc. as I expect it here early next week, & there is a lot to be done.' Later, on Monday 12th October he wrote, 'The Loco has arrived, & we landed her to the top of the bank safely on Saturday [10th October assumed]. She will not start for a few days, the incessant rain has hindered us so. We are nearly ground out of stone again because of the wet.' On Tuesday 20th October, he 'Was so busy with the Loco yesterday ... We had the loco out for first time under steam & again today, to try the road etc., & found all satisfactory. We shall not be in full swing for a few days yet.'

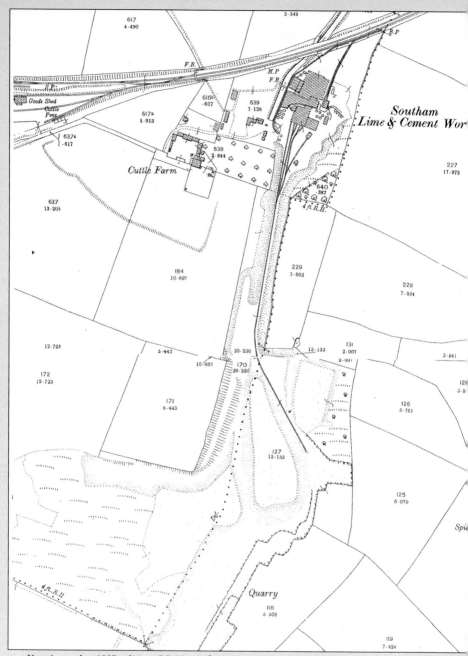

Kaye's works, 1905 edition OS 25 in. sheets 34.15 and 40.3. The recently constructed LNWR Daventry to Leamington branch crosses the top of the map. The tramway runs south to the quarry, with what is probably the original engine shed at the end of a siding. Note the independent tramway linking the east and west sides of the works with the canal and a loading bank beside a siding, effectively the headshunt for the goods yard. The presumed face of the old quarry extends further east than is shown on the 1887 map. The proximity of the old face (below Cuttle Farm) to both the works and the branch canal tie in with Oldham's early use of this site.

This first locomotive was very similar to the three which Peckett & Son had supplied to the nearby firm of Charles Nelson, but built to the slightly wider gauge of 1 ft 11½ in. Five more followed over the next 20 years.

There was a period in the mid-1900s, and possibly before, when the railway was laid on the lip of the quarry, with temporary tracks on the various levels. Wagons were then hoisted in and out of the quarry by steam cranes. It was probably the introduction of steam excavators in 1914 which caused the railway thereafter to be laid on the quarry floor.

The 1905 25 in. map shows four tracks entering the stone store. Just outside it, to the east, was a small building at the end of a siding which was probably the original engine shed. There was a weighbridge on the line from the quarry, about 250 yards south of the stone store. The narrow gauge layout does appear not to have been altered significantly following the construction of either of the new works in 1908 and 1936.

The quarry railway was situated right at the back of the works, on the eastern boundary, at a height of about 20 ft above the canal wharf and main works level. The line terminated in a large corrugated iron stone storage shed, about 75 ft by 150 ft, which was like two Dutch barns built side by side. The tipping level was reached by a long sloping embankment. Just outside the building the track divided in two, and each track then divided in two again, so that four lines ran the length of the building. They were supported by concrete pillars (originally wooden) about 10 ft high. The stone was stockpiled here in dry weather to avoid feeding the crushers with wet material. In addition, wet stone was tipped here to dry. More track was laid on the floor of the shed for wagons being loaded from the stockpile.

Immediately east of the stone store was the corrugated iron engine shed, approximately 50 ft wide x 25 ft long, and capable of holding all the locomotives on its three tracks. The single track section furthest from the stone store was probably the original building. A smoke vent ran the length of the ridge of each roof. Each track had a pit extending either side of the running rails, which were carried on girders, so that the motion outside the frames could be easily reached. Outside the back of the shed was a water tank, on a massive brick base, which supplied each road within the shed. At some date a lifting gantry was built on one of the tracks outside the shed. A coal siding ran into the ground floor of the stone store, presumably so that coaling could be done in the dry. Beside the stone store embankment was a sand drying oven.

Immediately west of the stone store was a row of three old lime kilns. Track was laid past their mouths so that they could easily be charged with coal or stone. Other sidings served the ground floor of the stone store. One line past the kilns terminated in a brick wagon repair shop that once employed three men. Situated on the western of three parallel loop tracks south of the old kilns was the crusher installed around 1937, near the site of the original crusher. South of these loops was a long siding, and south again was a loop with a weighbridge on one track.

Four sets of tracks converged at the south end of the narrow gauge yard. From west to east, they served (1) the weighbridge, crusher and old lime kilns, (2) the high level sidings in the stone store, (3) the locomotive shed and (4) the works coal yard. This line descended past the locomotive shed to the coal yard on the old loading bank, where narrow gauge wagons were loaded with fuel for the locomotives, steam excavators and kilns.

The coal yard line had once continued west then south to the canal wharf, as previously described. During the alterations and extensions in the mid-1930s this line was extended right through the works and was used to carry spoil to a tip beside

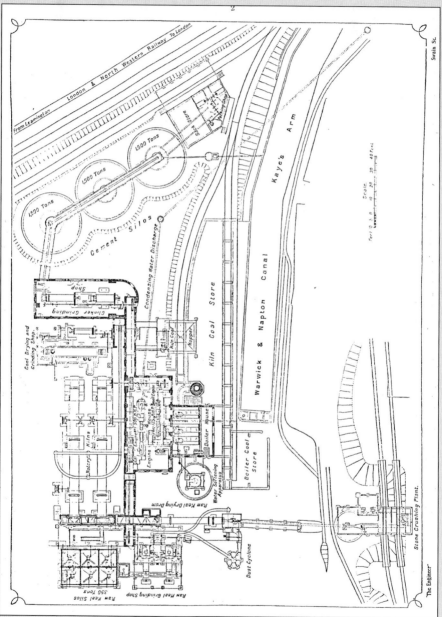

Plan illustrating the January 1909 article about the works in *The Engineer*, showing the new standard gauge sidings and two narrow gauge lines serving the

Southam cement works looking south-east on 12th September, 1938. The LNWR branch runs diagonally across the view, bridging the canal arm close to the left-hand edge. In the bottom right-hand corner is the wooded cutting of the former Cuttle tramway, seen in the illustration om page 78 (*centre*). A footpath from Long Itchington followed the diagonal hedge to reach the works near the silos by a footbridge over the railway. The 1908 works is behind the silos, and the 1936 RPC plant is to the right. The original works was on the further bank of the canal, in front of the later stone store, above the silos. The narrow gauge railway runs along the back of the site, with several rakes of skips visible. The quarry is in the top right corner, partially obscured by the plume from the chimneys. In the centre of the photograph there is a row of coal trucks, with *Southam* standing on a siding in front of them. The later narrow gauge and the standard gauge coal hoist are both visible behind the modern works building. Kaye's offices, built in 1913, stand at the end of the approach road. Coventry Road is in the right-hand corner, and the main road to Rugby is on the far side of the quarry, following the line of the diagonal hedge.

English Heritage, NMR Aerofilms Collection

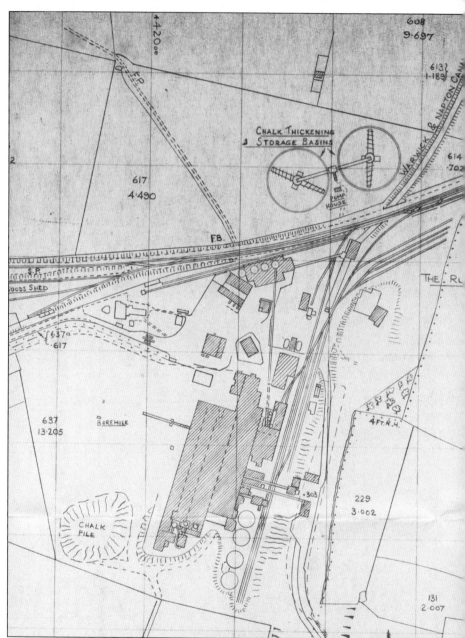

Southam works after 1972 track alterations. The narrow gauge engine shed and stone store still stand, and the dumper road leads south from the stone tip towards the quarry. Two tracks enter the standard gauge engine shed, and the coal hoist is by the scissors crossover at the south end of the yard.

Courtesy John Frearson and CEMEX/RPC Archives

the approach road, which explains why nothing is now visible of the old quarry served by the tramway to the kilns by the Cuttle. When the alterations were complete most of the line was lifted and replaced by a standard gauge siding. The remainder was removed when a new crusher was built in the early 1950s.

Proceeding towards the quarry, the railway climbed steadily. Soon it was joined by a line from the west which served the crusher (and its loop) installed in 1950. The later concrete road joined, and obliterated, the trackbed here. Still climbing, the railway ran through a deep cutting and ran along the base of an old spoil and clay tip. The ground to the east had been quarried and contained a lake. The summit was reached shortly before the entrance to the quarry, and the line then descended into the pit. A passing loop was provided halfway, near the quarry entrance, and another in the quarry near the face. Track within the quarry was laid and moved as required, and usually the line ran parallel to the face.

There had been a line up the clay tip, horse worked until the 1920s. Their stables were at the top of the tip. In later years a conveyor took the clay, picked by hand from the stone, to the top of the tip. The conveyor discharged into German wagons which were pushed along light track to the actual tip. The tip fell out of use in 1936 with the opening of the new kiln which could take all the stone and clay quarried, provided extra chalk was supplied to keep the correct proportion of calcium carbonate. The large German skips were scrapped when the tip closed.

Accidents happened from time to time. One involved John Cooke, a spare driver and mechanic who could also 'take a hand in any kind of mechanical work'. On Saturday 2nd April, 1904 he 'was bringing in an iron Tip Wagon from the Quarries to the Works, & had just descended an incline, at the foot of which are Points, he was riding on the back of the wagon & thought the wagon would open the points, but it did not & jumping off the rails, caused him to fall, & his leg caught on the Coupling hook, which went into his leg by the Shin Bone. The accident is not severe, & was brought about by the man's carelessness'.

A valuation of Kaye & Co. in 1909 included two locomotives and 90 wagons.

Although modernization undertaken by Rugby Portland Cement in 1936 did not greatly affect the quarry railway, the 1950s expansion and modernization of the works resulted in its closure. As the hump between quarry and works limited the loads that could be hauled, it was decided to remove it and lower the trackbed by some 12 ft. The work was done, but instead of the railway a single track concrete road 14 ft wide was laid on the new formation by G.R. Yeoman of Coventry. The narrow gauge railway closed on Saturday 20th October, 1956, being replaced by a pair of 6-wheel Foden dumpers carrying 15 tons, which were faster and cheaper than the railway. Three Volvo BM articulated vehicles, capacity 20 tonnes, driven by 186 hp turbo-charged diesel engine having hydraulic drive with automatic power shift transmission and full locks on all differentials, were in use by 1996.

At the time the railway closed the daily output of the quarry was 800 to 1,200 tons of stone, and the face was about 50ft high. The quarry floor was a 6 ft bed of clay. By 1960 only three men were employed at the quarry face, plus the dumper drivers, in contrast to some 200 when hand excavation was employed, although this figure includes those on haulage as well.

A week after the railway closed, on 27th October, 1956, members of the Birmingham Locomotive Club (Industrial Locomotive Information Section) - now the Industrial Railway Society - visited the works. All the locomotives were hauled out of the shed and positioned in the yard for the photographers. Various individuals, including the author, made visits over the next four years until all the narrow gauge stock had gone.

Above: Thought to be Kaye's quarry (or maybe Newbold RPC). A gang of quarrymen pose while loading a wooden open wagon with stone. Note the metal strapping, with lifting eyes at the upper end, near the corners of the wagon, and the way the strapping avoided the opening door. Also note the piece of light chain under the wheel to hold the wagon in position.

Alan Griffin, Feldon Photographic Archive

Right: The head of Kaye's Arm off the Warwick & Napton Canal on 4th May, 1975. The original works was along the left-hand bank, the 1909 works was off to the right, and the 1936 works is ahead. The tall structure in the left background is the coal tippler.

A.H. Faulkner

Illustration from *The Engineer*, January 1909, 'Quarry face showing stratification'. Note the skip wagons on the quarry floor, apparently loaded by the men with wheelbarrows from the plank bridges, and a steam crane hoisting a loaded wagon. *Author's Collection*

Another illustration from *The Engineer*, January 1909, showing the top of the quarry, with two locomotives, *Jurassic* and *Neozoic*, neither with nameplates. Note the iron tank wagons to carry water to the steam crane used to hoist the skips out of the quarry. *Author's Collection*

Stone store with elevated railway, and the three-road engine shed with a hoist on 3rd September, 1959. The frame of an old Motor Rail locomotive stands on the elevated track. Note the shape of the concrete supports for the elevated track. The line to the coal yard descended an incline at the far right.   *Author*

Shelter for the narrow gauge stone tip, with the standard gauge coal hoist behind. Note the wide steel channel supporting the bodies of the skips (*compare to top picture on page 103*).
Courtesy of Rugby Cement, Bob Darvill Collection

The track across the course of the replacement concrete road and at the crusher had been lifted immediately after closure and the road laid so that the concrete could set over the weekend. The line down to the coal yard was also lifted quickly, and the rest followed. Much of the track was lifted as complete panels with sleepers by W. Twigg, of Matlock, who sold them for re-use. Abelson of Birmingham also purchased a small quantity of track materials. By 1958 the only track left was in and around the locomotive shed, and that went soon after.

G.R. Yeoman laid only a single track concrete road, and quite soon afterwards RPC added a number of passing places. The narrow gauge yard became a dump for unwanted machinery, and nature reclaimed the rest. By 1996 only the larger part of the engine shed was still standing, used as a store, and ivy covered the water tower.

The railway was 1 ft 11½ in. gauge. In its later years it was laid using flat bottom rail in 18 ft lengths weighing 20 or 30 lb./yard. The rail leased from Oldham in 1870 appears to have been 40 lb./yd, which Kaye wanted to replace in 1904 with new 18 lb./yd rail. Kaye had a buyer for the old rails, but Oldham wanted the replacements to have the same total weight, and 90 tons (10,500 yards) was agreed. Most sleepers were wood, 3 ft 6 in. x 6 in. x 3 in., at 3 ft 3 in. centres, but there were some concrete sleepers 4 ft x 7 in. x 4 in. Some points were prefabricated with steel sleepers, the whole assembly then being laid on wooden sleepers. Parts of the main line and works yard had been relaid in 1939. An enthusiast who visited in November 1933 found that 'the 2ft-gauge track which was laid entirely on concrete sleepers afforded very smooth running' (*Railway Magazine*, March 1994).

Horses were used initially, and lasted on the spoil tip until the 1920s when they were displaced by locomotives, probably the petrol ones. There were then five or six horses. When they worked on the tip they learned to step from between the rails when the traces slackened at the summit. Wagons ran down the tip by gravity, with horse and driver in pursuit. Derailments at the bottom were not unknown! The horses were well cared for, and their drivers would return after work to have unofficial races! Trains up the tip comprised four wagons, but this may refer to locomotive haulage, using a petrol locomotive.

The 1909 article in *The Engineer* described the operation of the railway:

> Lines of light railway are run at various levels [in the quarry], and the materials are loaded into tipping trucks and hauled from the quarry by small locomotives [two at that time]. Some of the trucks which are filled at the intermediate levels are lifted bodily by jib cranes and dropped on to the rails at the upper level. Up till some little while ago horse haulage only was employed, but we understand that the introduction of the locomotives [in 1903] and cranes has very considerably reduced the cost of quarrying.
>
> The distance from the quarry face to the works is something over a quarter of a mile, and the railway line just before it reaches the latter passes over a weighbridge. Each separate truck of material is weighed, and as all the tare weights of wagons are known, an accurate record is kept of all the material going into the works.

An illustration accompanying the article showed a steam crane on the lip of the quarry hoisting complete wagons, frame as well as body, using a chain sling with two arms, attached to diagonally opposite corners of the wagon underframe. A second illustration showed a gang of six quarrymen at work on a level about 6 ft above the floor of the quarry. They were loading stone into wheelbarrows, which were pushed along a plank and tipped into V-skips on tracks on the quarry floor. Assuming the quarry had followed local practice and had always been worked on a number of levels, before the cranes were introduced there must have been one or

Ruston No. 30 steam shovel loading stone into a hopper for transfer into narrow gauge skips. The excavator and hopper are both mounted on rails to facilitate movement as the face receded. The excavator's fireman is standing on its rear platform.

Courtesy of Rugby Cement, Author's Collection

View of quarry face in 1920s. A steam excavator loads a hopper incorporating a screen. The stone is transferred to skips, while conveyors take the clay to a tip in old workings.

Courtesy of Rugby Cement (Aerofilms), Author's Collection

Screen 'Rumbler' in quarry, obscuring the excavator it serves (just the top of its jib is visible). On the left a conveyor transports clay to a tip. A shunting horse stands beyond the loaded wagons. Several skips stand on an intermediate quarry level beyond the steam crane. Note the curved supports for the skip bodies (*compare to lower picture page 100*). *Alan Griffin, Feldon Photographic Archive*

Summit of narrow gauge line at the entrance to the quarry, with the replacement concrete road some 12-14 ft lower, 11th July, 1961. *Author*

more inclines, presumably operated by steam winches, to transfer wagons in and out of the workings.

Steam locomotives took over main line haulage from 1903, while horses were retained for shunting at the quarry and works until there were sufficient locomotives for all purposes. At one time five or six locomotives had been in steam daily, but in the last years only two were required. One worked to and from the quarry and the other at the crusher. Each locomotive had a driver and 'rope runner' (shunter).

There were four rakes of 14 to 16 wagons, each train holding about 24 tons of stone. Trains were always pulled in each direction on the main line. The steep gradient down to the weighbridge by the crusher was a hazard, and trains sometimes had difficulty in stopping. To help ensure that the driver stopped in the right place for each loaded wagon to be weighed there was a series of 16 white pegs a foot high beside the track, spaced a wagon length apart.

The railway did not operate at night, except for a brief period during World War II. At this time of peak demand, mills designed to produce 15 tons per hour produced 21 or 22 tons. The cement was taken from the silos for bagging as soon as it fell in from the kiln, and the bags were then too hot to touch!

The stone was dug by hand until rail-mounted steam excavators were introduced in 1914. As in other local quarries, overburden and clay was taken in barrows along planks supported by wooden towers to be tipped in old workings, and the stone was loaded into the wagons. Until the mid-1930s, when the works used the clay as well as the stone, the steam shovels discharged into a portable rail-mounted steel hopper. The hopper fed a screen, so that stone dropped into the narrow gauge wagons and the clay was taken by conveyor to the tip. Coal and water for the steam excavators was brought into the quarry by rail. The track for the excavators had to be extended every seven to ten days as the face receded. Latterly there were three steam excavators, dating from the 1920s, but they fell out of use after 1956-57 when electric excavators were introduced. For a few years two of them stood derelict in the quarry.

One type of excavator used was the Ruston No. 30 Steam Shovel. This was supported on rails, apparently standard gauge, and was carried on two four-wheel bogies. The rear half of the body contained a horizontal boiler, with the fireman and water tank at the rear and the chimney coming out of the roof in the middle. The machinery was in the other half of the body, with the jib mounted on the end. The jib could be slewed, but for only about 80 degrees either side of the longitudinal axis of the excavator.

The nearby works of Charles Nelson at Stockton had introduced steam locomotives on its 21 in. gauge railway in 1897, and by 1901 three similar Peckett 0-6-0ST were working there. This obviously influenced Kaye, as no less than six very similar Peckett locomotives (but 23½ in. gauge) were delivered to Southam between 1903 and 1923. Over the years a number of petrol and diesel locomotives were also obtained.

Although a photograph taken in 1908 shows two locomotives, neither with nameplates, at quite an early date most of the steam locomotives were fitted with brass plates on their tanks with the names of appropriate geological periods. The Neozoic includes the Mesozoic; the Mesozoic includes the Jurassic and Triassic, and the Jurassic includes the Upper and Lower Liassic. The stone quarried at Southam belongs to the Lower Liassic period.

The locomotive fleet grew steadily, producing a fleet of very similar 0-6-0ST engines. *Jurassic* in 1903 showed the advantages of locomotive haulage and a second one, *Neozoic*, came in 1906. The first *Liassic* in 1909 could have been in response to the increased output obtainable from the modernized plant. *Triassic* was bought in 1911 and *Mesozoic* in 1913. The second *Liassic*, which carried no name until 1943, was the last Peckett and came in 1923. Then, for unknown reasons, but which could well have been the promise of rapid delivery to meet an urgent requirement, a nameless Bagnall 0-4-0ST was bought in 1924.

It is tempting to think that the second *Liassic* could have been ordered for the former Griffin limeworks at Stockton which Kaye had taken over (*see Chapter Nine*). Being the only locomotive on that site could then account for the lack of a name. If it had then been found unsuitable for some reason (for example by reason of weight, height or wheelbase), or if a second locomotive was immediately required, it could have resulted in the order of the Bagnall in 1924. Unfortunately for this theory, Kaye appears to have taken over Griffin's works by 1916 so there had been a number of years to use some of the Southam Pecketts there. The mystery remains.

The first petrol locomotive was bought second-hand in 1918, followed by a new one in 1920. They were used for sundry light jobs, which included displacing horses on the spoil heap. A third was bought in the 1930s. Once RPC Halling works in Kent no longer required its fleet of narrow gauge diesel locomotives they were transferred to Southam in 1955, but did little work as the system closed the following year.

Three locomotives, two Pecketts and the Bagnall, were scrapped in 1943. After the closure in October 1956 all of the four remaining steam locomotives found homes in preservation, and all still survive, unlike the diesels, all of which were scrapped over the next few years, even the one which went for preservation.

Triassic was the first to leave for preservation, going in August 1957 to J.B. Latham in Surrey. The other locomotives took some time to disperse, and were all still present when the author made his first visit on 6th August, 1958. Their unusual names made a strong impression! On the right-hand road of the engine shed were Motor Rail 1908, the two Orenstein & Koppel diesels, and *Jurassic*. *Mesozoic* was alone on the central road, and on the left-hand road were *Liassic*, Hunslet 2837 (frame and wheels only), and Ruston & Hornsby 168437. The red-painted frames of an old Motor Rail locomotive stood at the top of the embankment to the stone store.

By January 1960 both Motor Rail locomotives had disappeared, and the remains of the two Orenstein & Koppels lay outside the shed. Eighteen months later, in July 1961, *Mesozoic* was the sole occupant of the shed, *Jurassic*, *Liassic* and the Ruston having gone for preservation, while the remains of the Hunslet lay outside, leaning against one of the doors. Eventually it, too, went for scrap.

It is convenient to include the three Peckett locomotives at Charles Nelson's works when describing Kaye's locomotives. Nelson's locomotives were: *Gamecock* (No. 678 of 1897), *Niras* (785 of 1899), and *Jurassic* (918 of 1901), the names being painted on the tanks. Kaye's, latterly distinguished by cast brass nameplates, were: *Jurassic* (1008 of 1903), *Neozoic* (1119 of 1906), *Liassic* (1216 of 1909), *Triassic* (1270 of 1911), *Mesozoic* (1327 of 1913) and *Liassic* (1632 of 1923). In later years the two named *Jurassic* could be distinguished easily by the presence or absence of a nameplate.

Peckett referred to Nelson's locomotives as the 'Gamecock' class, although Nelson's *Jurrasic* is also referred to as the 'Jurassic' class, and was illustrated as such in their catalogue. The other locomotives were given variously as 'Jurassic' or 7 in. class. Whatever their name, these Pecketts were neat outside-framed saddle tanks with slender chimneys, having 7 in. x 10 in. outside cylinders which drove 1 ft 8 in. diameter driving wheels. Coal was carried in a bunker across the rear of the cab. The class was the first true narrow gauge design built by Peckett, the firm's previous

Jurassic, Peckett 1008, at an early date, probably 'as built', with the name painted on the tank. The whistle is mounted on the cab roof and the tank filler has a lift-out lid. Compare with the official photograph in Peckett's catalogue, on page 168. *Alan Griffin, Feldon Photographic Archive*

Jurassic, now with nameplates, whistle mounted on the front of the cab, and a hinged lid for the tank filler, with a wooden wagon for supplying coal to the excavators.

Alan Griffin, Feldon Photographic Archive

Jurassic in front of the ramp to the stone store, 1953.   *F. Jones*

Jurassic and Ruston & Hornsby 168437 in August 1962, just delivered to the Lincolnshire Coast Light Railway, Cleethorpes. Note the Ruston's 'keyhole' cab.   *J. Stancliffe*

Neozoic, Peckett 1119, at an early date without nameplates, with lift-out lid on the tank and whistle on the cab roof. Note the handle on the skip's body support frame for attaching lifting chains when being hoisted in or out of the quarry. *Allan Griffin Collection*

Liassic (1), Peckett 1216. Maybe delivery of this locomotive saw the introduction of nameplates and hinged lids on the tank filler, although the whistle is still on the cab roof. Note the sandboxes on the footplate of these first three locomotives. *Alan Griffin, Feldon Photographic Archive*

Mesozoic, Peckett 1327, in 1953, after its wartime rebuild (I have not seen a photograph taken before it). Note the deeper smokebox sandboxes, the square patch on its tank, and the unusual smokebox door. *F. Jones*

Mesozoic at work, 29th September, 1956. Note the support for the skip body. *G. Alliez*

Drawing of 'Jurassic' class 2 ft gauge 0-6-0ST *Triassic* Peckett 1270 of 1911. Note that this is the later design, 6 inches longer than the earlier locomotives, with detail differences (particularly the size and position of sandboxes) compared to other members of the class.

Narrow Gauge Railway Society www.ngrs.org

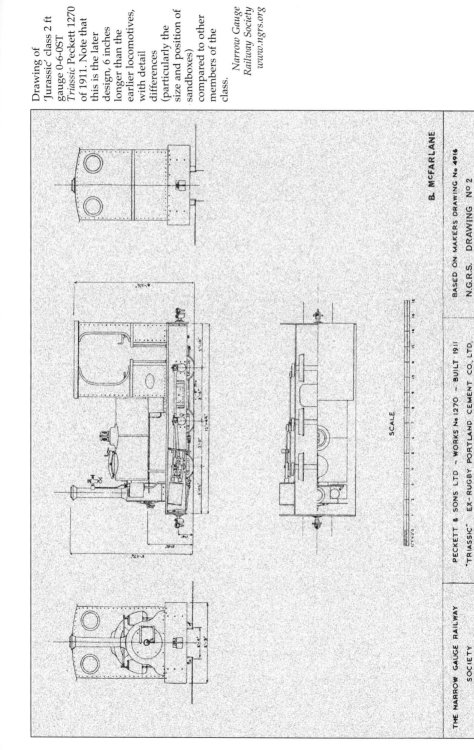

SCALE

B. McFARLANE

THE NARROW GAUGE RAILWAY SOCIETY

PECKETT & SONS LTD – WORKS № 1270 – BUILT 1911
"TRIASSIC" EX-RUGBY PORTLAND CEMENT CO. LTD.

BASED ON MAKERS DRAWING № 4916
N.G.R.S. DRAWING № 2

Triassic, Peckett 1270. Note small sandboxes on the smokebox and the whistle on the cab roof.

A. Griffin Collection

Triassic in the quarry, with a rake of skips for loading by the steam excavator. Note the wide steel channel supporting the bodies of the skips (*compare to top picture page 103*).

Courtesy of Rugby Cement

Triassic beside the embankment to the stone store in 1953, with the whistle mounted on the cab front.   *F. Jones*

Triassic outside the engine shed for the enthusiasts' visit, 27th October 1956. An elevated viewpoint shows top surface details, including the sandbox in the cab.

Photomatic, Author's Collection

narrow gauge locomotives having been adaptations of small standard gauge designs.

The two 'Gamecock' class, 678 and 785, were virtually identical with the first 'Jurassic' class ones, except for a slightly smaller grate area (2½ sq. ft against 2¾ sq. ft), a rivetted 'drumhead' type smokebox supported on a saddle in place of Peckett's more normal D-type, and minor differences in the cab and depth of the buffer beam. The tank filler on all of Nelson's locomotives lifted out, whereas on Kaye's it was hinged, and although Kaye's first ones were delivered with lift-out lids they were later given hinged lids. The first six locomotives (678 to 1216) were built 12 ft 0 in. long but the three later ones (1270 to 1632) were 6 in. longer. The visible differences between the two types are the distance between the cylinders and buffer beam, and the width of the rear sides of the cab.

There were minor variations between the engines as built. The 'short' ones had sandboxes on the running plate, while the later 'long' ones had sandboxes mounted pannier fashion on the smokebox, possibly in an attempt to keep the sand dry. (Sand was dropped on the rail to improve adhesion in greasy conditions.) The sandboxes on *Triassic* were almost cubes but on *Mesozoic* and 1632 (later named *Liassic*) they were approximately twice the height of those on *Triassic*. This was probably because *Triassic* had originally been fitted with rail washers, a clean wet rail being almost as good for adhesion as a clean dry one. The larger sandboxes on the later locomotives suggest that rail washing was not that effective in the quarry. Whistles were originally fitted on the cab roof but were later moved to the cab front sheet.

It is now necessary to explain why *Mesozoic* (1327), as existing at the closure, had a 12 ft frame, not a 12 ft 6 in. one as would have been expected. Two well known industrial railway enthusiasts recorded their visits. G. Alliez, on 15th April, 1938, had found all six Pecketts, although *Liassic* (1216) had 'frames only existing', which suggests that it had been withdrawn already, and 1632 was unnamed. Five years later, in June 1943, E.S. Tonks noted the following: *Jurassic* (1008) was spare, *Triassic* (1270) carried boiler 1248 (but as Peckett 1248 was a standard gauge 0-4-0ST supplied to a firm in Grantham (!) he did not know of the significance of the number, unless that particular boiler had been made by another firm), *Mesozoic* (1327) required no comment, and the un-named 1632 (later the second *Liassic*) carried boiler 1119, a small plate to this effect being (and is still in 2012) carried on the side of the cab, above the maker's plate. Outside the shed were a cab with plates 1119 of 1906 and a saddle tank named *Neozoic*. He assumed that a second cab, saddle tank and smokebox nearby were the remains of *Liassic* (1216). A workman told him that *Mesozoic* had switched identities with *Neozoic*.

In the early 1960s fitters at Southam told the author that in 1943 *Mesozoic* was in need of heavy repair and *Liassic* (1216) had a broken frame. Accordingly, the sound parts of each were combined, taking the name *Mesozoic*, and the remainder scrapped. Steam locomotives are comparatively simple machines, and at that time knowledge of their construction was widely available. As a result, all manner of firms, large and small, would undertake major repairs on their locomotives, and even built new ones. It was not uncommon, either, for a firm to take two or more run-down locomotives and construct a 'good' one from reusable components. The rebuilding of *Mesozoic* was not unusual, particularly for a firm with good workshop facilities and skilled staff.

The task now is to interpret the above information. In view of Alliez' observation that *Liassic* (1216) was dismantled in 1938 along with the statement made to the author, a broken frame could well have been the reason it had been dismantled around 1937/8. Tonks' observation that 1632 carried the boiler of 1119, *Neozoic*, and

Peckett 1632, later *Liassic* (2), as delivered with no name.   *Alan Griffin, Feldon Photographic Archive*

Liassic (2) and *Triassic* on 29th September, 1956. Note the distinctive smokebox door, formerly carried by *Mesozoic*, and the small plate above the maker's plate on the side of the cab giving the boiler number.   *G. Alliez*

Liassic inside the engine shed with *Jurassic* in the background on 6th August, 1958. Note the pit extends outside the rails to give ready access to the motion.   *Author*

Charles Matthews and his youngest son beside *Liassic* in Matthews' yard, Toronto, *c*.1964.
Author's Collection

Liassic, still in Toronto 30 years later, sharing a shed with a Welsh quarry Hunslet 0-4-0ST, *c.*1998.
D. Bray

Liassic, recently returned to England, beside *Triassic*, at the Statfold Barn Railway, near Tamworth on 15th September, 2012. Behind is *Michael* (Hunslet 1709), also recently returned from Charles Matthews' collection. *Author*

that other major parts from *Neozoic* lay outside the shed, show that it was then completely dismantled. There were also other unidentified major components nearby.

What actually took place and why in the early 1940s is uncertain. There are several unresolved questions. First, where was the rest of *Liassic* (1216) in 1938 if Alliez appears to have seen only the frames, but Tonks saw the (assumed) superstructure in 1943? Possibly it had been under a tarpaulin, but surely Alliez would have made enquiries. Secondly, what was wrong with *Neozoic* in 1942/43 if the boiler was good enough to be fitted to 1632 and the frames, presumably complete with cylinders etc., were suitable for use on *Mesozoic*, assuming the fitter's statement about the exchange of identities was correct?

My version of events, based on the evidence given above, follows - but it is only my supposition. Suppose 1632, the newest locomotive, required major boiler repairs around 1940-41, and *Neozoic* had received a new boiler in the 1930s. Maybe, as the second oldest locomotive, it had been dismantled as a potential source of spares and its boiler fitted to 1632 (both as noted by Tonks in mid-1943). Suppose subsequently *Mesozoic* required major overhaul, particularly to its cylinders, motion and/or wheels. During World War II a locomotive manufacturer would have been unlikely to be able to supply major spare parts without a considerable delay. As so much work was necessary, RPC decided it would be simpler, and far quicker, to use the existing, assumed sound, frames of *Neozoic*. This was a 'short' locomotive, so the cab from either *Neozoic* or *Liassic* would be required as well. It was very difficult to reach nameplate bolts in a small saddle tank. (One of *Mesozoic*'s later owners wrote to me, saying that while a small boy could be put into a standard gauge tank to unbolt nameplates 'a special spanner could be borrowed from Peckett's for smaller tanks). To save a lot of bother, the fitters decided to keep the name on *Mesozoic*'s tank and transfer the cabside works plates, which was very easy to do. *Mesozoic*'s owner also said that the locomotive's components were totally devoid of any works number stamped on them, only LH or RH as appropriate, except for the boiler, which was a crudely stamped 1216 – the first *Liassic*. But if *Liassic* had been withdrawn with broken frames its boiler could still have been serviceable, and possibly in better condition than *Mesozoic*'s original one.

If this approximates to the truth, then *Mesozoic* comprises *Liassic*'s boiler on the frames of *Neozoic*, with the cab from either *Neozoic* or *Liassic* (now carrying *Mesozoic*'s works plates) and the tank from *Mesozoic*. This leaves the tank of *Neozoic* for Tonks to see, with a cab nearby. Even lacking plates, it would be reasonable for him to assume it belonged to *Neozoic*, but in fact it came from *Mesozoic*. In addition, there is the unidentified tank and cab assumed to belong to *Liassic*, whose nameplate had been removed for future use on 1632. The works plates could have been in the stores or gone for scrap. That leaves two frames, belonging to *Liassic* (assumed broken) and *Mesozoic* unaccounted for, not noted by Tonks, but if Alliez could miss a cab and tank then equally Tonks could have missed two frames. Maybe they had gone for scrap, but if so, why had the other surplus parts not gone as well? All that is certain is that the present *Mesozoic* is not the locomotive that Peckett built and delivered in 1913! (To determine whether an undated photograph is before or after the rebuild, count the number of rivets across the base of the rear cab side sheet. The early locomotives, and *Mesozoic* after the rebuild, had four rivets, later locomotives including *Mesozoic* as built, had six.)

The distinctive smokebox door on *Mesozoic* with the ribbed cross, seen by Tonks in 1943, may date from this wartime rebuild. The rebuilt *Mesozoic* retained the large pannier sandboxes on the smokebox carried by the original *Mesozoic*, so maybe the original smokebox was used on the reconstructed locomotive. It is curious that there was an almost square patch rivetted on to the rear lower part of the saddletank on each side, as though some fitting had been removed. None of the other locomotives have either these patches or any fitting here.

Nelson's works was purchased by RPC in 1946 and closed. The locomotives were scrapped but some parts went to Kaye's as spares. For example, the left-hand connecting rod now fitted to *Triassic* carries the number 918 instead of the expected 1270. It has been said that one locomotive, probably *Gamecock*, was considered for possible use at Southam but the cost of gauge conversion was prohibitive.

The individual locomotives can now be described. *Jurassic* (1008) was the third to go for preservation, leaving in June 1961 for the Lincolnshire Coast Light Railway (LCLR), at Humberstone, south of Cleethorpes. This line had opened on 27th August, 1960, and *Jurassic* saw regular use there. It is now at Skegness Water Leisure Park, the new home of the LCLR.

Neozoic (1119) was rebuilt in 1943, with its frame emerging as *Mesozoic* (as described above), and its boiler was later observed on *Liassic* (1632). This rebuilding was perhaps the reason for the hoist outside the shed. A collection of parts called *Neozoic* was scrapped by Jackson of Coventry in 1943.

Liassic (1216) had been dismantled in the late 1930s with a broken frame. Its boiler was fitted to *Mesozoic* (as described above) and the remains were scrapped in 1943 by Jackson of Coventry. Its name, and maybe the tank as well, bearing in mind the difficulty of attaching nameplates, was transferred to 1632.

Triassic (1270) was dispatched from Peckett's works on 14th August, 1911. It was the first locomotive to go for preservation, being chosen since it was said to have been the last one steamed at Southam and it appeared to be in the best condition. A new firebox had been fitted at Southam by the fitter F. Hodges, recorded by a plate 'Rebuilt Southam 1951'. The locomotive left Southam by low loader on 22nd August, 1957 and arrived at the home of the Industrial Locomotive Society's Secretary, J.B. Latham, at Kettlewell Hill, Woking, Surrey, the following day, having spent the night at Edgware. Latham's book *Railways & Preservation*, published in 1975, has a whole chapter entitled '*Triassic* and its problems'. It was occasionally steamed at Woking, running on a length of mixed gauge track shared with the 3 ft 2 in. gauge 0-4-0T *William Finlay* from Dorking Greystone Lime at Betchworth. After Mr Latham's death *Triassic* moved around, and by 2003 was at the Bala Lake Railway awaiting work as the boiler (safety) certificate had expired some three years previously. It arrived at the Statfold Barn Railway near Tamworth in August 2011, 'being cared for on behalf of the Bala Lake Railway while the intentions of the locomotive's owner are being ascertained' (*Statfold Guide Book & Stock List Update*, September 2012).

Mesozoic (1327) had been rebuilt in 1943, exchanging identity with 1119 (as described above), and was also completely rebuilt shortly before closure. It was the last locomotive to go for preservation, languishing in the otherwise empty shed until the autumn of 1961, when it was acquired by E.L. Pitt & Co, locomotive dealers at Brackley, Northamptonshire. It moved to Pitt's yard sometime between 12th July and 4th November, 1961. It is now on the private Bromyard & Linton Railway in Herefordshire, completely stripped down to its frame, and has been in this state for many years.

Liassic (1632), built 1923, was nameless until 1943 when it took the name and maybe the tank of the recently scrapped 1216. The lack of a name may have been due to initial use at Griffin's works at Stockton. By June 1943 a small plate on the cab stated that the boiler number was 1119, so more than nameplates had been transferred by then. Sometime after 1951 it acquired the distinctive smokebox door previously carried by *Mesozoic*. After closure it left for foreign parts - literally. C.H. Lambe collected it with a low loader on 4th July, 1959 and took it to his depot at Bromsgrove, Worcestershire, where the locomotive was checked over and steamed at 120 psi. It was then dispatched by road to Liverpool on 27th July, 1959, and loaded on to the German vessel *Concordia*, a small ship able to travel up the St Laurence River to Toronto on the Great Lakes, enabling *Liassic*'s purchaser, Charles Matthews, to avoid heavy overland transport costs.

Charles Matthews Ltd, of 99 No. 7 Highway East, Thornhill, Ontario, Canada advertised, 'buildings moved, heavy machinery, float crane'. Charles Matthews collected steam vehicles and had several engines. His widow wrote, 'My late husband bought them for pleasure. We had one of the largest collections in America at one time but my husband sold most of the collection about 5 years ago (c.1964). He kept all the English engines and locomotives. We also have a couple of steam wagons'. He had previously obtained a Kerr, Stuart 'Wren' class 0-4-0ST from Avonmouth Smelting, two Hunslet 0-4-0STs from each of the Dinorwic and Penrhyn slate quarries, and he also owned a Canadian Pacific locomotive weighing 120 tons. As the plates had been stolen from the Kerr, Stuart while in transit, Lambe removed them and sent them separately. *Liassic* stood at Toronto Docks for about a fortnight then Mr Matthews 'just paid the customs and sales tax and brought it home'. He had hopes of running it from time to time, and may have done so initially, but after Charles died in 1966 his two sons ran the family's successful business and they appear to have ignored their father's steam collection. Certainly the only narrow gauge track in 1998 was that under the locomotives.

The *Narrow Gauge Railway Society Newsletter* No. 60 (August 1969) listed the six 2 ft gauge (nominal) British engines owned by Charles Matthews. Sometime after Matthews' death in 1966 the two Penrhyn locomotives went to Toronto Science Museum. *Narrow Gauge News* No. 224 (January 1998) had a photograph of *Liassic* and two of the others stored in a large shed. However, in August 2012 *Liassic* arrived at the Statfold Barn Railway (near Tamworth), along with Dinorwic Hunslets *Michael* and *King of the Scarlets*, having spent almost half its life in Matthews' collection.

At the time the Southam narrow gauge system closed an unidentified boiler lay outside the engine shed. Perhaps this came from *Triassic*, but I regret that I never looked for any identification number. Inside the shed were a chimney and three sets of driving wheels and axles.

The last narrow gauge steam locomotive bought for the works was an 0-4-0ST built by W.G. Bagnall Ltd of Stafford, No. 2148, delivered new in 1924. It is not known why this smaller, less powerful, locomotive was bought. It was slightly lower in height than the Pecketts (8 ft 3¼ in. against 8 ft 5 in.) but its minimum curve and weight of rail was similar (70 ft and 16 lb./yard, Peckett 60 ft and 18 lb./yard). While it may have been intended for shunting in the quarry or on the tip, the most attractive explanation is that it was intended for use at Stockton limeworks (Griffin) which Kaye had taken over some years earlier.

The use of Bagnall instead of Peckett is surprising, too. Perhaps fast delivery was required, and Peckett was unable to oblige. Delivery on 10th November, 1924 was within a few days of the order being placed. Bagnall often built batches of small standard narrow gauge locomotives for stock, so that they could be completed quickly once a firm order gave the required gauge. Kaye's was one of six (2144 to 2149) eventually completed as four 2 ft gauge and two 2 ft 6 in., sent to Kent, India, Malaya and South Africa. Two preserved examples of the same type as Kaye's locomotive are *Leonard* (2087) at Abbey Pumping Station, Leicester, and Revd 'Teddy' Boston's *Pixie*

'Jurassic' class boiler dumped near the engine shed, 3rd September, 1959.   *Author*

No photograph is known to survive of Bagnall 2148, but *Pixie* (2090) and *Armistice* (2088) were built to the same design. Compare the low and exposed position of the return crank and combination link (attached to the crosshead) of the Walschaert's valve gear with the almost hidden similar components of the Bagnall-Price valve gear on *Mercedes* (*see page 40, top*). Amerton Railway, near Stafford, 17th May, 1997.   *Author*

(2090) at Cadeby near Hinkley, Leicestershire. Kaye paid £550 (about £17,000) for his new engine. Unlike the Pecketts which had inside Stephenson's valve gear and conventional fireboxes, the Bagnall had outside Walschaert's valve gear and a circular section firebox (as described for the Harbury locomotives – *see Chapter Four*). The cab was open above the waist, having the roof supported by an iron pillar in each corner. G. Alliez observed it without comment in 1938, so it was then presumably in working order, but by 1943 it was red with rust from long disuse, and along with two Pecketts was scrapped on site by Jackson of Coventry. This locomotive never carried a name, although there is the suggestion it was known as *Nonsuch*.

The first of a number of petrol and diesel locomotives came in 1918, second-hand from the Slough Trading Estate. It was a 'Simplex' petrol locomotive, built by Motor Rail of Bedford. Painted red, it was called unofficially *Old Red Indian*, and was scrapped at an unknown date. As 20hp 'Simplex' locomotives were light (2½ tons) and of rugged construction it would have been suitable on the tip or for light shunting, or to take coal to the steam excavators.

The 20 hp Motor Rail Simplex was the first British internal combustion locomotive to be built in quantity, over 600 being produced for the Ministry of Munitions for use on War Department Light Railways serving the front line in World War I. They were a simple and robust design. The 'boat-shaped' girder frame was intended to minimize overhang on sharp curves. A 2-cylinder 20 hp petrol engine was mounted centrally across the frame and drove a patent 2-speed Dixon Abbott gearbox, from which the final drive was taken to each axle by a chain. The driver sat sideways at the rear, and the radiator was mounted longitudinally at the front, in both cases so that they were equally effective in either direction. After the war many of these locomotives were available as army surplus, and others were reconditioned by Motor Rail. Large quantities of spares were also available, and some competitor companies bought both surplus locomotives and spares which they used as a basis for their own production. While Motor Rail's post-war production soon used straight girder frames, the basic layout was unchanged for years over a range of designs.

Possibly as a result of satisfaction with the previous locomotive, a new 20 hp petrol one was ordered from Motor Rail on 16th February, 1920. No. 1908 was delivered by 15th April, 1920. The price was £700 (about £15,000). The builder's records show it was 24 in. gauge (half an inch wider than the nominal gauge at Southam, but quarry track was rarely that well laid!). It weighed 4 tons nominal (3 ton 16 cwt actual) and survived until the line closed. Like the two other Simplex locomotives it had two speeds in each direction and no cab. The maker's records note 'spring buffers 11.625 in. from rail'. This probably refers to the standard buffer bar bolted loosely across the face of the multi-slot coupling block. The locomotive had straight frames of steel channel, with cast-iron weights bolted underneath at each end to augment adhesion by increasing the weight from the basic 2¼ tons. Sand boxes were much larger than the normal Motor Rail fitting, and were obviously the result of experience with the Pecketts. The engine and gearbox were covered by the standard Motor Rail curved bonnet, hinged on the locomotive centre line.

Another 'Simplex' petrol locomotive was purchased in 1936 from a contractor, apparently to handle spoil during the extensions to the works in the mid-1930s. It was known unofficially as *Smokey Joe*, which could well refer to the exhaust! It was probably painted the builder's standard green. When the works railway closed in 1956 the remains of a 'Simplex' stood on the bank to the stone store. As this locomotive had a green body on a red frame it is possible that at some date the two second-hand locomotives were rebuilt at Southam into one unit.

Motor Rail, 1908, on the enthusiasts' day, 27th October, 1956. Note the extra large sandboxes at each end, and the ballast weights under the buffer beams.   *Photomatic, Author's Collection*

Orenstein & Koppel 20178, from Rochester, in the yard on 27th October, 1956.

Photomatic, Author's Collection

There is the suggestion that a 10/12 hp Ruston & Hornsby diesel locomotive, No. 183427 of 1937, was borrowed in the summer of 1938 from the company's chalk pits at Totternhoe (*see Appendix Two*). However, employees at both Southam and Totternhoe doubted whether such a loan occurred, particularly as the locomotive would have required regauging, Totternhoe being 2 ft 6 in. gauge. Maybe some sort of trial was planned, but the organizers had been unaware that the two railways had different gauges. The locomotive weighed 2½ tons, and was fitted with a Ruston 2JP engine developing 10 hp at 600 rpm.

Four diesel locomotives were transferred to Southam in June 1955 following the closure of the narrow gauge railway in RPC Halling works, Kent. The newcomers comprised two by Orenstein & Koppel, one Hunslet and one Ruston & Hornsby. They were in poor condition and saw little use at Southam except for the Ruston, which received a new engine soon after it arrived.

The Orenstein & Koppels, Nos. 20178 and 20227, type RL2a, looked quite large machines. The angular bonnet almost entirely covered the sturdy fabricated chassis. A 2-cylinder 4-stroke diesel engine developed 20 hp at 1,000 rpm. The drive was through a two speed cone clutch and a chain drive to the leading axle, the axles being coupled by a second chain. A cab with small square windows was fitted at one end. The radiator was protected by a panel of expanded metal, and the side panels of the bonnet lifted out for access. The Babelsberg works, Berlin, had dispatched 20178 to RPC Rochester works, Halling, Kent, in July 1931. The London dealer, Wm Jones Ltd, had received 20227 in May 1932, and it too went to RPC Rochester works. RPC Halling works was constructed after World War II on a site very close to the former Rochester works. The remains of these locomotives were noted outside the shed in January 1960 and they had been scrapped by July 1961. There is an illustration of one at work at Halling in *Industrial Railways of the South East* by Chalk Pits Museum (Middleton Press, 2000).

The Ruston & Hornsby, No. 168437 of 1933, had a 3-cylinder Lister engine developing 22/28 hp with a three-speed gearbox. It weighed about 3½ tons, and was fitted with an all-over cab having Ruston's distinctive 'keyhole' entrance. A new engine was fitted after arrival at Southam, and it was quite popular. Following closure of the Southam railway, it was offered to the Lincolnshire Coast Light Railway, at Humberstone near Cleethorpes, and so it accompanied *Jurassic* into preservation in June 1961. During the winter of 1961/62 it was overhauled by the new owners, ready for use in the 1962 season, but it was found to be too slow and so it was not much used. The LCLR gave it the name *John*, but later it became No. 3 *Southam*. It was taken out of use in September 1966 and scrapped in 1968.

The Hunslet, No. 2837 of 1944, was one of large numbers of similar locomotives built for the Ministry of Supply. It was later reconditioned and sold to RPC. The design was a development of the pre-war Hudson-Hunslet range covering 20, 25, 30 and 50 hp types. The engine of the Southam locomotive developed 20 hp at 1,200 rpm. As built, the locomotive weighed 3 tons 6 cwt in working order. A cab was fitted. During mid-1959 the locomotive was partly dismantled. The frame and wheels remained in the shed in October 1959, but by July 1961 the frame, marked 'for scrap' was dumped outside against the shed doors across the track. Parts of the Hunslet were the last of the narrow gauge locomotives to survive at Southam.

The Pecketts were painted dark green, lined black edged each side with cream. The outside frames, cylinders and motion were red. Latterly they all had a brass nameplate mounted on the tank, but in their early years at least *Niassic* and *Liassic* (1) carried no name, and *Jurassic's* name was painted on the tank. The livery of the

THE HUNSLET ENGINE CO. LTD *Engineers* LEEDS England

0-4-0 TYPE

20 H.P. "HUNSLET" DIESEL LOCOMOTIVE

Gauge of Railway (can be modified to suit requirements)		2′ 0″
Dia. of Coupled Wheels...		1′ 6″
Wheelbase		2′ 11″
Height Overall		5′ 2¼″
Width Overall		3′ 6″
Length over Buffer Beams		8′ 3″
Power and Speed of Engine		20 h.p. at 1,200 r.p.m.
Speed 1st Gear		3·5 miles per hour
,, 2nd Gear		7·0 ,, ,, ,,
Fuel Capacity		5 gallons
Weight in Working Order		3 tons 6 cwts.
Maximum Axle Load		1 ton 13 ,,
Tractive Effort 1st Gear		1,820 lbs.
,, ,, 2nd Gear		910 ,,
Ratio. Adhesive Weight ÷ Tractive Effort		4·06 to 1
Minimum Radius of Curve Engine will traverse with ease		30 ft.
Weight per Yard of Lightest Rail advisable		12 lbs.
		Level 1 in 100 1 in 50
Load Engine will start and haul in 1st Gear		98 tons 42 tons 25·5 tons
,, ,, ,, haul in 2nd Gear		72·5 ,, 23 ,, 13 ,,

Loads hauled are based on 18 lbs./Ton Starting Resistance and 12 lbs./Ton Running Resistance

Code Word—**LINPA**

B I 248   400—1/41   Order 48000

Specification sheet including official photograph of 20 hp Hudson Hunslet design.

Author's Collection

Bagnall is not known. The operational Simplex (1908) was black and the second-hand ones were red and green. The locomotives from Kent were all painted orange except for the Ruston which was green. All the frames were black.

Gauge 1 ft 11½ in.

Jurassic	0-6-0ST	OC	P	1008	1903		New	(1)
Neozoic	0-6-0ST	OC	P	1119	1906		New	(2)
Liassic	0-6-0ST	OC	P	1216	1909		New	(2)
Triassic	0-6-0ST	OC	P	1270	1911		New	(3)
					rebuilt Southam 1951			
Mesozoic	0-6-0ST	OC	P	1327	1913		New	(4)
					rebuilt Southam 1943			
Liassic	0-6-0ST	OC	P	1632	1923		(a)	(5)
Nonsuch?	0-4-0ST	OC	WB	2148	1924		(a)	(2)
Smokey Joe	4wPM		MR		rebuilt J.C. Oliver		(b)	(6)
Old Red Indian	4wPM		MR				(c)	(7)
	4wPM		MR	1908	1920		New	(8)
	4wDM		RH	183427	1937		(d)	(9)
R No. 6	4wDM		OK	20178	1931		(e)	(10)
	4wDM		OK	20227	1932		(e)	(10)
R9	4wDM		HE	2837	1944		(e)	(11)
R10	4wDM		RH	168437	1933		(e)	(1)

Note: Some of the Pecketts probably worked for a time at Kaye's Stockton limeworks after Kaye took over from Griffin & Co. (by 1916).

(a) Ex-Griffin's works, mid-1920s?, otherwise New
(b) Ex-?, contractors, 1936
(c) Ex-Slough Trading Estate, 1918
(d) Ex-Totternhoe Lime & Stone Co. Ltd, Beds - alleged loan, summer 1938
(e) Ex-RPCM Halling works, Kent, c.6.55 (by 8.1955), but little used at Southam
(1) To Lincolnshire Coast Light Railway, Humberstone, Cleethorpes, June 1961
(2) Scrapped on site 1943 by Jackson of Coventry. Frame of Neozoic used to rebuild Mesozoic
(3) To J.B. Latham, Woking, Surrey for preservation, 22.8.1957
(4) To E.L.Pitt & Co. (Coventry) Ltd, Brackley, Northamptonshire after 27.7.61
(5) To C. Matthews, Toronto, Canada via C.H. Lambe & Sons Ltd, Bromsgrove, 4.7.59
(6) Dismantled 3.1954, remains on stone store viaduct 10.59, scrapped 1961
(7) Scrapped at unknown date, parts possibly used to repair Smokey Joe
(8) Scrapped during 1961, after 1.1961
(9) To Totternhoe Lime & Stone Co. Ltd, return after alleged loan, summer 1938
(10) Remains outside shed, gone by 7.1961
(11) Dismantled between 4&9.1959, frame & wheels in shed 10.1959, frame seen marked 'for scrap' 12.7.61

The first wagons had three fixed sides, each made from a single plank about 18 in. wide, with the fourth side hinged so it could drop down. The body was fastened to the wooden underframe by steel strips. On the closed side these strips extended above the side in an eye, and the strips extended under the end of the frame. The ends had similar steel strips with eyes fitted close to the opening side. The eyes enabled the wagon to be lifted in and out of the quarry by crane. They had been described to me as 'wooden side tippers', but they could have been emptied easily

Skip (*third from left*) having an extra strut to secure its body.

Courtesy of Rugby Cement, Bob Darvill Collection

enough by tipping sideways - like the tubs at Napton brickworks (*see Appendix Eight*). Wooden wagons with hinged tipping bodies would not have been strong enough to lift by crane. Their last duty was on the clay tip, where they were used until about 1915 and were then broken up for firewood. They could well have been made at the works; there was a wagon shop employing three men near the stone store. The later wagons used on the tip were light German steel side tippers, which appear to have been scrapped when clay tipping ceased in 1936.

The wooden wagons used on the main line were replaced by steel either-side tippers. This seems to have been in two phases, small wagons and then their replacement by larger ones of double the capacity. The small wagons could have been the German ones mentioned above. The larger wagons could have been introduced as a result of Lister-Kaye's 'enquiries out for suitable wagons' in July 1903, and suggests they were introduced at the same time as the locomotives.

Some if not all of the later steel wagons were made by Howard of Bedford. There were between 80 and 100 wagons (90 at a valuation of Kaye & Co. in 1909), each carrying about 30 cwt of stone. A typical body was triangular in section, 5 ft 3 in. wide, 5 ft 6 in. long (both over a 2 in. wide flange) and 2 ft 7 in. deep with 1 cubic yard capacity. They had an oval steel frame of 5 in. x 2½ in. channel steel, 8 ft 6 in. long, 3 ft wide with 13 in. wheels at 32 in. centres. The body was supported on a curved channel steel frame, with a handle either side of the actual point of support for attaching the crane or shunting horse in the quarry, or to give a handhold for manual shunting. In later years the body of many wagons was supported on a piece of wide steel channel mounted across the frame, the simple alteration probably being done on site. Latterly the wagons used for stone had a steel angle fitted a few inches below the top of the body sides, to give additional strength, particularly when the excavator loaded large lumps, but the ones used for excavator coal were not strengthened. Loading by excavator imposes greater strain on a wagon's body than loading by hand.

At least one wagon was fitted with a strut to make its body more secure when loading, to prevent unexpected tipping following an accidental knock from the excavator bucket. A steel bar was attached by a link to the body support frame and had the upper end formed into a hook which went over the lip of the wagon body. While the experiment may have been successful the hooked bar was not fitted to the other skips.

The majority of wagons were scrapped or possibly sold for reuse soon after closure. In September 1959 about a dozen bodies and a few frames were still scattered about the site, but they subsequently disappeared. In 1909 the tipping wagons each carried a running number painted in large white figures on the body, but in later years the wagons seem to have been devoid of any identification.

The company built three wooden open wagons in 1914 to carry coal to the three steam excavators. All three survived at the closure but then began to disappear piecemeal; by 1959 one frame and one body remained, and their measurements differed slightly. The body was 5 ft 6 in. (or 6 ft) long by 4 ft 4 in. wide, and was made of three planks giving a side height of 2 ft 9 in. The sides were all fixed; the wagon was just a box on wheels, but that would have been sufficient to carry coal to the quarry and store it before use. The wheels were 15 in. in diameter with seven curved spokes on a wheelbase of 2 ft 10 in. (shorter bodied wagon). The wooden underframe was outside the wheels, which ran in plain bearings. A D-shaped block of wood in the centre of each end acted as a buffer, and gave an overall length 8 in. more than the body.

There were also several water tank wagons to supply the steam cranes and excavators. They had cylindrical iron tanks mounted horizontally on what appears to be a skip chassis. Possibly they had been made by Howard's as well.

When Oldham had set up the business in 1854 he acquired a fleet of about 10 narrow boats, but later the firm relied mainly on outside carriers. Kaye's own fleet never exceeded half a dozen boats. In 1900 it acquired the topically named *General Roberts* and *General Buller* (Boer War). *Coronation* and *Edward VII* followed in 1901. William Nurser & Sons, of Braunston, eight miles away, built *Blue Lias* in 1923. The entire fleet was horse-drawn.

The LNWR had opened a branch from Rugby to Leamington in 1851. For years this line was the closest railway to Kaye's works, so cement for dispatch by rail had to be carted about two miles to Marton station. The Warwick & Napton Canal (W&N) ran past the works and six miles away, just outside Leamington, it went under the railway, so in August 1881 Kaye approached the canal company for transhipment facilities. A railway siding was laid close to the canal bridge to serve a canalside wharf. The work was completed in March 1883. A year later the LNWR erected a shed on W&N land so that transhipment could take place under cover (SP 324650).

A similar connection with the GWR was provided by the W&N at Leamington in the autumn of 1892, to meet the expected competition following the proposed extension of the LNWR Weedon to Daventry branch to Marton Junction, where it would join the existing Rugby to Coventry line. Land for the new facilities was purchased at Clapham Terrace, Leamington, near the LNWR siding, and a new canal basin was built with a warehouse to store lime under cover. Although the canal continued to be used until 1969, the new branch line, opened 1st August, 1895 and passing right beside the works, increasingly took the traffic.

Horse-drawn canal craft used to deliver cement in 2 cwt jute sacks to Sampson Road wharf, a mile south-east of Birmingham city centre, the journey taking some 15 hours. One hundredweight sacks were introduced in the 1920s. The sacks were wheeled into the boats and Kaye employed packers to help with the loading. Kaye's fleet was disbanded after the RPC takeover in 1934, and instead arrangements were made with the Grand Union Canal Carrying Co. (GUCCC). A mechanized conveyor to the canal transhipment shed was installed at Southam in 1935 and mechanized unloading equipment was provided at Sampson Road. The GUCCC provided a shuttle service of craft to carry 2,000 tons per month. Boats had to reverse into, or out of, Kaye's arm as there was insufficient space in it to turn.

British Waterways (BW) continued to carry the traffic after the canals were nationalized but tonnages gradually declined. *Banstead* and *Tow* made the last 50 ton delivery in March 1969, although the writing had been on the wall for some time. The subject of a BW internal memo in June 1963 was about maintaining 'the pair of boats running between Southam and Sampson Road' on the 'Cement Run'. Motor boat *Pinner* and butty (unpowered boat) *Belmont* were on this duty. They were inspected at the end of September 1963. *Pinner* was in 'generally reasonable condition' but the plates of *Belmont* were very thin and a replacement boat was suggested. At this time 'the steerer is continually complaining of the state of the canal particularly at Leamington and by the BSA [factory, at Small Heath, Birmingham]. He is continually dragging the bottom and if the canal level is down an inch or so he has extreme difficulty in passing through the bridges. I understand that last week it took 5 hours to travel 2 miles … some consideration should be given to immediate dredging of this length.' A month later, following inspection of other possible boats, the Engineer reported that they were in much the same condition, and there were three immediate alternatives:

1. Repair *Pinner* and *Belmont* 'to make them into reasonably good boats',
2. To do first aid repairs as necessary while continuing to run them until they were no longer safe to operate at which time major repairs would be undertaken or the trade terminated,
3. To 'terminate the trade now'.

The upshot is not recorded, but I suspect it was option 2. Southam cement was the last commercial traffic on this stretch of canal.

Memories of two people who were on the 'Cement Run' have been published in *Midlands Canals - Memories of the Canal Carriers* by Robert Davies (Tempus, 2006). Joe Safe's memories date from the early 1930s.

Many runs for the GUCCCo with the *Mizar* and *Merak* were involved with general cargoes, but included a regular cement haulage run, going from Southam and into Birmingham. Other boatmen on the same routine of around four trips per week included Ike Merchant and his brother Jim, who had a boat each, and Tom Smith. At first the bagged cement - which got everywhere - was taken to a warehouse near Old Turn Junction, and then later to Sampson Road. Every kind of material carried had its idiosyncrasies, but cement, due to its nature, had to be kept bone dry. This meant in practice that the flooring had to be kept bone dry, which was not always easy. For this, the clothing up [tarpaulin sheets to cover the load] had to be thoroughly done to prevent rain spoiling the cement.

Ellen (Nellie) Harris remembered 'When I was a teenager [late 1930s] ... we also did regular cement runs from Southam up to Camp Hill. Even though this material was bagged, cement was still dreadful stuff to handle, and the fine powder seemed to get into every nook and cranny.'

Joe Safe also featured in *Tales from the Old Inland Waterways* by Euan Corrie (David & Charles, 1998).

We went on the cement run from Southam to Sampson Road in Birmingham. About 1936 that was. There was five pair on that, doing four trips a week each. If you loaded during the night and come out of the basin at, say, two o'clock, you would empty that day at Sampson Road [a trip of 31½ miles involving the operation of 40 locks]; we used to average between twelve and thirteen hours for that run from Southam to the depot at the top of the Camp Hill Locks. As soon as the men at the works had finished loading you'd be away - sheet up the boats and gone. And when you was empty you had to keep the floors dry in the boats, so you had to turn them up to stop any rain getting on them ...

Since the beginning of 1982 the northern 700 yards of Kaye's arm has been leased by the Warwickshire Fly Boat Co. as moorings, and the southern 200 yards has been dammed off to use as a reservoir and settling pond for water, to catch oil and dirt pumped from the firm's quarries and brought in by chalk slurry (45 per cent water by volume), before discharge into the River Itchen. This part had been filled in by 1994.

In September 1925 Kaye responded to a letter from Garrett about the performance of two steam lorries which had been purchased for deliveries within a radius of about 40 miles. These 'undertype' lorries, with the cylinders under the body instead of being on top of the boiler, had been found far more economical and reliable than the petrol lorries previously used. 'These two wagons are in constant daily use (except Saturdays, when they are at home for cleaning purposes)'.

Above: Horse-drawn canal boat *Blue Lias* belonging to 'Kaye & Co Ltd/Portland Cement Manufacturers/Southam Works Rugby' at Drawbridge Road, Shirley (south-east Birmingham) on the Stratford-upon-Avon Canal, *c.*1923. The horse is just visible above the bow of the boat.

T.J. Edgington Collection

Right: Covered canal boat loading bay, constructed at Southam works in 1935. Grand Union Canal Carrying Co. boat.

Courtesy of Rugby Cement, Author's Collection

The original siding arrangements by the main line are shown in the LNWR book *Diagrams of Private Sidings: Rugby to London and Branches* under Southam & Long Itchington. In 1908 Kaye was experiencing problems, as Dr M.W. Oldham wanted to retain some rights to the sidings, but they were eventually resolved. Kaye agreed to pay Oldham £400, Oldham granted a rebate of 2*d*. per ton on royalties, to a maximum of £460 in total (equivalent to 55,200 tons), and Kaye agreed 'to pay half the cost of connecting our siding up to their boundary if they ever require it'. Siding plan 975, dated January 1909, refers to the grant made by the LNWR to Kaye & Co. Ltd, dated 2nd June, 1896, and shows Messrs Kaye's tramway and loading bank, situated 670 yards east of Southam & Long Itchington station. On LNWR land there were 105¼ yards [*sic*] of tramway 'maintained by Trader at own cost'. The plan shows a standard gauge siding, an extension of the headshunt for the nearby goods yard, on the south side of the single track main line. It passed the 15 mile post, then crossed the canal arm to terminate beside the loading bank. The narrow gauge tramway entered LNWR property beside the canal and curved east beside the main line siding. A siding was thrown off to the right just inside the boundary fence. At the east end of the loading bank a trailing connection was made to a second line into the works.

An undated LNWR plan shows a long siding on south side of the main line branch, extending approximately 180 yards east of the canal bridge. West of the canal were points and a gate into Kaye's works. Two parallel sidings were labelled 'Coal & Lime' and 'Coal', while a third siding, parallel to LNWR, was labelled 'Cement' and passed the packing shed, sack store and three cement silos. This siding continued to the bridge carrying the footpath from the Cuttle to the works. An undated plan for proposed additional siding accommodation, probably associated with the construction of the new works in 1908, showed only the 'Coal & Lime' and 'Cement' sidings, each of which was entered by a curve of 200 ft radius. In addition, immediately east of the canal bridge, there was a short spur to an engine shed about 35ft long, easily long enough for a single locomotive. This spur was protected by its own gate. The layout described earlier in *The Engineer* corresponded to that in the LNWR siding plan.

A Grand Union Canal map in British Waterways' Archives, BW58/11/7/30, dated 26th March, 1930, showed two sidings east of the canal bridge, one along the bank and one on the far eastern side of works, and none west of the canal. A Siding Modification plan dated 1938 showed the 'firms new siding' on the east bank of the canal, and on the west bank points gave access to the silos and another siding.

In 1973 a capstan remained in the sidings, just east of the canal bridge. Although none were mentioned in the 1909 article, it seems likely that in the absence of a works shunting engine one or more were installed around that time to move standard gauge wagons. Horses would not have been very suitable on gantries over hoppers, neither would it have been convenient to have to rely on the services of a main line locomotive. A capstan consisted of a circular steel body about 30 in. high, about 15 in. diameter at the ends but with a waist about 12 in. diameter at approximately 18 in. from the ground. A foot switch caused an electric or hydraulic motor housed in the base to rotate the capstan body. Wagons were moved by attaching a rope to the wagon underframe and putting two or three turns around the capstan body. While the rope was loose it slipped as the capstan rotated, but if the operator provided a gentle tension on the excess rope it gripped and the wagon was moved. The operator coiled down the rope as it left the capstan. Provision of a fixed pulley near the further end of a siding enabled the capstan to haul wagons in either

Above: Standard gauge engine
shed, Southam, 20th June, 1996.
Author

Right: Wagon on coal hoist.
*Courtesy of Rugby Cement,
Author's Collection*

direction. Capstans were once common in yards and warehouses where locomotives could not be used.

Horses were also used for shunting to supplement the capstan(s) until replaced by a diesel locomotive which was included in the 1936 modernization.

In the late 1950s the standard gauge layout had a long loop extending either side of the canal bridge, with connections to the main line at each end and near the canal bridge. A siding left the loop east of the canal, and this served two trailing sidings into the coal storage yard. It then joined the other coal hoist sidings near the locomotive shed. On the west bank of the canal one track curved away from the loop beside the main line, immediately throwing off two sidings to the silos before continuing south to a loop serving the coal hoist. After a wagon had been shunted on to the platform of the hoist, the platform was lifted to raise the wagon to the top of the concrete tower, where both were tilted to empty the coal into the hopper within. The concrete hoist tower still stood in 1996.

Opposite the coal hoist was the stone crusher on the other loop track. Beyond the hoist and crusher the two tracks were joined by a scissors crossover. Near the hoist was the engine shed made of corrugated asbestos sheeting on a steel frame. It had two roads, each with a smoke hood, so was presumably constructed after the second locomotive came in 1942. It was used only by the diesels, any steam locomotives on site being kept outside. By 1996 it was used as plasma welding shop.

Although many sidings were relaid in 1972, the layout remained very similar to the 1950s, except that there was a siding at the east end of the main line loop, presumed on the site of the original loading bank, for incoming chalk. This line led round a sharp curve along the east bank of the canal and made trailing connection to sidings serving the coal yard. North of the former narrow gauge engine shed were four sidings. At the end of the canal the line divided into four parallel tracks which served the coal hoist and chalk tippler, the latter by then disused. On the west side of the canal there was still a pair of sidings serving the silos. Covered vans were loaded on the track nearer the silos but Presflo cement hoppers could be loaded on either. A sharply-curved point by the canal bridge led from the silos line, over the fire dropping pit, to the coal tippler.

Southam & Long Itchington station had been closed in 1958, and the Rugby to Leamington line was closed to passengers in June 1959. The line eastwards from Southam to Weedon was closed completely in early 1964 (chalk then travelling via Rugby), and the line from Marton Junction to Leamington followed in 1966. However, the works retained main line rail access for incoming coal and chalk and some outgoing cement. Freight travelled along the former Leamington branch from Rugby, then reversed at Marton Junction (where the locomotive ran round its train) for the remainder of the journey to Southam. The former route to Weedon was retained as far as the bridge under the Long Itchington to Stockton road near the Blue Lias inn (SP 427646), being used as one, later two, sidings for empty chalk tipplers.

The chalk traffic finished in 1965 following the opening of the pipeline for chalk slurry, but coal and some outward cement continued by rail until June 1984. The track from Rugby to Southam was then lifted, and the bridge under the main road near the former station was strengthened by having a 6 ft diameter steel tube laid through it with the space around it filled solid. By 1996 most internal track, a mixture of bullhead and flat bottom rail, had been lifted, although sundry lengths remained embedded in concrete.

From 1895 rail transport had been available to carry coal inwards and cement outwards. Until the mid-1930s, shunting was done by horse, capstan and the

A Hudswell, Clarke official photograph of *Southam*, D604, taken well towards the bottom of the works yard. This locomotive was ex-works on 6th February, 1937. The signals are on the MR main line into Leeds which is below the low wall visible on the left. The connection which served the works of three locomotive builders - Hudswell Clarke, Hunslet and Manning, Wardle - came up a steep gradient in the cutting behind the wall, with the junction serving Hudswell, Clarke to the right of this picture.   *Ron Redman Collection*

Southam shunting, with RPC internal open wagon behind, 6th August. 1958.   *Author*

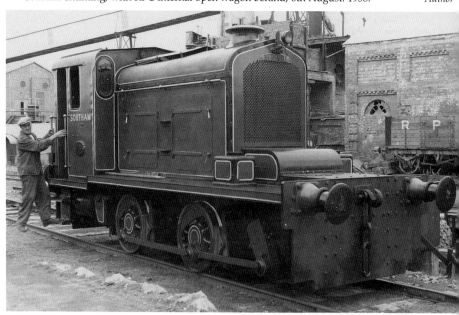

locomotive on the main line goods train. Although some chalk had been brought in from around 1920, from 1936 it came by the trainload from quarries at Totternhoe, Bedfordshire, on the Leighton Buzzard to Dunstable branch (*see Appendix Two*). This great increase in rail traffic probably accounted for the introduction of a diesel standard gauge shunting locomotive as part of the modernization of the works. In 1973 standard gauge traffic inwards was coal and gypsum, and cement outwards. There were three outwards trains per week, each comprising twenty 22-ton Presflo hoppers, in addition to sundry van loads of bagged cement. By then much more cement was being dispatched by road, both in bulk and bags, and until 1969 a little bagged cement was still sent to the Birmingham area by canal. By the early 1980s the only standard gauge rail traffic was inwards coal, all cement being sent out by road. During the miners' strike in March 1984 coal was brought in by road and the railway was mothballed. RPC decided to continue with road haulage when the strike ended, so the internal railway did not reopen.

Both steam and diesel locomotives have been recorded at Southam works, but there have rarely been more than two at any time. The first one was a standard Hudswell, Clarke 120 hp 0-4-0 diesel-mechanical, No. D604, dispatched from the maker's works in Leeds on 6th February, 1937. The tall bonnet had a steam locomotive type chimney, and the final drive was by side rods from a jackshaft at the front. The name *Southam* was painted on the cab. It was rebuilt by Hudswell, Clarke in 1953, and eventually withdrawn due to thin tyres on the wheels and the big ends needing replacement. *Southam* was sent in 1966 to the scrap dealers J.& H.B. Jackson, Coventry, who used it occasionally in their yard. Twenty years later it passed into preservation in the hands of the Coventry Steam Railway Centre at Baginton airport on the outskirts of Coventry although it received no restoration or protection. In 2000 the locomotive was bought by the proprietor of the Great Western public house and restaurant at Bishop's Itchington, close to the former Southam Road station. *Southam* came from Coventry on 9th June, 2000 and stood on a short length of track in the car park beside the road. During the autumn of 2007 it was taken away, and its present whereabouts are not known.

A second, very similar 120 hp 0-4-0DM locomotive, Hudswell, Clarke No. D625, named *Southam 2*, was obtained in 1942, ex-works on 21st October. This became the spare when a new diesel, No. 3, was delivered in 1966, being then used monthly while No. 3 was being serviced.

During 1943 Southam works borrowed 0-6-0ST, Manning, Wardle No. 2047 of 1926 (the last locomotive built by that firm) from Rugby works. Presumably one of the diesels was undergoing extended repairs and a second, or at least a spare, locomotive was required. This locomotive was borrowed again for a short time in 1966. A discarded Peckett 0-4-0ST, No. 9 *Whitby*, was obtained, dismantled, from the nearby APCM Harbury works in 1961, but it was not reassembled and was scrapped in 1963.

In 1966 a new diesel-hydraulic locomotive was supplied by Thomas Hill of Rotherham, No. 164V. It developed 157 hp and had four wheels coupled by chains. The bonnet was much lower and the cab had large windows giving good all round visibility. Unlike the other two diesels it faced west, not east.

When No. 3 had been ordered but not yet delivered and No. 2 was waiting for a gearbox, a 100 hp Sentinel steam locomotive was temporarily borrowed from Rugby works.

The Hudswell, Clarke diesel locomotives were painted green, lined black and white, and had red rods. The name was painted in white, shaded black and red. The

Southam 'stuffed and mounted' outside the 'Great Western' public house, Bishops Itchington, 29th March, 2005. The sign had a good representation of a GWR branch line train.　　*Author*

Southam 2 shunting past the site of the former narrow gauge yard, with the remains of old kilns behind it in the mid-1960s. Although the storage shed for stone had been demolished some of the concrete supports for the high level tracks remain. Beyond are the former narrow gauge engine shed and its water tank.　　*P.J. Wiles, J. Frearson Collection*

Southam 2, Hudswell, Clarke D625, having been hauled out of the shed by No. 3, Thomas Hill 164V, 31st July, 1973.   *Author*

No. 3 with a rake of BR 'Presflo' wagons near the silos, 31st July, 1973.   *Author*

Thomas Hill was painted unlined green with red wheels, with black and yellow warning chevrons on the buffer beams.

When it became clear that the railway was no longer required, the two remaining locomotives went to Rugby works in July 1985. No. 3 went under its own power and saw further use. *Southam 2* was towed to Rugby by a BR class '08' 0-6-0DE shunter. Later it went to Leeds Industrial Museum for preservation, as part of the museum's collection of Leeds-built locomotives. At the time of a visit in 2008 it had not yet been restored, and nearby was a Fowler 2-4-0DM from Harbury.

Standard Gauge

Southam	0-4-0DM		HC	D604	1936	New	(1)
					Rebuilt HC/53		
Southam 2	0-4-0DM		HC	D625	1942	New	(2)
	0-6-0ST	IC	MW	2047	1926	(a)	(3)
No. 9 *Whitby*	0-4-0ST	OC	P	1505	1918	(b)	Scr. 1963
No. 3	4wDH		TH	164V	1966	New	(4)
No. 1	4wVBT	VCG	S	9559	1953	(c)	(5)

(a) Ex-New Bilton works, Rugby, loan 1943
   Another steam locomotive, possibly this one, had been borrowed from Rugby works for a few days in October 1940 while *Southam* was under repair.
(b) Ex-APCM Harbury, *c*.1961 (in dismantled condition)
(c) Ex-New Bilton works, Rugby *c*.3.1966

(1) To J. & H.B. Jackson Ltd, Coventry *c*.9.1966, to Coventry Steam Railway Centre 1986, by 11.1986, to Great Western public house, Bishops Itchington 9.6.2000, to unknown location after 5.8.2007, by 15.10.2007
(2) To Rugby works, 4.7.1985
(3) To New Bilton works, 1943. To Warwickshire Industrial Loco Preservation Group, Severn Valley, Bridgnorth, 22.10.1967, where named *Southam*
(4) To Rugby works loan 26.6.82, returned 22.7.1982, to Rugby works 4.7.1985
(5) To Rugby works *c*.5.1966

A number of wooden open wagons, painted blue with 'RPC' in white letters, were used for internal coal traffic. Six remained, out of use, in 1973. Ordinary wood or steel mineral wagons were used for incoming chalk from around 1920, but latterly chalk was delivered in British Railways 27 ton tipplers (robust all-steel open wagons with no doors) (*see Appendix Five*). RPC had its own main line wagons which will have served this works. They are described under Rugby works (*see Chapter Twelve*).

Chapter Eight

Greaves, Bull & Lakin,
Stockton Limeworks

Late 1830s	Richard Greaves
1855	Greaves & Kirshaw
1860s, by 1868	Greaves, Kirshaw & Bull
1870s, by 1880	Greaves, Bull & Lakin
1900s, by 1904	Greaves, Bull & Lakin Ltd
1927	Greaves, Bull & Lakin (Harbury Works) Ltd
1927	Red Triangle Group
1931	Associated Portland Cement Manufacturers Ltd

Closed by 1936

The Blue Lias limeworks operated by Greaves, Bull & Lakin at Stockton was situated on the south bank of the canal, just east of the bridge carrying the Stockton to Long Itchington road, close to the Blue Lias inn (SP 429647).

The works appears to have been started in the late 1830s, as Greaves began to manufacture artificial cement here in 1840. An advertisement in *The Builder* in 1843 reads 'A depot is opened in London for the sale of Blue Lias Lime and Cement from Mr Greaves' celebrated quarries at Southam [*sic*], Warwickshire.' Two years later *The Builder* praised Stockton Lias Cement as 'it is of a beautiful stone colour ... does not crack and is well adapted for every description of modelling and casting'. The names of several large properties where it had been used were given. Wilmcote Lias Cement was reported as 'of inferior quality to the above from containing oxide of iron, but is of superior quality for Tunnels, Sewers and Hydraulic purposes.' The Ground Lias Lime was suitable 'for concrete and every description of hydraulic work, for which purposes it has been used at Woolwich and Chatham dockyards, the London Docks, Hungerford Suspension Bridge, Westminster Bridge, Regent and Grand Junction Canals, London & Birmingham Railway Co', ...'

An 1850 trade directory states 'The blue lias limestone abounds in this parish [Stockton], and is considered to be the best in England. The lime works are very extensive, and are the property of Mr Richard Greaves, and Mr Richard [*sic*] Griffin.' The proprietor is shown as Richard Greaves in 1854 'Blue lias lime and cement, and at Wilmcote'. As described under Harbury Works (*see Chapter Four*), he had been joined by Kirshaw in 1855, who himself was replaced by Bull by 1866. The firm continued as Greaves Bull & Lakin until 1927, when it became Greaves Bull & Lakin (Harbury Works) Ltd. The company was taken over by APCM on 30th October, 1931, and the works had closed by 1936.

Lime was made in kilns at western end of the site. For a time in the early days cement was also made (the 1888 25 in. OS map shows this as the Blue Lias Lime & Cement Works) but latterly only lime was produced. The works was enlarged eastwards in 1898, with the date in a disused chimney still standing in 1961. Beside the road are two rows of cottages, dated 1873 and 1899.

APCM never modernized the works and eventually, when the supply of stone was exhausted, production was transferred to Harbury. Reliance Aluminium took over the site in 1942 or 1943 and used it to cast scrap aluminium into ingots. The aluminium was melted in the former slurry shed. Later Stockton Metal & Alloys operated here but they closed in 1972.

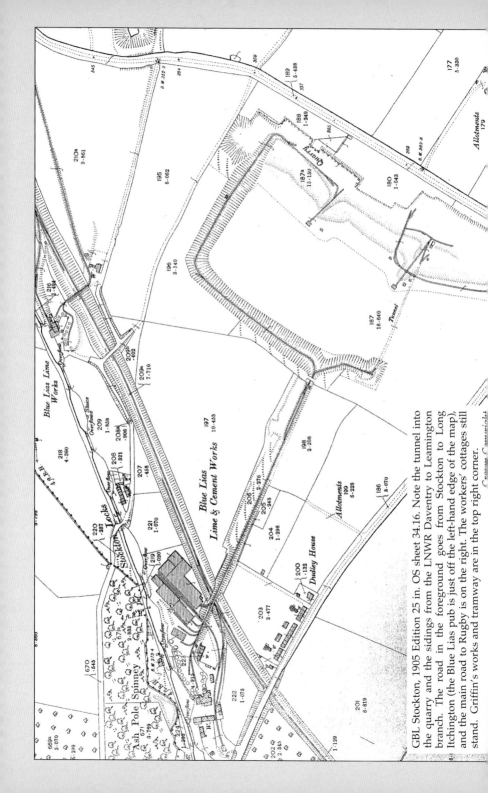

GBL Stockton, 1905 Edition 25 in. OS sheet 34.16. Note the tunnel into the quarry and the sidings from the LNWR Daventry to Leamington branch. The road in the foreground goes from Stockton to Long Itchington (the Blue Lias pub is just off the left-hand edge of the map), and the main road to Rugby is on the right. The workers' cottages still stand. Griffin's works and tramway are in the top right corner.

The 1888 25 in. map shows the Blue Lias Lime & Cement works beside the canal east of the Blue Lias inn. There were then 15 kilns, in a row going west from the lock then curving south through a semicircle. A tramway is shown serving the top of the kilns before heading south-east on an embankment. The 1905 edition showed the 1898 extension, two large buildings constructed near the next lock eastwards. The tramway had been extended to serve both of the new buildings, joining the earlier line near two new bridges which carried the tramway over a siding and the LNWR branch, opened in 1895.

About 190 yards south of the bridge over the LNWR there was a loop 50 yards long, and the entrance to the quarry was about 120 yards further, a total distance of about 360 yards. A bridge, probably carrying a farm track, spanned the line at the quarry entrance where the tracks divided. One line ran north-east for 350 yards along the edge of the quarry, then 170 yards across the end before turning south for 100 yards along the east side of the pit, about 100 yards from the main road between Southam and Stockton. The other branch turned south-west for 70 yards then turned south-east and entered a brick-lined tunnel about 100 yards long which served a face adjacent to that reached by the first branch. The tunnel was presumably to shorten the distance to the face. The quarry continued to be worked eastwards, towards the main road. The tunnel was still shown on the 1951 2½ in. OS map, although by 1966 the ends had been bricked up and the approach cuttings partially filled. There was another quarry north of the tramway, between the LNWR and the quarry with the tunnel, but this appears to have belonged to Griffin (*see Chapter Nine*).

Gangs of men dug the stone, as at other local quarries. Overburden was removed in barrows which the men ran along planks supported on trestles and boxes at heights of up to 60 ft above the quarry floor. The runways were 2 ft 3 in. wide, being three 9 in. planks side by side. Another former workman gave the maximum height as 30 ft, with the runways made of planks 21 in. wide by 21 ft long, with up to 13 spans (270 ft total). He added that barrows had to be loaded carefully! Neither type of run would find favour with modern quarry inspectors! Stone was loaded into wagons to be taken to the kilns, while clay was picked out by hand and dumped by the road.

There was a single crane to hoist wagons out of the pit. A 'traction engine' (more likely a portable engine, which looked like a traction engine but which was not self propelled, being just a power plant on wheels) anchored to a concrete block was also used to haul wagons up a quarry incline. As the works was about 50 ft lower than the entrance to the tunnel, the gradient (average about 1 in 24) was sufficient for gravity to be used to move loaded wagons through the tunnel down to the works. A horse hauled the empties in rakes of five wagons back to the tunnel, where they were pushed through by hand. There was one horse on the main line, and one or two on the clay tip. Some ponies were kept in a shed in the pit, but the main stables holding three horses were on the canal bank at the works.

A locomotive came in 1922, not many years before the works closed. A corrugated iron shed was built for it in a corner of the quarry field. The locomotive was used only on the main line and did not go through the tunnel, and even after it had been bought some horses were still used. Indeed, it does not seem to have been heavily used at all, as IRS records show that for a time the locomotive was lent to the Ham River Grit Co. in Surrey. The tramway was lifted when the works closed in the early 1930s and the equipment scrapped or sold.

The locomotive was a tiny 0-4-0ST of Kerr, Stuart 'Wren' class, No. 4266 built in 1922. It was ordered in June 1922 and delivered on 20th July to Greaves Bull & Lakin

GBL Stockton works beside the Warwick & Napton Canal, looking east.

Mrs B.G. Otway Collection

Remains of GBL Stockton works on 11th July, 1961, looking east. The brick arch bridge used to carry the tramway over a standard gauge siding. To the right of the roof of the small brick building is the pale abutment of the former girder bridge over the LNWR.   *Author*

Greaves quarry. At the right-hand end of the furthest barrow run is a steam crane, and to the right of it, on the quarry floor, is a low open wagon which is probably standing near the end of the tunnel. The hut with large door near the centre of the picture could house a winding engine for the nearby incline. Waste clay covers the foreground, along with some unused trestles for the barrow runs.   *Mrs B.G. Otway Collection*

Illustration of a horse-drawn train from *Portrait of a Parish* (A. Payne, Roundwood Press, Kineton, 1968), thought to be at the GBL works. Note the lifting eyes on the wagon so it could be hoisted in and out of the quarry by crane.   *Author's Collection*

GBL canal boat in use for an outing, comprising mainly adults.   *Mrs B.G. Otway Collection*

Kerr, Stuart 4256 of 1922, a 'Wren' class locomotive similar to the one used by APCM at Stockton (4266 of 1922). They may even have been under construction at the same time. This engine was originally No. 114 *Peter Pan* in the Devon County Council fleet, the small plate low on the cab side carries the name of the county surveyor and the DCC number. Photographed at the Amerton Railway near Stafford on 15th June, 2013.   *Author*

at Southam & Long Itchington station (which probably means the firm's private siding). It had cylinders 6 in. x 9 in,. and driving wheels 1 ft 8(9) in. in diameter on 3 ft 0 in. wheelbase. The boiler had a steel firebox and tubes and worked at 140 psi. Total heating surface was 86 sq. ft and the grate area was 2.2 sq. ft. Empty weight was 3 tons 7 cwt 3 qtr, increasing to 4 tons 5 cwt in working order, then carrying 2½ cwt fuel and 85 gallons of water. Height to the top of the chimney was 7 ft 8 in., overall width 4 ft 2½ in., and it was about 11 ft long. The maximum axle load was 2 t. 17 cwt, tractive effort (75 per cent) 1,700 lb, and the minimum radius curve it could negotiate was 35 ft. Haulage capacity on the level was 90 tons, falling to 45 tons up 1 in 100 or 25 tons up 1 in 50. It cost £675 new and was painted grey, although it was remembered as black at Stockton. It was scrapped in 1936. Stephenson Locomotive Society records state that it went to Ufton before being scrapped, possibly on a brief loan when the quarries were being opened in early 1934 (*see Chapter Five*).

2 ft gauge

| 0-4-0ST | OC | KS | 4266 | 1922 | New | (1) |

(1)   To Ham River Grit Co. Ltd, Surrey, and returned. Lent to Ufton Quarries *c*.1934 and returned. Scrapped 1936.

Originally there were about 20 wooden open wagons. They had a square body about 12 in. high having one side removable, and held between 30 and 40 cwt of stone. The stone was stacked carefully above the low sides. Lifting eyes on the ends of the bodies enabled the wagons to be slung from a crane into the pit. Iron V-skips were introduced after the locomotive came. In 1913 the boy employed weighing wagons earned a wage of 4s. (approximately £11) per week.

Michael H. Lakin made a siding agreement with the LNWR on 27th April, 1893, two years before the extension from Daventry was opened! A siding plan dated November 1909 shows the works' siding comprised a very short loop on the north side of the main line, about 1¼ miles west of Napton & Stockton station. The 14½ mile post was opposite the lime kilns. The loop was entered by a two sets of crossover points, each of which served a headshunt beside the running line. The siding into the works close to the western loop crossover. It led to a short loop, and a siding ran back, through a brick-arch bridge carrying the narrow gauge tramway, split into two and finished between the buildings of the 1898 extensions. The main line loop was spanned by a girder bridge carrying the narrow gauge tramway. Shunting was by horse or the main line locomotive.

In 1961 the kilns still stood by the canal basin immediately west of the lock (the second of six in the Stockton flight), with a disused BR siding on the south side. At the east end of the site the skew brick tramway bridge spanned a works road laid on the former siding, and the abutments of the girder bridge carrying the tramway over the main line remained with their approach embankments.

The main line siding was not used much, most traffic going by canal. GBL owned some narrow boats, but no details are available. A 'coke gang' of three men used to earn 8d. (about £1) unloading a pair of boats bringing 40 tons of coke from Leamington on Saturday mornings.

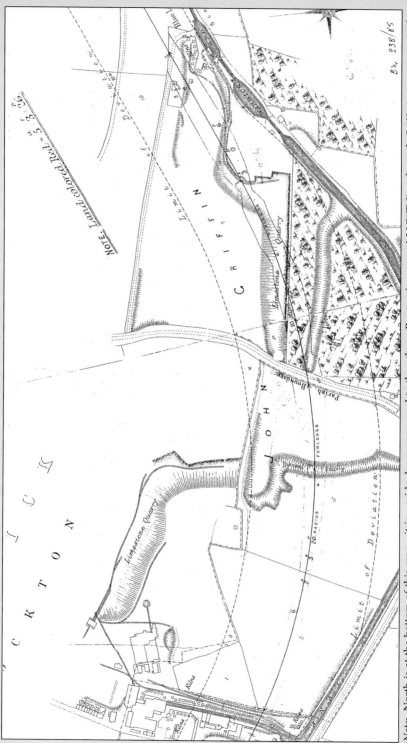

Note: North is at the bottom of this map - it is upside down compared to the others. Route of proposed LNWR line through Griffin's quarry, 1890. The quarry and its tramway are virtually on the centre line of the route, as also is the building marked 8 which is probably the manager's house. The 'Limit of Deviation' is the tolerance permitted by the railway's Act of Parliament. East of the road are Nelson's quarry and a disused pit from earlier workings.
British Waterways Archive - Gloucester, BW92/5/5

Chapter Nine

Griffin's Stockton Limeworks

After 1834	Capt Thomas Lamb
1841	William Griffin
1862	Executors of Wm Griffin
By 1866	Mrs Ann Griffin
By 1868	Executors of Wm Griffin
By 1888	Griffin & Co.

Closed c.1906, equipment sold 1910

By 1916	Kaye & Co.

Closed mid-1920s, c.1928?

By 1929	Watson Nelson

Closed mid-1930s

Griffin's Blue Lias Limeworks was on the canal bank between the second and third locks from Stockton top lock, about 600 yards south-west of Birdingbury Wharf, just before the long bend which turned the canal from north-east to south-east for the three mile section to Napton Junction (SP 435649). A minor road from near the Blue Lias inn, half a mile away to the west, also gave access to the works.

The 1854 trade directory shows Richard Greaves as a blue lias lime burner and Wm Griffin as a farmer, but Bartlett states that William (1791-1861) was definitely the lime burner as there is no trace of a Richard Griffin in contemporary records. In 1862 his executors were listed as blue lias lime and cement manufacturers as well as farmers.

William Griffin was a tenant farmer at Stockton Fields Farm (renamed Stockton Hill Farm after World War II), situated about halfway between Stockton village and Birdingbury Wharf, almost due south of Nelson's later works. The owner of the farm, Captain Thomas Lamb of Leamington Spa, signed an agreement with William Griffin on 22nd June, 1841 for 21 years, leasing him 'his lime rock' at Stockton, on land adjoining the Warwick & Napton Canal. Lamb was guaranteed a minimum annual royalty of £100 (approximately £4,600) calculated on 4,000 tons at 6d. per ton 'whether excavated or not'. Griffin paid Lamb £150 for tools, waggons, etc., while the 'Railway, Iron Rails, Buildings and Fixtures' remained the landowner's property. Lamb had retired from the Army due to ill health in 1834, and the lime works with its railway had been started soon after. Maybe he leased the business to William as he was then too ill to run it himself, dying aged 51 three months after signing the agreement.

Following Lamb's death, the 168 acres of land farmed by William, plus another 17 acres which included the lime kilns and quarry (of which about 2 acres had been excavated), was put up for auction. The auction, held on 14th May, 1844, was advertised in *The Times*, the description including '[quarry] communicating (by means of a tram road) with kilns situate on the banks of the Warwick & Napton Canal'. The map of the smaller plot showed it was immediately south of the 'Church Land'. There were three kilns by the canal, just below the second lock, and a single track 'tram road'

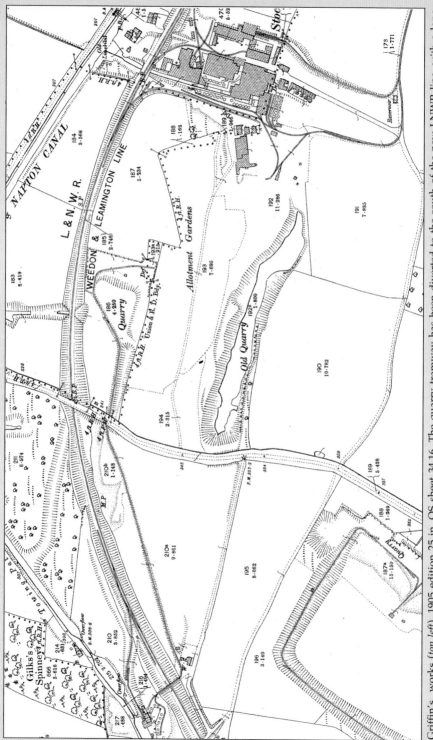

Griffin's works (*top left*), 1905 edition 25 in. OS sheet 34.16. The quarry tramway has been diverted to the south of the new LNWR line, with a long embankment to raise it to the level of the bridge over the LNWR close to the manager's new house. East of the main road is Griffin's quarry, with Nelson's old quarry and his works on the right-hand edge of the map. The former line along the canal bank now serves the LNWR siding. The GBL ran near the southern boundary about 300 yards to the eastern end of the quarry, which was still about 100 yards short of the main road. Bartlett states that no information about the sale was given in local papers, although by 1850 William was in possession of the kilns and quarry while the farm land had passed to the Nelson family. It seems that William did not actually own the works until June 1850, so maybe he had some sort of arrangement with Lamb's executors until he had acquired sufficient capital.

A surviving sales ledger for 1849-54 shows that lime was sold locally for about 10s. (£30) per ton but in London it sold for 18s. 6d. (£55), which included the cost of transport. Raw limestone (mainly sold to lime burners in north Warwickshire) fetched about 2s. per ton, while cement was sold for 16s. (£48) locally or £1 5s. 0d. (£75) in London. Most of the cement sales were to Messrs Ashby & Sons, Roman Cement Works, Isleworth, Middlesex who took 340 tons in 1852, 204 tons in 1853 and 655 tons in 1854.

William Griffin died in 1861 and his executors took over. According to a trade directory, by 1866 the business was being run by his widow Mrs Ann Griffin, but his executors were still shown as 'Lime burners & Merchants' in 1872. *White's Directory* of 1874 has separate entries for 'Griffin, William, (executors of): blue lias lime and cement manufacturers' (one of the few known printed references to cement manufacture here); 'Griffin, Thomas, executor & manager' (William's son, farmer at Birdingbury Fields) and 'Archer, Thomas, executor & manager' (William's son-in-law, chemist, of Southam). However, Thomas Griffin died in 1874, aged 42, reputedly of measles, and while his brothers William, John and George may have assisted running the firm they were primarily local farmers. Their sister, Sarah Jane, married her cousin John Griffin, son of George the brother of William (senior). George was a wine and spirits merchant in Southam - and also supplied top hats to Rugby School. The 1881 census for Southam shows John Griffin as 'farmer, wine and spirits merchant, lime merchant' and the 1888 trade directory shows Griffin & Co. being run by him. William's widow Ann had continued to live in her home, and although her landlord, Charles Nelson, had felt it necessary in January 1877 to serve her with notice to quit within the next 12 months, he died before the time had elapsed and the Griffin family continued to live in that house for another 90 years spanning three generations!

Although John Griffin had inherited his father's wine merchants business, he was described in the 1881 census only as a lime merchant, and it is certain that he had long played an important role in the business. When he died in 1906, being the last of William's sons, his executors eventually closed the works. There was no entry in the 1908 directory, and they arranged the company's 'Machinery, Plant, Tools, Buildings &c' to be sold by auction on 1st December, 1910. The Breaking-Up Sale was advertised in the *Leamington Spa Courier* on 18th November, 1910 'By direction of the Executors of the late Mr John Griffin'. The plant advertised for sale on 1st December comprised:

25 HP Engine and Boiler, by Danks; Vertical Engine, by Tangye; Two Steam Pumps, by Tangye; Steam Winch and Platform Hoist, Large Quantities of Trolley Rails, 8 Tons of Pine Baulks, 12 Trolley Wagons, 2 pairs of Grinding Stones, Large Quantity of Tools, 2 Canal Boats, 5,000 New Blue and Brindle Bricks. The Whole of the Buildings Forming Engine House, Grinding Mill, Boiler House, and Shaft; the Brickwork forming 11 kilns, and a very large quantity of Quarried Stone &c. &c.
NOTE - The above plant lies handy for removal, there being a Canal Wharf and L. and N.W. Railway Siding on the Premises.

Then, in 1916, there is the first entry in a trade directory for a limeworks operated by Kaye & Co. (of Southam cement works – *see Chapter Seven*). The last entry for

Griffin's works beside the Warwick & Napton Canal, in 1938, looking west. To the right of Griffin's chimney, in the background is the chimney of APCM Harbury works (4½ miles away), with the chimney of RPC Southam works in the central distance (1 mile away) and the two chimneys of APCM Stockton works on the right, above the canal (½ mile away). The new wide lock is under repair so the pair of boats is using the original narrow lock. The motor boat will pass through the lock while the unpowered butty boat remains at the higher level. The butty will then be hauled by manpower into the lock to rejoin the motor boat at the lower level. (When passing through wide locks the two boats would be 'breasted up' so that they could go through the lock together, in a single operation. *Alan Faulkner Collection/Canal & Rivers Trust Waterways Archive*

Bridge under the Southam to Rugby road giving access to Griffin's quarry east of the road, close to the LNWR bridge, 11th July, 1961. *Author*

Kaye's lime works was in the 1921 edition, although Kaye's name appeared in the 1928 & 1932 editions, being replaced by Rugby Cement in 1936. These later entries related to the Southam cement works itself. One informant said Kaye's closed here about the end of World War I, but Kaye's presence here until the mid-1920s would help explain the purchase of the two newest steam locomotives at Southam. Unfortunately, soon after they were delivered, Kaye was forced to close these works in order to concentrate production at Southam. This decision may have been brought about by a combination of problems, such as coal strikes, the 1926 General Strike, and increasing competition in the cement industry.

Summarizing, it seems that William Griffin began lime burning on a small scale in 1841 and ran an existing lime works, constructed by Thomas Lamb a few years earlier, alongside his farm. After William's death in 1861 his widow Ann and his executors continued the business. The family continued the business until around 1906, although the closing sale was not until 1st December, 1910. There was then a gap of about 10 years when the works appears to have been closed, until 1916 by which time it was owned by Kaye, who had it until the mid-1920s. By 1929 Watson Nelson was using the site to dispatch the products of Napton Brickworks, which he owned (*see Appendix Eight*). The 1929 edition of the *Railway Clearing House Hand Book of Stations*, which listed every private siding, had an entry for Watson Nelson's Siding between Napton and Southam stations.

The 1905 25 in. OS map, published a year before the firm closed, shows 12 kilns, although the advertisement for the sale in 1910 says there were 11 kilns. A chimney was still standing in 1970 and the kilns were used as pigsties. Despite occasional references to cement, very little cement was made here; the site was primarily a lime works. As usual, clay was picked out of the quarried stone by hand.

The quarry was east of the kilns, served by a 2 ft gauge tramway. The earliest workings seem to have been immediately east of the canal, working towards the main Southam to Rugby road which had just been reached by 1886. The northern edge of the quarry followed the southern boundary of the L-shaped workings previously described at Birdingbury Wharf (*see Chapter Six*), while they stretched southwards to the GBL quarry.

A brick bridge was built under the main road in 1894, presumably by the LNWR, giving access to a new quarry east of the road, the new railway going through much of the existing quarry. The bridge had a passage 50 ft long, 10 ft wide and 8 ft high (when measured in 1961). This quarry was eventually about 250 yards long, cutting through the disused quarry associated with the former lime works at Birdingbury Wharf. It was on the north side of the area known as 'Calley Gardens', which itself had been quarried and then filled in again using waste from the quarries on either side, so that it was recovered for agricultural use. Although plans drawn up for the construction of the LNWR branch (*see below*) show Griffin owned land on this side of the road as far as Nelson's cement works, which may have been the reason why Kaye became involved, competition from larger local firms and the quarries becoming worked out were reasons proposed by Bartlett for the closure around 1906. The disused quarries were used as a refuse tip after World War II until the 1980s, and were then covered with soil for agricultural use.

The works would have been connected to the proposed Marton Tramway of 1889, whose route went through the quarry but avoided the kilns. Although the authorized line of the extension of the LNWR Daventry branch to Leamington (Act obtained 1890, line opened 1st August, 1895) passed south of the working area it was diverted south, within the 'limits of deviation' to avoid the kilns. However, the manager's house lay on the direct line of the railway so the railway company built a red brick replacement known as 'Griffin's House', north of the original quarry. The house still stands, with the date 1893 in blue brick in the south wall (SP 434648). The

LNWR built a bridge near the kilns to carry the tramway to the quarry over their new line. This bridge was not demolished until the late 1950s. The tramway ran straight for about 400 yards, parallel to the LNWR, to a bridge under the main road. This bridge, of blue brick, was probably built by the LNWR as compensation for occupying much of the old quarry. Its parapets are still visible, immediately south of the LNWR bridge.

The tramway was horse operated, but no other details have survived. Kaye is said to have used at least one of his Peckett 0-6-0ST locomotives here, as the run of 500 yards to the road, plus the quarry, would justify their use, although the bridge under the main road shows no sign of soot under the arch. These locomotives are described in Chapter Seven. Any experimental use of locomotives was probably after World War I. As a result of successful trials it could be that he decided to obtain one for permanent use here, taking delivery of No. 1632 of 1923. The engine having been delivered and proved invaluable, a second one could then have been required in a hurry for extra work, or even to cover the other when it was receiving routine maintenance. However, if Peckett quoted too long a delivery date Kaye may have tried elsewhere, hence the order to Bagnall, a firm which often built small standard locomotives for stock and so could provide quick delivery. Bagnall No. 2148 was an 0-4-0ST, ordered in November 1924 and delivered within a few days. This is all supposition, but would account why this Peckett initially had no name (later it became the second *Liassic*), because it was the only engine on site, and also for the purchase of a small Bagnall when all the previous locomotives had been Pecketts. Unfortunately, soon after they were delivered, these works were closed to concentrate production at Southam, where the two virtually new locomotives were transferred.

2 ft gauge

| 0-6-0ST | OC | P | 1632 | 1923 | New | To Southam Works mid-1920s |
| 0-4-0ST | OC | WB | 2148 | 1924 | New | To Southam Works mid-1920s |

The advertisement for the sale in 1910 includes '12 Trolley Wagons'. These were probably wooden wagons with fixed bodies to carry the stone, similar to neighbouring lines. The advertisement also listed two canal boats, assumed horse drawn, one being named *John*.

According to the 1906 25 in. OS map and the LNWR siding plan (No. 973, dated January 1909, referring to the agreement with J. Griffin dated 6th March, 1896), there was a short loop on the north side of the single track Daventry to Leamington line near the 14 milepost. At each end of the loop was a headshunt about 200 ft long. The single siding ran from the west end of the loop to terminate on the canal bank close to lock 2 of the Stockton flight. The OS map shows a narrow gauge tramway running from beside this siding about 200 ft to the works building, although the 1909 LNWR plan shows the siding continuing over the narrow gauge route to the building, which must have been much more convenient. A horse, or even men, was probably used to move wagons on the siding, assisted by the main line locomotive when it collected or delivered wagons.

After the limeworks closed in the mid-1920s the site was used until the mid-1930s to transfer tiles and pipes made at Napton brickworks to rail, the brickworks itself having no rail access (*see Appendix Eight*). Griffin's abandoned site, having a siding beside the canal, offered good transhipment facilities, including space to store goods.

Chapter Ten

Nelson's Stockton Lime and Cement Works

Late 1850s	Nelson & Rutland	
1859	Charles Nelson	
1886	Charles Nelson & Co. Ltd	
1945	Rugby Portland Cement Co. Ltd	closed 1946

Stockton Lime & Cement Works was shown on the 1834 and 1862 one inch OS maps. It was located on the south side of the canal near Birdingbury Wharf, where the canal began a long curve to the south-west (SP 440649 – *see Chapter Six*). The works was marked disused on the 1888 25 in. map. It is probable that a narrow gauge tramway connected the works with quarries to the west and with a canal wharf to the north.

The 1889 6 in. map showed Nelson's works a few hundred yards further east, half a mile north of Stockton village. It was then situated on both sides of the canal arm (SP 442647), with a Y-shaped quarry west of the works. The western branch, 'No. 1 Quarry', was marked 'old quarry' and the northern branch 'No. 2 Quarry'. North of it, marked 'disused', was the quarry used by the earlier works. Although the private canal arm had been built, Nelson's tramway still went as far as the canal bank. The map showed a footbridge over the canal giving direct access to the works from the Napton to Birdingbury road. By August 1958 this wooden footbridge on brick piers was in dangerous condition, and was it demolished soon after, some years before the rest of the works.

The 1906 edition 6 in. OS map showed the quarry west of the works as closed, replaced by a new quarry immediately west of the road from Stockton village to Napton & Stockton station. It could well be that the change was a consequence of the construction of the main line railway, opened in 1895. This quarry was worked steadily westwards until eventually it was almost south of the works.

This company's history is linked to the firm of George Nelson, Dale & Co. Ltd, Emscote Mills, Warwick, timber merchants and makers of gelatine and isinglass (a kind of gelatine obtained from fish). The firm had been founded by George Nelson and John Dale in 1837. The original gelatine works was at Rock Mill, but in 1842 they moved to larger premises nearby, on the south bank of the canal on the eastern outskirts of Warwick. Gelatine manufacture requires a large quantity of lime, and accounts for George Nelson establishing a lime works at Stockton in 1844.

An article in *Waterways World* (March 1988) stated that this lime works was beside the canal 'nearly a mile east of Stockton top lock'. This location is clearly wrong because it is just east of Napton & Stockton station, where no works was ever shown on a map. However, quarter of a mile east of the top lock would site it at Birdingbury Wharf, where there was an early but short-lived lime works. This location is about 10 miles east of Emscote Mills, with a direct canal link. In view of this, it is surprising that Nelson is not mentioned in the 1850 trade directory, although the entries for Warwick in the 1856 edition includes a reference to Nelson supplying Portland cement. The 1860 edition listed Charles Nelson at Stockton making Blue Lias Lime and Cement, 'and at Southam'. Under Stockton, this directory also states 'The Blue Lias is extensively manufactured here by Greaves and Kirshaw of Warwick, and Messrs Oldham & Nelson of Southam'. It looks as though Nelson's original works

Nelson's works, looking south-east, 25th May, 1937. In the lower left corner a short stretch of road is visible beside the Warwick & Napton Canal. Trees cover the site of old kilns at the junction with the canal arm into the works. The LNWR branch is roughly parallel to the canal. A disused quarry, possibly supplying Nelson's former lime works at Birdingbury Wharf, is in the right foreground. The cottages with their outbuildings are beside the approach road. In front of them is the ramp to the later tip. Near the water tower (still standing) is the engine shed, with an engine beside it. On the far side of the works, near the square chimney, is the older narrow gauge tipping gantry, its access track being marked by a row of poles. The quarry is in the distance with a steam crane on the lip to hoist skips. There is a rake of skips by this crane and a second rake headed by a steam locomotive is nearby. Below and to the left of this crane there are about half a dozen skips on the intermediate level of the quarry. In the corner of the quarry nearest the waste tip is another crane, mounted on a concrete structure, with about a dozen skips to the left of it. There are two more cranes on the quarry lip, either side of the right-hand tree in the group of three above the pair of smoking chimneys. In the centre, old workings are filled with waste clay. The derrick is on the near side of the quarry, beside a single tree. Apart from five vans on the curved siding, all the rolling stock visible comprises open wagons, most of those by the main line appearing to be loaded with coal.

English Heritage,

edition 25 in. OS, sheet 34.16. Note the 'old limekilns' at the canal junction, the rows of kilns either side of the canal arm, the locomotive shed served by a triangle of lines, the row of cottages by the works' entrance, as well as numerous standard gauge sidings in the works, with wagon turntables where lines cross. The railway to the quarry ran beside the private road to the works. The building at the southern end of the quarry was the winding house for the incline into the workings. Quarrying later extended over fields 161, 162, most of 171, and other fields to the south. The later lorry loading point was near the windpump, and the line to the later stone tip was beside the road to the cottages. The hand derrick was near the reservoir. *See also map on page 140.*

Crown Copyright

was at Southam, probably at High Clays Farm, which was close to Stockton bottom lock, and was marked disused on the 1886 OS map.

Expanding his business, and probably finding transport difficult (High Clays required smaller boats, *see Chapter Six*), Charles Nelson transferred to Birdingbury Wharf, and then in the early 1860s opened a new works on a virgin site beside the canal at Stockton Fields several hundred yards further east. The first kilns had been built on the bank of the main canal, and later there were more kilns beside the short branch canal which served the works.

George Nelson died in 1850, and the two main enterprises were then separated. The eldest son Charles had the lime works while a younger son had the gelatine business. The Nelson family, trading as Nelson Brothers, became increasingly preoccupied with overseas business interests, particularly developing the Canterbury Lamb and meat refrigeration business in New Zealand. The gelatine business was eventually absorbed into Davis Gelatine.

Charles Nelson expanded production and introduced the manufacture of Portland cement, which supports the supposition above about the moves to new sites. While the 1860 trade directory refers to Messrs Nelson, the 1866 edition lists Charles Nelson & Co. According to 1866 copies of the *Southam Parish Magazine*, Charles Nelson had already started a coal club and in October he gave donations to the Southam clothing and shoe clubs.

In 1870 Charles Nelson took his brothers George and Montague into partnership, together with Thomas Blyth and William Blackstone, both London lime and cement merchants. Blyth was living in Stockton House, situated at the crossroads on the western side of the village, in 1874. Unfortunately, Charles Nelson died from Bright's (kidney) disease in 1877, aged only 43, leaving a widow and 10 children, but his partners carried on. One son, George Herbert (baptised in August 1867) managed Harp Brickworks, Banbury Road, Southam, in 1910.

By 1880 brick and pipe making had been added to the firm's entry in trade directories. The 1904 edition mentioned tiles as well, following the link with Napton Brickworks in 1901 (*see Appendix Nine*). In 1886 the firm became Charles Nelson & Co. Ltd. The Directors in 1904 were Sir Montague Nelson and two sons of Thomas Blyth, George and Howard. G.B. Blyth became a member of the parish council in 1894, and its chairman from 1906 until 1934. Nelson's son 'went to France and had an accident', so he left the business, handing it over to the three Blyth brothers, George, Charles and Harold. George Blyth, Chairman of Charles Nelson & Co., had no descendants which may have been a contributory reason for the sale to Rugby Portland Cement in 1945.

By 1905 the works was entirely on the east side of its private canal branch, the kilns on the bank of the main canal west of the branch being then disused. A rotary kiln was introduced around 1910. It was about 30 ft long and 6 ft diameter, and made 3,528 tons of cement clinker in three months in 1911. A second rotary kiln was built in 1913. The first ball mill was constructed in 1920, and the quarry itself was modernized 1923. The works was powered by two large Sulzer uniflow steam engines, and later a British Thomson-Houston steam turbine.

The Blue Lias Co-operative Society had been formed by 1904, operating a store in Stockton. (Independent retail co-operative societies were once common, even in small communities. It is only in comparatively recent years that significant numbers have merged or closed. For example, in the early 1960s, within a 20 mile radius of Northampton, there were 18 independent co-operative societies with sizes ranging from less than 100 members to over 20,000, and premises ranging from a single travelling van to town centre department stores with 20 or more branches).

Charles Nelson & Co. Ltd gave money in 1904 to construct Stockton Methodist Church, which is still in use. The Nelson Working Men's Club was built in Napton Road or Victoria Terrace (the opposite sides of the same road). A copy of the original rules, dated 1914, hangs in the bar. The primary object of 'The Nelson Club' was 'for the accommodation and benefit of the employees of Messrs Chas Nelson & Co. Ltd. And Messrs Watson Nelson Ltd [Napton Brickworks]…' The present premises were built in the mid-1920s at a cost of £20,000 (about £600,000). The works telephone number was Southam 5 in 1928, and a second line was added in the late 1930s.

Following an unsuccessful attempt in 1923 or early 1924, a major strike took place in August 1924, to try to obtain seven fully-paid days of annual holiday, and for overtime rates. The strike lasted 13 weeks, and as a result 44 of 247 employees (18 per cent) lost their jobs. The company paid a halfpenny (about 6p) an hour less 'than certain other manufacturers' but it had a profit sharing scheme which 'more than cancelled this out'. The workmen said their rate was a penny halfpenny (19p) less, and that the employees of Kaye and Greaves Bull & Lakin were much better off. The company denied treating their employees badly, pointing out that they had built a chapel and working men's club, as well as many houses.

The firm's entry in the 1928 *Concrete Year Book* stated that because its Blue Lias Lime would set under water, it had been extensively used in the London tube railways (Bakerloo, Central, Piccadilly, Waterloo & City), the Thames Tunnel (probably Blackwall built 1897 or Rotherhithe built 1908), and extensions to Waterloo station. Cock Brand Patent Selenitic (quick setting) Cement was also manufactured.

During World War II (and probably before), schoolchildren with a father, brother or other relative in the works had an extra half-hour for lunch so they could take them a hot meal. It was about half a mile from the village to the works, along a direct footpath. The works was well away from local roads, so the two nearest were linked by an east-west private road over half a mile long, with a branch northwards 200 yards long to the works itself joining near the mid-point.

Charles Nelson & Co. Ltd was not in the cement federation. The works was closed in 1946 following its purchase by Rugby Portland Cement Co. Ltd in 1945, possibly due to lack of trade, but more probably because the plant had become out of date and so was uneconomic to operate. The machinery was dismantled in 1950. After standing derelict for many years the empty buildings were finally demolished around 1970/71. The quarry became a reservoir for nearby Southam works.

In the late 19th century Charles Nelson & Co. Ltd appears to have been technologically ahead of some other companies, for example in the introduction of steam locomotives on its quarry railway. As an independent manufacturer it had outlasted Kaye & Co. by 11 years. There were branches in London, at 16 South Wharf, Paddington; in Manchester at 2 Mount Street; and Birmingham at Cambria Wharf Crescent.

Visits in 2007 and 2008 found a 2.4 metre-high steel security fence erected right round the quarry. The concrete water tower still stood on the edge of the works site, but little else recognisable remained. The whole area was very overgrown. There was no sign of the locomotive shed, but there was a half-buried concrete building which might have been an air raid shelter. Near the main road and the course of the LNWR branch there was a flooded quarry, and brick and concrete ruins which might have been kilns. Several sleepers with chairs marked 'LNWR 1900' were nearby. The Blue Lias Ring Walk passes through the site. At the east end of the former approach road the lorry loading point could be seen through the security fence, and several

The Nelson Working Men's Club, Napton Road, Stockton, 20th June, 1996.   *Author*

Stockton Methodist Church on 20th June, 1996, it was built by Nelson in 1904.   *Author*

industrial units, one building canal narrow boats, had been built on the western half of the road. The Nelson Club in Stockton village was still functioning, 60 years after the company had closed.

The 1886 6 inch OS map shows a railway on the west bank of the canal branch, serving a group of five kilns on the bank of the main canal at the junction, where there was a small wharf, long enough for a single boat. It seems probable that these were Nelson's original kilns, which were disused by 1905. There was a loop beside the north end of canal branch. Towards and beyond the southern end of the canal branch were 18 kilns on its west side and another 11 on the east side. Just beyond the southernmost kiln a track entered a building, which possibly housed a tip serving a stone crusher. The main line then turned west towards the quarry.

In 1887 the quarry was about 150 yards south west of the end of the canal arm, running westwards 350 yards to the main road from Southam to Dunchurch. About 50 yards of double track, presumably a winch operated incline, went from a building on the edge of the quarry down into the pit, with lines onward to the faces. Another track ran from the presumed winch house along the northern lip of the quarry, possibly for tipping the waste clay which interleaved the beds of limestone. After this quarry was abandoned, perhaps as a result of the construction of the LNWR branch, it filled with water and was used as a reservoir to supply the works. Additional water came from the canal. Grand Union Canal Accounts show that Nelson took 1,408,840 gallons @ 9d./1000 in the year ending 31st December, 1942 at a cost of £60 15s., about half as much again as had been taken in 1936.

The 1905 map shows the works narrow gauge railway terminating in a pair of sidings between the canal branch and a standard gauge siding. From the presumed crusher building, still rail served, one line bore west to the old western quarry while another continued south, parallel to the works approach road. The track serving the engine shed joined from the west, creating a triangle of lines, and then there was a long loop. The main line continued south along the edge of a field until it reached the main private road, where it turned east to run beside it. Shortly it was joined by a branch serving the original stone tip, latterly disused, on the eastern side of the works. The railway continued eastwards through fields for about 500 yards to the quarry. The first face had been close to the road from Stockton village to the station when the quarry opened around 1900. The railway then turned south for 200 yards, and finally turned northwards through a semi-circle to serve a winding house with double track incline into the quarry itself. There was a loop just before the winding house, and another at the foot of the incline, to accommodate full and empty wagons. The winding house probably contained a stationary engine, as the gradient was against the load, with, the map suggests, a boiler house and chimney at the western end of the building.

This remained the basic layout for the next 40 years, modified of course as the quarry was worked gradually westwards. The incline into the pit was superseded by steam cranes on the quarry lip which hoisted wagons in and out of the workings. Temporary tracks were laid to serve the faces and also on the tip.

The corrugated iron engine shed had been constructed in two if not three stages. The original building was about 18 ft long with a pit and curved roof, and would have held one locomotive. At some date, probably around 1900, it was extended eastwards by 24 ft, which would have accommodated the other two steam engines. This part also had a curved roof, but was narrower than the part with the pit. Later still a westwards extension 33 ft long was built, presumably to house the petrol locomotives obtained in the 1920s. This extension had a ridged roof. No smoke pots

Nelson's quarry. Wooden side-door wagons are on the quarry floor, while iron V-skips are on the bench below the left-hand crane and a skip body is being hoisted by the right-hand crane. Note the long barrow run in the foreground - the three men are all pulling their empty barrows.

Mrs B.G. Otway Collection

Concrete structure in a corner of quarry (just above the derrick in the aerial photograph on page 154). It was the base of a fixed steam crane (visible in the aerial photograph), having a workshop or quarry locomotive shed at the bottom, with access stairs inside the left-hand end. Photograph taken after a drought, when the water level had dropped significantly on 2nd October, 1965.   *Author*

remained in 1961 but aerial photographs suggest they were fitted to the eastern and central sections.

In the late 1930s a concrete ramp with a double track was built to serve the new western stone tip. A winch hauled wagons up to the tip from a loop protected by a shelter with a roof but no sides. There was a weighbridge at the foot of the incline. The disused eastern branch terminated on an elevated but level tipping dock.

By the time the works closed the quarry was some 500 yards from east to west and 700 yards from north to south. Old workings near the road were filled with clay which was surplus to the amount required for cement making. Unlike several local works, Nelson never imported chalk or limestone from elsewhere.

Latterly the excavated rock was mechanically screened to separate the stone and clay. The stone went into wagons for transport to the works, while the clay was put on a conveyor which brought it up out of the pit to a hopper, where it was loaded into wagons for transport to the tip.

In the early 1930s improvements made to the adjacent canal, by then called the Grand Union. This work was partly financed by a Treasury grant of £500,000 (£18m), given to provide work to the unemployed, as many as 1,000 men being employed. The improvements included widening two canal bridges on the main Daventry road at Lower Shuckburgh (four miles away). Lorries taking clay from the waste tip for use as fill were loaded at a concrete tipping dock constructed beside the eastern end of the private road. Other improvements to the canal involved the construction of new wider locks and lining the towpath bank with concrete piles to counter erosion caused by the wash of motor boats. The contractors for the locks and bridges were L.J. Speight Ltd.

The quarry had a hand-operated derrick at the north-west corner, provided for bringing in equipment and materials but apparently not much used. Its jib was 28 ft long, made from 10 in. x 3½ in. channel. The remains of a concrete structure nearby could have been a hoist for stone. The holes in the concrete base, 64 in. x 39 in., were too small to permit a quarry wagon to go through but they could have been used by skips. Assuming one wagon (27 cu. ft) filled a skip, and the hoist's skip was 12 in. smaller than the hole in each direction to accommodate its guides, then the skip would have been about 33 in. deep. An aerial photograph shows a train here, which helps to confirm this possibility.

On the south-east corner of the quarry was another large concrete structure which contained a long flight of stairs from the lip of the quarry to its floor. At the bottom was a room described in my notes as 'possible garage', which could have been the shed, or workshop, for locomotives used in the quarry. An aerial photograph confirms that the massive construction of the building, with a loop across the top of it, was the base for a crane for hoisting wagons from the pit.

The gauge of the railway was 21 in. (1 ft 9 in.). The rail used weighed about 20 or 24 lb./yard. Sleepers were 40 in. x 6 in. at 2 ft 6 in. centres. When the works closed, old rails were taken to Southam, cut into 6 in. lengths, and used in the grinding mills in place of metal balls. Two permanent way men were employed.

The quarry was a large hole below the surrounding level fields and always had to be pumped to keep it dry. After the works closed it became a reservoir supplying Southam works. One seam of stone, a uniform 8 in. thick, was known locally as 'The Builder' as it was ideal for construction purposes, and was worked for this purpose where it outcropped. The works only used the limestone; the clay between the seams of stone was extracted and dumped on the tip.

The men worked in gangs of about 12, taking out a column of stone from top to bottom, typically 12 yards wide by 8 to 20 yards long. The column was worked in

Engine shed on 27th July, 1961. Note the two different sections of the building.   *Author*

Peckett official photograph of *Gamecock*, 678. Note the riveted smokebox.   *F. Jones Collection*

steps about 3 ft high. The tonnage dug was booked against the gang. When inclines were used to take the railway into the quarry, stone was probably dropped down chutes from higher levels into the wagons at the bottom. Later, when wagons were hoisted to the working levels by steam cranes on the quarry lip, they were loaded direct.

When all the excavation was done by hand stone and clay were separated and loaded into different wagons at the face. The quarry was modernized in 1923 and this probably marks the introduction of steam excavators. The dug material was taken to 'rumblers' (mechanical screens) which sorted it into stone and clay, loading the stone in wagons which were hoisted out of the pit and taken to the works. Fine clay was blown along a steel pipe by compressed air to a hopper, to which small stones were taken by conveyor, where the waste material was loaded into wooden wagons for tipping.

In the 1920s, quarrymen worked a 6-day week, 6 am to 5 pm, with 30 minute breaks for breakfast and lunch, for 4¼d. per hour (i.e. 60-hour week for £1 1s. 3d., or about £30 today). If it was too wet to work they were not paid! There were then four gangs of men and six steam cranes. Another two men worked on the clay tip. Overburden could be removed by grab crane.

Two steam locomotives were in daily use on the main line up to the closure, hauling trains of 10 to 12 wagons. The Simplex petrol, later diesel, locomotives were used first in the pit bottom. Similar locomotives, used when the nearby canal locks were widened in 1931-32, had been called 'dinkum' by all concerned and the name stuck. There was a Simplex locomotive on each step in the quarry, lifted in and out when required by crane. They were not as powerful as the steam engines, and could only haul six to eight wagons. In addition to those used in the quarry, these small locomotives also worked on the tip and did sundry odd jobs on the main level.

Cranes lifted the wagons out of the quarry by a chain fastened to an eye in each corner. The wagons held 20 to 25 cwt, and were always pulled to and from the quarry. On arrival at the works the wagons of stone were weighed, and single wagons were then winched up the concrete ramp to be tipped into the crusher. The winch was at the top of the ramp, opposite the crusher. The ramp was double track, to separate full and empty wagons. It had been built around 1937; previously wagons had entered the works area past the cottages, had been weighed, and then had to be worked out again to the tip on the east side of the works. This tip had served the crusher for the lime and the old cement works, and had been abandoned when the new one opened.

Locomotives were introduced in 1897, probably to cope with the much longer haul to the new quarry near Napton & Stockton station. The first, *Gamecock*, was followed by *Niras* in 1899 and *Jurassic* in 1901. *Gamecock* was the first really small narrow gauge locomotive built by Peckett of Bristol, whose previous narrow gauge designs were adaptations of small standard gauge engines. All three were neat 0-6-0ST. They are described in Chapter Seven, alongside the very similar 2 ft gauge locomotives on Kaye's system at Southam.

The three steam locomotives were scrapped in 1949 when the works were dismantled. After closure there was talk of sending one of them, probably *Gamecock*, to Southam, but the cost of rebuilding to 2 ft gauge was prohibitive. However, parts from Nelson's Pecketts were used in repairing those at Southam works, although one former driver maintained that nothing had gone to Southam when they were cut up. In 1961 E.S. Tonks wrote: 'A lovely little line, [Southam] and Nelsons too. Their little Pecketts used to puff over the cornfields - a wonderful sight.'

Gamecock at work. Note the hole cut in the top corner of the skip body for ease of lifting it by crane.   *IRS Collection*

Gamecock with a short train, including a tank wagon to supply water to the steam cranes on 30th July, 1938. Note that these skips have inside frames, while all the skips on the other photographs have outside frames.   *D. Clayton*

In addition to the steam locomotives the firm used a total of five Motor Rail of Bedford (Simplex) petrol and diesel locomotives. All were cabless. The first, No. 1899, was purchased new in July 1919. This was followed by two more new petrol locomotives, Nos. 3657 and 3794 in 1924 and 1926 respectively. A new diesel locomotive, No. 5917, came in January 1936. Presumably as a result of observing the economies of a diesel at first hand, the three petrol locomotives were soon converted to diesel by Motor Rail staff. There was one other, unidentified, diesel locomotive, presumably obtained second-hand in the late 1930s or early 1940s. All the Simplex locomotives were scrapped in 1950, except for 5917 which was eventually obtained as a source of components by an enthusiast.

Motor Rail 1899 was ordered on 31st July, 1919. It was a 20 hp petrol locomotive weighing 4 tons and of 21 in. gauge. It cost £650 (£16,200) plus £6 (£150) for different buffing and drawgear, probably similar to that fitted to 5917, *see below*. Later it was fitted with an exhaust whistle. This comprised a whistle mounted on a hinged box which could be pulled across the exhaust pipe, thus deflecting the gases through the whistle itself. The locomotive was converted to diesel 16th February, 1937, reducing the weight to 3 t. 14 cwt in working order.

Motor Rail's records for 3657 show that it was ordered by Charles Nelson Blue Lias Lime & Cement on 24th January, 1924. It was a reconditioned 20 hp petrol locomotive weighing 4 tons costing £430 (£13,200). The basic locomotive was probably one built originally for the War Department for front line use in World War I. Reconditioning involved new ballast weights attached to the ends of the frame (to bring the weight up from the standard 2½ tons) and new running gear (the standard unit was for 60 cm/2 ft gauge). The power unit, gearbox, radiator etc. was taken from 3653 under a pooling agreement with Wm Jones. The records noted that 'Everything on this locomotive to be a duplicate of that supplied to the above firm in July 1919 Works No. 1899'. It had been delivered by 5th February, 1924. This locomotive was later converted to diesel. Motor Rail records for Charles Nelson show unspecified locomotives being converted to diesel on 16th February, 1937 and 15th March, 1938, and that a fitter was sent to overhaul 3657 on 23rd March, 1938. This suggests the conversion was in 1938, particularly as the tractive effort was altered, presumably by fitting a new gear box. The tractive effort was reduced from 1,100/2,300 lb. (2nd, 1st gear) to 865/1,730lb. Calling the maker's fitter a week after the conversion would have given enough time to show that all was not well with the converted machine.

Records for 3794 show it was ordered on 9th April, 1926 and delivered on 30th April. It was another 20 hp reconditioned petrol locomotive, weighing 4 tons, and again cost £430. The locomotive required a new engine, underframe, etc and the only reconditioned material was the gearbox, radiator and possibly the wheels. This was the first of Nelson's petrol locomotives to be converted to diesel, on 28th April, 1936. Special sprockets were fitted on conversion, involving reduction of the wheel boss at the driver's end, gearbox side, to accommodate them.

No. 5917 was ordered on 6th January, 1936 and delivered on 7th February, 1936. It was a larger 32/42 hp diesel locomotive weighing 5 tons, and cost £510 (£18,600). Frames were straight steel channel; the earlier locomotives probably had bowed frames, which were steel channel, parallel in the centre of the locomotive and tapering at each end. Basic measurements of 5917 were length of frame 8 ft 7 in. and width 4 ft 10 in., with 16½ in. wheels on a wheelbase of 39½ in. Although the records make no mention, it seems to have been built with an unusual central buffer/coupler. A 'top hat'-shaped frame was fastened to the buffer beam and supported the coupler, whose

Niras, Peckett 785, near the derrick. Note the riveted smokebox.   *IRS Collection*

Niras outside the shed (note the painted name), a glimpse of a Motor Rail diesel, and the cab of either *Jurassic* or *Gamecock* (probably the former) on 15th April, 1938.   *G. Alliez*

spring was inside the top hat. The coupler head was circular, and carried a hook on a link for coupling. In early 1939 a Motor Rail fitter had to be called out twice to overhaul this locomotive, on 18th January and again on 24th April. When E.S. Tonks visited the railway in June 1946 this was the only one he did not see, possibly being in a locked shed. By the late 1950s it lay upside down on a V-skip body on the quarry floor beneath the hand derrick. The remains were later given to R. Weaver who removed them from the quarry in late 1969. Some parts were taken for use on other preserved Motor Rail locomotives but the wheels and brake gear were re-gauged for use on Jack Marshall's 2 ft steam locomotive, the 'first steam locomotive to be built in Warwickshire since 1877'. As some of Nelson's rails had found their way to local enthusiasts' railways, it could be that its wheels, at least, may still run on its old rails!

There were entries in Motor Rail's records for 'mechanic to overhaul loco' (unspecified) on 23rd June, 1931 and 27th June, 1932. The last order to Motor Rail for spares was on 21st March, 1945. None of these locomotives carried a name or number.

Gauge 1 ft 9 in.

(*Gamecock*)	0-6-0ST	OC	P	678/97	New	(1)
Niras	0-6-0ST	OC	P	785/99	New	(1)
(*Jurassic*)	0-6-0ST	OC	P	918/01	New	(1)
	4wDM ex-PM/37		MR	1899/19	New	scr. 1950
	4wDM ex-PM/38		MR	3657/24	New	scr. 1950
	4wPM ex-PM/36		MR	3794/26	New	scr. 1950
	4wDM		MR	5917/36	New	(2)
	4wDM		MR		(a)	scr. 1950

(a)   Ex ?, second-hand
(1)   Scr. 12.49, some parts to Southam works as spares
(2)   Dismantled 1950, some parts e.g. wheels to J. Marshall, Hockley Heath 1969 (for his home built locomotive), frame still in quarry 6.68, removed late 1969

The original wagons were wooden, with a capacity of about 30 cwt. The body was fixed but the sides could be lifted out. The majority - perhaps as many as 200 - had inside frames, and there were 20 'Banjo' wagons with outside frames. They were replaced on the main line, probably following the introduction of locomotives, by steel V-skip tipping wagons, but some of the wooden ones lasted on the clay tip until later. An inventory in 1910 listed 28 wooden wagons for quarry, 60 steel tip wagons for quarry, 20 steel clinker wagons (for carrying clinker from the kiln to the grinding and bagging plant), and four 'moveable steam cranes'. There were also a number of wagons to carry coal and water to the steam excavators and cranes at the quarry.

Eventually there were about 100 iron V-skips, holding about 25 cwt. Some, apparently the more numerous type, had outside frames and the others had inside frames. Both types had lifting eyes fitted at each corner of the chassis. The frame of an outside frame wagon found abandoned in the quarry was made of 3 in. x 6 in. channel, forming an oval 8 ft 3 in. long by 2 ft 9 in. wide. The 15 in. diameter wheels had six spokes and had a wheelbase of 3 ft. The V-section wagon body which supported the frame of Simplex 5917 was 6 ft long by 4 ft wide and 2 ft 4 in. deep. In the last years the number of wagons fell to about 60.

Although former employees spoke of whole wagons being lifted in and out of the quarry, this practice must have been quite hazardous, as normally a V-skip body just rests on bearers at each end. Later, wagon bodies had a hole cut in each corner to

Cylinders, 7-in. diameter × 10-in. stroke ; Wheels, 1-ft. 8-in. diameter ; Wheel Base, 6-ft. 6-in. Weight in full-working order, 7½ tons.   Gauge 1-ft. 9-in. to 2-ft. 6-in.   Tractive force, 3,330-lbs.

'Jurassic' class 0-6-0ST illustrated in Peckett's 1938 'Abridged illustrated list of Tank Engines'. It shows Nelson's *Jurassic*, Peckett 918 - the number of rivets on the front of the cab shows it is not Kaye's locomotive. Note the different smokebox compared to *Gamecock* and *Niras*. This picture was the basis for the decoration on my 60th birthday cake. *Author's Collection*

Remains of Motor Rail 5917 on the floor of the quarry. This skip body also has a hole for hoisting by crane, 27th July, 1961. *Author*

attach the chain sling from the crane for hoisting in and out of the quarry, presumably leaving the underframe behind ready to receive the next body. A permanent way trolley in the works in 1961 had a body 5 ft 6 in. long by 3 ft 9 in. wide. The frames were made of 3 in. by 6 in. wood, 2 ft 6 in. apart, and extended 4 in. beyond the body at each end. The 14 in. diameter wheels were set at a wheelbase of 3 ft 2½ in. The body had six longitudinal planks resting on four beams 3 in. by 4 in. high. A large wooden block forming a dumb buffer and a hook were in the centre of each end.

In its early days the company felt the lack of rail access. The LNWR main line ran very close to the canal at Weedon, so an agreement was made with the Grand Junction (later Grand Union) Canal dated 26th February, 1877. This authorized the construction of a new siding with a crane, on land built up to form a wharf on the north side of the entrance to Weedon Military Dock (SP 624590), but this arrangement was hardly convenient as it required a journey of about 16 miles and the passage of 16 locks.

Accordingly, in 1881 the company began negotiations for a railway siding 'near Marton'. First it had to acquire a piece of land from Sir Theo. Biddulph, and then to negotiate with the LNWR. Nelson's had to find half of the cost of the siding, £311. What became known as Nelson's Siding was located about ¼ mile east of Marton station, on the Rugby to Leamington line which had opened in 1851. Although it was about 3½ miles from the works by road, it would then have given a railhead much more easily accessible than Weedon. The siding was shown on the 1889 6 in. OS map on the south side of the bridge over the Marton to Birdingbury road (SP 420684). Although this siding was no closer than Birdingbury station, it was probably more convenient as it avoided the twisting road through that village. (Marton station would have been much more difficult to reach.) A signal box on the south side of the line controlled a trailing crossover, and there was a pair of sidings with headshunt on the north side. Later renamed Marton Siding, it fell out of use following the opening of the Daventry to Leamington branch in 1895, and the track was lifted.

The extension of the Daventry branch to Leamington ran past the works. According to LNWR private siding plan 972, dated January 1909, C. Nelson & Co. Ltd made agreements for private sidings on 5th March, 1897 and (presumably for extensions) on 29th February, 1908. It is curious that the date of the first agreement was about nine months later than the similar agreements at neighbouring works on the newly opened branch. Perhaps there was a dispute over the facilities to be provided, or a period of notice had to be given to discontinue using Nelson's Siding.

The works was situated some 500 yards west of Napton & Stockton station, at the 13½ mile post. In 1909 there was a loop either side of the single track Daventry to Leamington line. The northern loop, not shown on the 1905 OS map, and so possibly the cause of the 1908 agreement, had trap points at each end. The southern loop had a headshunt at each end, and had three points giving access to the works, two east of the bridge over the canal arm and one west. A second bridge under the railway gave pedestrian access to the works from the north via the footbridge over the canal.

The two sidings east of the canal arm converged at a wagon turntable within the works and formed a triangle. Later the turntable was replaced by a point, but another turntable remained in 1961 by the loading bay. A weighbridge was provided on the western arm of the triangle. At some date, presumably when the wagon turntable was replaced, a line was laid from the apex of the triangle down under the railway to a wharf on the main canal bank. This siding was probably to handle products from Napton brickworks, taken to Nelson's works for loading into railway

Shunting horses in Nelson's main line sidings. The lack of visible brake gear on the MR wagon on the extreme right suggests a date no later than 1910. The wagon on the extreme left has 'NELSON' in white lettering shaded black on the top plank of the door. The horse was attached to the wagon by a chain from the stretcher bar behind its rear end. The purpose of the stretcher was to prevent the side chains of the harness from rubbing against the horse and chafing it.

Mrs B.G. Otway Collection

Nelson's canal arm, full of boats, with a rake of coal wagons on the bridge. One wagon on the bridge is owned by Exhall Colliery, Bedworth, near Nuneaton, Warwickshire. The white diamond on other wagons is the logo of the LNWR, and the coal wagons are probably LNWR vehicles as well. As several of the wagons appear to lack brake gear the date is again likely no later than 1910. The left-hand boat appears to be loaded with bricks which could well have come from Napton, which dates the photograph to 1901 or after. Note the cock trademark on the chimney.

Pope/Parkhouse Archives Collection

wagons in the absence of any rail connection at Napton, and as such was probably laid in the early 1900s after Nelson had become associated with Napton (*see Appendix Eight*). It probably fell out of use in the late 1920s once Griffin's site (*see Chapter Nine*) was used to transfer Napton's products. There was also a siding, later two, along the west bank of the canal arm.

Main line shunting was always done by two or three horses, right up to the time the works closed. Lame horses were sent to convalesce on Griffin's land at Stockton Hill Farm, about halfway between the works and village and close to the footpath connecting them. The standard gauge track by the canal wharf was laid in concrete containing iron plates set on end forming ridges for the horses to grip. The stables were situated between the LNWR and the canal. There were other stables just outside the offices, possibly originally for horses used on the narrow gauge.

For 'conveying Cement over Railways', the firm had a number of privately-owned wagons, mainly 8 or 10 ton vans so that the lime or cement was kept dry. The wagon livery was light blue, or maybe grey, with white lettering shaded black. A valuation made in 1910 listed the main line stock of 42 wagons: eighteen 10-ton covered steel wagons, two 10-ton open steel wagons, eighteen 8-ton covered timber wagons, four 6-ton open timber wagons. Two wooden van bodies 'covered timber wagons' remained beside the canal wharf in 1961. One body was 14 ft 7 in. long and 5 ft 6 in. high, made of nine planks, with a central door opening 4 ft 1 in. wide, and a curved roof. It was braced by a pair of external timbers up each end and an internal iron strip from each corner of the roof to the base of the door opening. Tare weight was 5-5-3. The name 'CHAS NELSON & Co Ld' was painted the whole length of the body. Nelson's ordered four 10-ton steel vans from Birmingham Railway Carriage & Wagon Co. on 28th December, 1911. They were painted medium grey with white letters shaded black, and the Cockerel trade mark was black on a white circle. The firm also had some coal wagons, Nos. 89-92 being built by Thomas Hunter, Rugby (LNWR registration Nos. 15531-34). Maybe these were the four 6-ton open wagons mentioned above. The Gloucester RC&W Co. supplied at least three 4-wheel delivery carts (of different designs) to Nelson's Paddington depot in 1897. Their livery was probably light grey with black wheels and lettering.

The track layout in the works, particularly the central wagon turntable, and the fact that the siding points leading from the main line loop faced both eastwards and westwards, probably accounts for the lack of a locomotive and use of horses (two in 1910), although in view of the use of petrol locomotives in the quarry it is perhaps surprising that a small locomotive, such as the 40 hp Motor Rail design, was not used on the standard gauge.

(A standard gauge 0-4-0ST named *Charles Nelson* was supplied by Peckett to the Pelaw Main Collieries in 1928, number 1748. However, it was named after one of the Directors and he had no connection with Stockton Cement Works. On the formation of the National Coal Board on 1st January, 1947, *Charles Nelson* became No. 66 in the stock of No. 6 North West Durham Area, and was eventually scrapped in July 1973.)

Coal was brought in by canal, mainly from pits near Hartshill and Polesworth in north Warwickshire, and boats took away the lime and cement manufactured. George Nelson had begun to operate his own canal narrow boats from early 1844. The division of the family businesses following George's death in 1850 saw the transfer in 1854 of all his canal boats to Charles Nelson, then aged 20. Charles soon bought about eight more so that by December 1855 he probably had about 15, including those inherited from George, and the George's toll credit account with the Oxford Canal Co. (OCC) was transferred to him on 16th November, 1854. He

Birmingham Railway Carriage & Wagon Co. Ltd official photograph of Charles Nelson's van 740, 1912. Note pair of wooden-framed cupboard doors and the ventilator on the end.

Ian Pope Collection

At least three 2-horse pole wagons were purchased from the Gloucester Railway Carriage & Wagon Co. Ltd in 1897, order 1478. This one was delivered in August 1897, the photographs of similar but not identical vehicles being dated February and May 1897. Note the seat, foot rest and hand brake for the driver. The two horses were harnessed either side of the pole seen leaning against the wall. Henry Perkins was presumably the contractor for Nelson's haulage in London. *Ian Pope Collection*

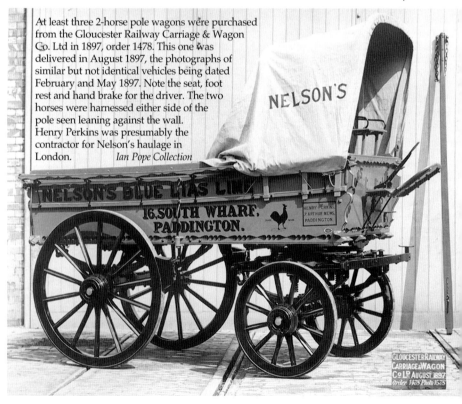

continued canal carrying and other businesses, and took control of Stockton lime works in 1856. On 27th January, 1857, George Nelson Dale & Co. was granted its own toll account with OCC and soon after Charles formed a partnership with Birmingham merchant Joseph Rutland, trading as Nelson & Rutland, manufacturing lias lime and cement. The partnership did not last long, being dissolved by mutual agreement on 13th May, 1859. Rutland retained works at Tipton while Nelson held Stockton. Moreover, Rutland agreed to sell Nelson's lime and cement and not to manufacture either within 25 miles of Stockton for 18 years.

Nelson's growing fleet was registered at the Thames Waterman's Hall on 19th January, 1860, and by March 1862 he had about 16 boats. Some were named after members of the family while others used Greek mythology, e.g. *Achereon, Cerberus*. A number of boats took the name of older ones they had replaced. At one time Nelson owned 20 boats, but the opening of the LNWR branch past the works in 1895 was the probable reason for the fleet to contract, not least because it was no longer necessary to take cement to Weedon for transhipment to rail. By the 1920s the output was dispatched about equally by rail and canal.

A dock was built at Stockton to repair boats in 1870. It was later extended to form an arm 200 yards long, permitting craft to load and unload within the works. Most of the firm's early boats were built at Emscote boatyard, close to the gelatine factory at Warwick. This yard had a number of owners in the second half of the 19th century, finally closing around 1900. Construction and repair of the company's boats was then transferred to William Nurser at Braunston, about eight miles east of Stockton by canal. However, at least three craft, including the steamers *Janus, Jason* and *Jupiter*, were built in 1885 by William Green at Polesworth near Tamworth. These three were used almost exclusively on the run to Nelson's depot at Paddington Basin, London, where Nelson's had two warehouses, although one was given up in 1909. *Janus* and *Jupiter* were sold in 1908 to the Jees Hartshill Granite Co., Nuneaton, and *Jason* was sold to Lawrence Faulkner of Linslade, Buckinghamshire, probably after 1910 as the valuation that year recorded '1 Steam Barge and 13 Horse barges'. Faulkner later purchased *Janus* and *Jupiter* as well so the three boats were together again. Nelson's three steam boats burnt coal instead of coke, having Cochrane type vertical boilers which protruded above the cabin top.

Nurser built several new boats for Nelson: *Edward VII* (1901) and *Alexandra* (1902), named after the new king and queen. Although *Orangia* was converted to a motor boat in the autumn of 1920, horse boats continued to be built including *Rhodesia* (November 1921, cost £190), two in 1922 and the final one, *Geneva*, in October 1924. The first new motor boat, *Gamecock*, was launched in 1923. It had Kitchen's 'Reversing Rudder' speed control system with tiller steering, which included a pair of curved vanes either side of the propeller. *Jason II*, of more conventional design, followed in September 1924. These two boats were unusual in having the living cabin forward of the engine room, giving greater space to the occupants. They were the last additions to the fleet apart from a single horse boat *May* bought in the mid-1930s from Lees & Atkins of Polesworth.

Analysis of boat repairs in British Waterways' Archives suggests that the fleet was down to about eight boats by 1932. *Jason II* and *Gamecock* were sold to Samuel Barlow Coal Co. Ltd in 1935, who renamed it *Nelson*, after the firm's practice of using admirals' names, and not after its former owner. *Jason II* later became simply *Jason*, and was converted in 1951 for pleasure trips on the Regents Canal, London, as part of the Festival of Britain. It continued on this work until 1959 when it was replaced by another boat of the same name.

A steam narrow boat and its butty moored by the junction of Nelson's cut, where there is another boat moored. The original lime kilns were on the bank near the further boat. Judging by the clothes the photograph commemorates a special occasion, possibly a wedding. Probably early 1900s.   *Mrs B.G. Otway Collection*

The horse boats continued operating to the company's depot at Cambrian Wharf, Birmingham until they were sold in 1941 and 1942. The Manchester depot was always supplied by rail. The main traffic by canal was loose lime to Paddington, which had virtually ceased by 1923, and bagged cement to Birmingham. At first, returning boats brought back coal, but latterly it all came in by rail, so instead the boats returned from London with wheat for the mills at Warwick or Coventry. In 1905 18,000 tons of Nelson's raw materials and finished products were carried by canal (i.e. about a dozen boatloads each week).

Later the fleet was reduced to six boats, two horse drawn and two pairs of a power boat (*Gamecock* and *Jason II*) each with an unpowered boat or butty. Further details of Nelson's boats are in *Appendix Seven*.

Nelson's steam boat *Jason* towing a butty on the Grand Junction (later Grand Union) Canal, probably near Linslade, in the 1920s.   *The Waterways Archive - Gloucester*

Chapter Eleven

Small Works in the Newbold and Rugby Areas

General

The opening of the Oxford Canal in 1774 accounted for the development of the lime burning industry in the Rugby area, mainly around Newbold-on-Avon, a village about 1½ miles north-west of Rugby. A report to the Parliamentary committee examining the Bill for the proposed canal in 1768 mentioned the large quantities of limestone near Newbold 'which were at present useless for want of coal to burn it'. The first edition of the 1 in. OS map in 1834 shows a works near Little Lawford, a short distance west of Newbold, and another one near Newbold church. The works will be described moving from west to east. The canal as built was excessively circuitous, and parts were shortened in 1828-34. Some parts of the original route were left as branches to serve specific wharves, and other sections no longer needed became dry cuts, the remains often still visible today. Two relevant sections which were retained were 0 miles 4 furlongs (½ mile) to Finnis Fields and 1 mile 1 furlong to Newbold Lime Works. Over the years there were at least four limeworks in Newbold, with others not far away.

Church Lawford

By 1863   H. Townsend   Closed c.1890

The 1834 1 in. OS map shows two works at Church Lawford, a village about four miles west of Rugby and about three miles by road from the Oxford Canal. One works was by the junction of the road running south to Rookery Hall (SP 446762) and the other was about half a mile along this road (SP 441753). A building, Limestone Hall, is shown here on modern maps and is just north of the site. The 1887 25 in. OS map shows small earthworks by the road junction but no kilns - obviously long gone - but marks two near Limestone Hall. The southern one had an L-shaped stone pit, with the kiln in the angle, and there was a much smaller lime kiln with its stone pit 140 yards north-east of the Hall (SP 442754). The 1863 trade directory shows limeworks owned by H. Townsend at Church Lawford and Kings Newnham but no entries on other dates. Together, this suggests that both works here were small, serving local needs, and while one reopened for a time in the 1860s it closed around 1890. Like other works in the area, there could well have been short narrow gauge tramways to connect the quarries to the kilns, although none are shown on the map.

Harborough Parva

1852   W.S. & J.Harris   Closed

On 20th April, 1852, J.W.Boughton Leigh Esq. leased to Messrs William Smith Harris & Joseph Harris, both of Craven Colliery in County of Warwick, '5 acres of land at Little Harborough [now Harborough Parva] Parish of Newbold upon Avon in the

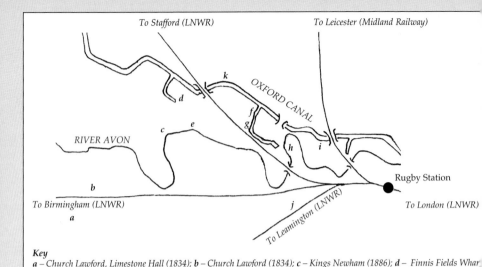

Key

a – Church Lawford, Limestone Hall (1834); *b* – Church Lawford (1834); *c* – Kings Newham (1886); *d* – Finnis Fields Wharf
e – Little Lawford (1834); *f* – Hinton Parva?, Newbold (1852); *g* – North & South of Canal Bridge (1834);
h – Walker-Church (1834); *i* - Walker, later RPC (1886); *j* - New Bilton, Rugby (1886); *k* – Canal Wharf

Newbold area, showing lime kilns marked on 1834 edition OS 1 in. map and 1886 edition OS 6 in. sheet 23SW.

A poor quality image of Kings Newnham Lime Works, from the 1887 edition 25 in. OS sheet 23.13. The works, with its kilns near the river and its quarry tramway, are lower left. Fennis Fields and a stub of the Oxford Canal are upper left, old stone pits (some flooded) and Brown's Spinney are in the centre, and the LNWR Trent Valley line is top right. *Crown Copyright*

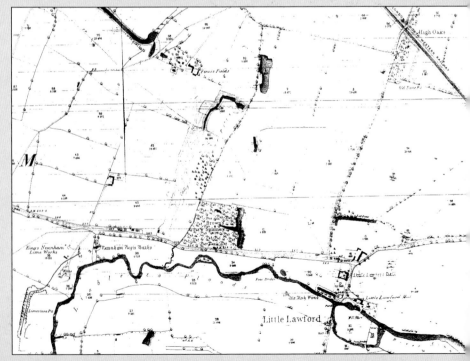

County of Warwick with the liberty of working the Limestone Mines hereunder for 21 years determined as within, beside Oxford Canal'. The rent was £62 10s. pa (£3,700), plus 10d. (£2.45) for every ton of raw limestone and 4d. (£1.00) per quarter (28 lb.) for lime. Mentioning Little Harborough, Newbold and the canal suggests that this enterprise was situated near the bridge which carries the road from Harborough Magna and Parva to Newbold over the canal (SP 482778). The 1834 OS map shows an area which might have been quarried or contained buildings on the inside of a loop in the old canal (SP 481778), and on the 1887 25 in. map field number 150 (but 7.7 acres) at the same location has indications of quarrying. However, there is no caption 'Old Stone Pit' or 'Old Lime Kilns', so any industrial activity had finished long before 1887. As the firm did not appear in any trade directories of the period, the enterprise appears to have been very short lived, assuming it traded at all. Maybe in 1852 it took over earlier workings and ceased trading soon after.

Kings Newham Area

| By 1850 | H. Townsend | |
| After 1863, by 1868 | Mrs A. Townsend | Closed by 1898 |

About 1½ miles west of Newbold, the 1887 25 in, OS map marks a limeworks with two groups of kilns (five and three) beside the Newbold to Kings Newnham road, just west of the Elizabethan Newnham Regis Baths (SP 459773), whose site was occupied by a modern house in 1994.

The kilns were served by a tramway about 400 yards long running south to a limestone quarry about ¼ mile from the road. The works were disused by 1898. The first entry in the trade directory for Kings Newnham and Newnham Regis was in 1850 which stated 'Here are extensive limeworks wrought by Mr Henry Townsend'. Henry Townsend had entries in 1854, 1860 and 1863 as 'farmer and lime burner', and in 1860 there was also an entry for John Holmes coal & lime merchant, Newnham. Townsend also had works a little over a mile away at Church Lawford in 1863, but by 1868 he had died and Mrs A. Townsend was listed, but only for Kings Newnham.

The tramway was presumably narrow gauge and horse- or man-operated. The output from the kilns was probably carted to the canal wharf by the bridge on the outskirts of Newbold, about 1¼ miles away (SP 480774), or perhaps to the wharf half a mile away serving Finnis (or Fennis, maps show both spellings) Fields (*see below*).

In October 1974 the quarry was a mass of thorn and briars. Mounds showed the site of the kilns.

Little Lawford Limeworks

| Before 1828 | Owner not known | |
| By 1868 | James Thurland & Son | Closed after 1876, by 1887 |

The 1834 and 1853 OS maps show a limeworks in Finnis Fields, about ¼ mile north-west of Little Lawford Hall (SP 466776). They predate the straightening work on the Oxford Canal because the 1834 map shows a ½ mile stub of the old canal finishing at a wharf (SP 462780), presumed then in use by this limeworks (and perhaps later used by Kings Newnham works as well). The works and quarries had

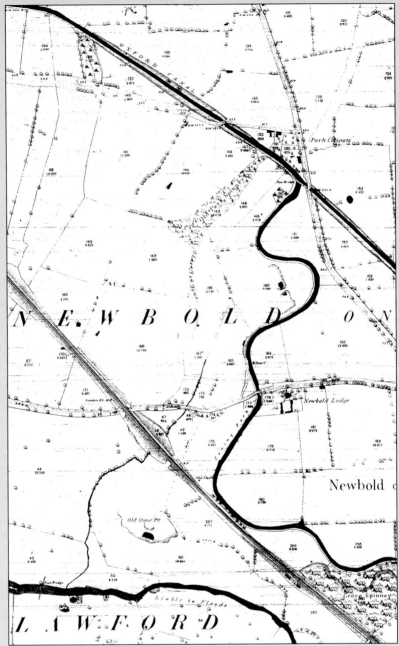

A poor quality map of the area immediately west of Newbold, from the 1887 edition 25 in. OS sheet 23.14. The straightened Oxford Canal runs diagonally across the top half, and the LNWR Trent Valley line is roughly parallel below it. The canal's former main line follows its meandering course down the middle. From north to south along it, there appear to have been lime works within the canal's eastward loop (field 150), immediately north of the lane from Newbold to Little Lawford (field 165 - opposite the wharf) and south of the lane (field 257 - now isolated by the LNWR). *Crown Copyright*

closed by 1887, when the 25 in. OS map shows 'old stone pits' covering much of the area between the canal wharf at Finnis Fields and the road east of the Elizabethan baths, with several long narrow flooded areas including one on the eastern edge of Brown's Spinney (SP 466773) which had probably served the same kilns. If or when the wharf on the old canal was no longer used, then the works probably carted lime to the wharf at Cathiron Lane (SP 422783), a little over ½ mile away. The 1834 map shows a narrow road heading due north and crossing the canal - the bridge (SP 467782) was still shown on the 1954 edition 1 in. OS map. The old stone pits were used as a tip by the council from 1945 to 1975.

The maps show no traces of a railway but in view of the distances involved a narrow gauge line was probably used to carry stone from the quarry to the kilns, and to carry lime to the old wharf.

This limeworks was probably operated by James Thurland & Son, who had trade directory entries from 1868 to 1876. The address is given as Long Lawford, but that much larger village is only ¾ mile from the site of the limeworks, connected by a direct road crossing the River Avon by a ford.

Newbold Canal Bridge

There were three limeworks on the bank of the old route of the Oxford Canal where it passed round the western and southern edges of the village of Newbold, and two of them are described in this section. The road west from Newbold to Little Lawford crosses the canal by a bridge (SP 481774), and maps show limeworks on the west bank of the canal both north and south of the bridge. An unpublished thesis states that in 1841 there were three limeworks in Newbold, owned by Thomas Norman, William Umbers and Thomas Walker. Umbers died in the early 1840s - the Warwickshire Record Office has miscellaneous accounts for his executors showing lime was sold in 1846-47 at 2s. per quarter (28 lb.) (i.e. £8 per ton - £400 today). In 1854 'limeworks to some extent are carried on here' by the executors of Thomas Norman (his widow Mary) and Thomas Walker. After 1860 only Walker remained, and was trading as Walker & Co. from 1871 (see below). Norman had operated the works just south of the bridge, and Umbers' works had been immediately north of the bridge. Using this information, maps, and trade directories the histories of these works can be derived.

By 1841	William Umbers	Closed by his executors late 1840s
Mid-late 1840s	Thomas Norman	
By 1854	Executors of Thomas Norman (his widow Mary, and Thomas Walker)	Closed before 1860

This small works was situated 'immediately north of the bridge'. Nothing is shown here on the 1834 1 in. OS map, and the 1887 6 in. map marks a possible quarry immediately north of the road bridge, running parallel to the canal, but the only caption is 'Wharf' about half way along it (SP 480775). This limeworks appears to have been very small, operating after 1834 and closing well before 1887. Umbers died in the mid-1840s and his executors traded for a while. The works was then probably taken over by Thomas Norman in the late 1840s, finally closing before 1860. This agrees with the statement above and evidence from maps.

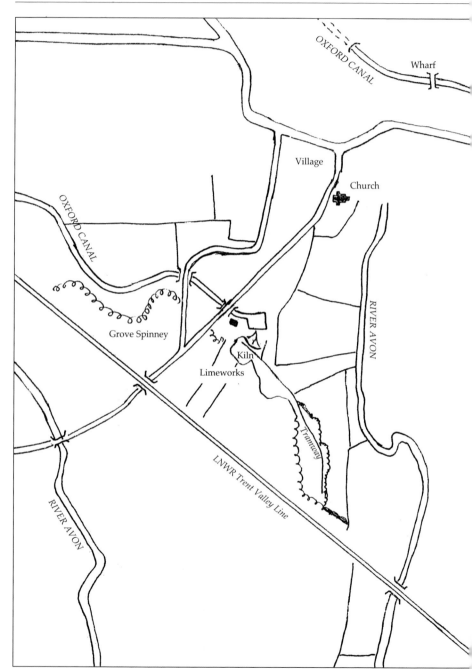

Newbold Church Limeworks, based on 1887 25 in. OS sheets 23.14 & 28.2. Note the LNWR Trent Valley line and the river, both limiting expansion.

By 1834   Thomas Norman   Closed c.1845

The 1834 map shows a limeworks on the west bank of the canal (SP 479772) south of the bridge, which supports the statement 'Norman had operated the works just south of the bridge. The 1887 25 in. map marks an old stone pit about halfway between the canal and a stream, but the LNWR Trent Valley line (Rugby to Nuneaton, opened 1847) passed through the site of the works itself and had obliterated it. Therefore Norman's works can be assumed to have closed no later than 1845. How, then, to account for the statement above that in 1854 'limeworks to some extent are carried on here'? I think the most likely explanation is that following the closure of his works by the LNWR, Norman took over Umber's former works, recently closed. If he died in the early 1850s, his executors could have continued operation in a small way for a few years, closing before 1860 when Thomas Walker became the only local operator. This later operation of Umber's works does not alter the account above.

Although maps do not show any tramways around either works, they could well have been used to carry stone to the kilns.

Newbold Church Limeworks

By 1828   Thomas Walker
1856   George Walker
1868   Walker Tatham Kaye & Co.
1871   Rugby Portland Cement   Closed c.1895

One works shown on the 1834 map was still marked in 1887. It was owned by Thomas Walker. Surveys for the straightening the Oxford Canal in 1828 show that he owned a limeworks near Newbold church (SP 485768). Just over a mile of the old canal was left intact to serve it and the small works mentioned above. The branch joined the canal's new main line about three-quarters of a mile north-west of the village; previously it had continued by tunnelling under the churchyard, where one entrance is still visible. About 170 yards east of the bridge carrying the lane to Home Farm the stub canal was widened to form a basin where boats could be turned. The works was on the southern bank. The quarry was to the south-east, situated between the River Avon and the embankment of the LNWR Trent Valley main line. It was connected to the works by a tramway about 300 yards long which divided into three tracks to serve the five kilns. A separate low level line linked each kiln with a large building on the canal bank - presumably a warehouse and packing shed. By 1905 all this had disappeared, and production was concentrated at the works at the east end of the village (see below), and at New Bilton to the south, which had opened in 1865 (see Chapter Twelve and illustration on page 192).

In October 1974 the kilns at the back of the church were a few humps beside the canal, used by local lads for motor cycle scramble practice. The quarry was overgrown. It appeared to be downhill from the kilns so it is very likely that horses hauled the wagons of stone up to the works.

Thomas Walker (1781-1856) was succeeded by his son George Henry Walker. In 1868 the partnership Walker Tatham Kaye & Co. owned works at New Bilton and Newbold, and had offices at 14 & 16 Wharfs, Paddington Basin (south side). Tatham and Kaye had taken over works at Southam in 1870 (see Chapter Seven) but the

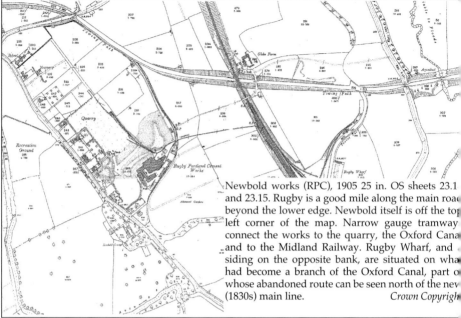

Newbold works (RPC), 1905 25 in. OS sheets 23.1 and 23.15. Rugby is a good mile along the main road beyond the lower edge. Newbold itself is off the top left corner of the map. Narrow gauge tramways connect the works to the quarry, the Oxford Canal and to the Midland Railway. Rugby Wharf, and a siding on the opposite bank, are situated on what had become a branch of the Oxford Canal, part of whose abandoned route can be seen north of the new (1830s) main line. *Crown Copyright*

RPC Newbold Quarry, with empty *flat* wagons being returned to the face in the distance, while loaded *open* wagons are being pushed towards the hoist. Probably taken by the Rugby photographer Edward Hall Speight prior to 1882. *John Frearson and CEMEX/RPC Archives*

business remained a partnership until George died in 1871, when the Rugby Portland Cement Co. was formed to acquire George Walker's business.

This works appears to have closed around 1895, having been replaced by a new works east of the village (*see below*).

Newbold Works (RPC)

c.1878	Newbold Lime & Cement Co. (Warwickshire) Ltd
1889	Rugby & Newbold Cement Co. Ltd
1898	Walker Bros i.e. Rugby Portland Cement Co.

Closed *c*.1925

The construction of the LNWR Trent Valley line in 1847 would obviously eventually limit the existing quarrying area near Newbold church. Perhaps this was the reason for the purchase of a new site on the east side of Newbold (SP 495767) in 1874. The Newbold Lime & Cement Co. (Warwickshire) Ltd began production around 1878. The new works was situated close to the main road from Rugby, behind cottages which flanked each side of the entrance. It was linked by a tramway 350 yards long to the Midland Railway (MR) branch from Leicester to Rugby. (This had been the main line from Derby to London when it opened in 1840, but it had been displaced by a more direct route via Bedford in 1857.) Perhaps surprisingly, initially there was no link from the works to the Oxford Canal, less than 300 yards to the north. The new business was not very well managed, and by 1882 it was trying to sell. No purchaser was found, so there was a major restructuring in 1889 and the Rugby & Newbold Cement Co. Ltd was formed. By this time there was a large quarry, and with plans for extensions additional land was bought 1893-96. Financially, things were still precarious, and the firm decided to wind up in 1896. A receiver was appointed in 1898, culminating in the sale to Walker Bros (i.e. Rugby Portland Cement) on 30th June, 1898.

The 1928 trade directory shows RPC having works at Rugby (New Bilton) and Newbold, with no mention of lime burning, only cement. If Newbold works was indeed still then functioning, it closed soon after. Other sources suggest it had closed by 1925, having struck a spring in 1923 which rapidly flooded the quarry, allegedly too quickly to remove the equipment. Who knows what interesting relics may still lie there, submerged! Production was then concentrated at New Bilton, the quarry (SP 494770) becoming a reservoir for the canal.

The site of the works was covered by a housing estate in the 1950s. In 1974 the quarry was a wilderness and the abandoned MR line nearby was used as a tip. A length of stone wall in the canal bank, about a boat length long, may have marked the remains of the wharf. Later, in 1994, the quarry became a nature reserve as Newbold Quarry Park, with a car park in Norman Road. There is a network of paths, one going right round the lip of the quarry. The flooded quarry attracts many water birds and the clean limey water also supports increasingly rare native crayfish, which look like small lobsters. There are viewing platforms along the blue lime-rich spoil banks, and picnic sites with splendid views.

The 1887 25 in. OS map shows two sidings west of the MR line, about 150 yards south of the bridge over the canal. Cemex Archives contain a lease from the Revd Egerton Broughton Leigh, with a 'Liberty to construct a tramway…' for seven years from 25th December, 1893, to connect the Rugby and Newbold Cement Co. works in

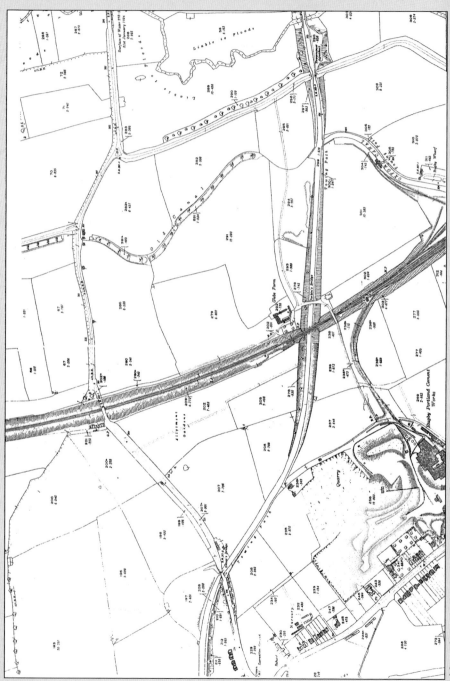

Newbold works, 1925 edition 25 in. OS map sheets 23.14 and 23.15. The tramway to the canal has been lifted, and the standard gauge connection to the

Newbold to the Midland Railway, at an annual rent of £37 10s. (£2,400). As both the 1889 and 1905 large scale maps show this tramway in the same position, it is likely that this was one of a series of seven-year leases, with the first starting in December 1879, reinforcing the date the works opened 'around 1878'.

(A siding east of the MR served Rugby Wharf (SP 501767), situated at the end of a 300 yds-long branch canal, but this probably had nothing to do with the limeworks. The wharf could have been used to supply materials during the construction of the Midland Counties Railway, as it had been in 1840, with the siding a relic of those days.) A single track, later doubled, ran west from a loading bank beside the westernmost MR siding to the works, a distance of 300 yards. At the works the line served both sets of kilns and some other buildings. Another line, possibly at higher level, ran north for 100 yards to the quarry, which was apparently quite small.

There was another tramway, featuring on plans drawn in November 1893, which ran from a junction on the eastern edge of the works northwards to the canal, 280 yards away. At that time there was a winding house at the north end of the quarry. By 1905 a shed had been built over part of the railway loading bank, presumably to keep cement dry while it was transhipped to the main line wagons. The quarry had been worked north and west, and there was a tramway 200 yards long on its lip.

The 1925 25 in. map showed a number of changes. The tramway to the works had been converted to standard gauge and now joined the MR sidings, the agreement between RPC and the MR being dated 8th May, 1907, superseding one dated 9th January, 1900. Each company would bear the cost of the new railway on its land. The junction was just behind the signal box controlling the sidings. The new connection was slightly the north of the narrow gauge alignment, in a curved cutting, and rejoined the original route on the edge of the works, where there was a loop. Besides the actual siding arrangements, RPC agreed to use the Midland Railway wherever possible for transporting their cement and any incoming materials. The map suggests that a locomotive shed was provided, probably built in 1909 following the arrival of the Peckett. Although a standard gauge siding ran a short distance towards the canal, the line to the wharf itself had disappeared. The map shows a separate set of lines serving the quarry, which had been worked further to the north-west. The main line connection remained for about 20 years after the works closed, notice being given in 1945 that 'the premises of RPCC at Rugby Wharf have not existed for a number of years and the siding connection provided ... is being removed.'

The distances suggest horse operation would have been used between the works and either the main line sidings or the wharf, and probably between quarry and works. Within the quarry, however, hand operation was the rule. As usual, the stone was dug by hand in a series of steps. A photograph shows men loading stone and clay into wheelbarrows. The stone was then tipped, or more likely carefully stacked, in a wagon which was then pushed to a steam crane on the quarry lip. Surviving concrete bases suggest that some of these cranes were fixed, but a photograph also shows one mounted on rails. The crane hoisted the wagon out of the quarry for onward passage to the works. The barrows of clay were pushed along planks about 18 in. wide supported on trestles and tipped in worked out areas. The trestles were 10, 20 or even 40 ft tall.

Photographs show that the quarry tramway was approximately 2 ft gauge, so it is likely that the lines to the MR and canal were 2 ft also. Quarry rolling stock comprised wooden open wagons or flat wooden trolleys. The sides and ends of the open wagons were single planks. One side opened, possibly hinged along its lower

Hillmorton works, 1887 edition 6 in. OS sheets 28NE and 28SE. Rugby station is about 2½ miles off the top of the map. On the right-hand edge the 'Northampton Loop' is just separating from the main line which is heading south towards Kilsby and Weedon. The Oxford Canal goes under the railway and then passes the Royal Oak where there are lime kilns but no obvious quarry. Although the area served by the nearby tramway is not labelled, it appears more likely to have been a sand pit (several are marked nearby) than a limestone quarry, and certainly it did not appear to have been associated with the kilns.

Crown Copyright

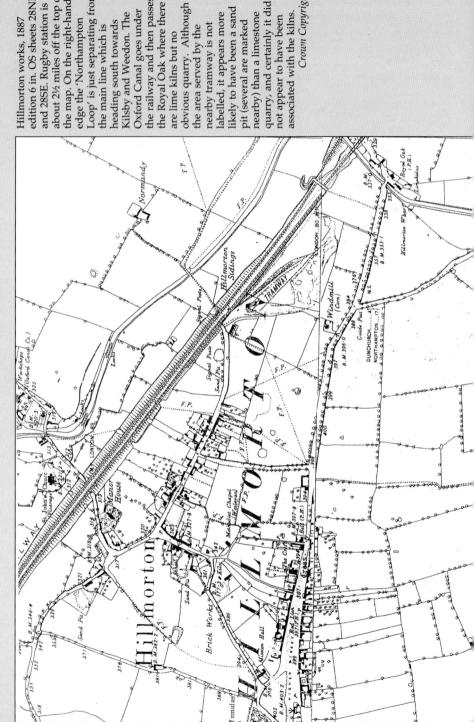

edge or possibly lifted out being secured by hooks at floor level. Either method used a catch pivoted near the top open corner of the end. There were probably open wagons for incoming coal, and flat wagons to carry bags of lime and cement to the MR sidings.

The later standard gauge railway used ordinary main line wagons. Although a horse was undoubtedly used initially to haul the wagons to and from the works, after two years a locomotive was purchased to haul the heavier main line rolling stock. It was a Peckett 0-4-0ST of class 'M4', coming second-hand from the contractors Foster & Dicksee around June 1909. It was painted black, and had neither name nor number. When Newbold works closed the engine was transferred to nearby New Bilton works, and it was eventually scrapped at Totternhoe Quarries around 1952 (see *Appendix Two*).

Standard Gauge

0-4-0ST	OC	P	947/03	(a)	(1)

(a)   Ex-Foster & Dicksee Ltd, Ewell Asylum contract, Surrey *c*.6.1909
(1)   To New Bilton works 1925

Hillmorton

1874	H. Simms?	Closed

Early maps do not mark any lime works beside the Oxford Canal east of Rugby. Large scale maps show lime kilns at Hillmorton, about 2½ miles south-east of Rugby, in 1887 and 1900. They were marked 'Old Limekilns' in 1926. The kilns were on the canal bank opposite Hillmorton wharf, just south of the Royal Oak (SP 544733). In 1874 Mr Harry Simms of Hillmorton Old Wharf was described as 'victualler, coal, lime & salt merchant, boat owner' so he might have owned the kilns. A visit in 1996 showed that extensions to the Old Royal Oak and the workshops for a nearby marina had obliterated the site.

The 1887 six inch map shows a quarry with a tramway about 180 yards north of the main Rugby to Northampton road (SP 543736). It was in the space between the road and the LNWR, an area now occupied by Hillmorton Sidings, just north of the railway's 80 mile post. The tramway, presumed narrow gauge and hand operated, linked the quarry with one of the sidings. The layout shown was a narrow Y-shape, with one arm approximately parallel to the standard gauge siding, running south east to a headshunt. The other arm joined just beyond the end of the siding and ran nearer the workings. The tramway did not reach either the main road or the canal, so this quarry did not supply the Hillmorton kilns. It might even have served a sandpit, as one was marked elsewhere along the road from the village which passed this quarry. There was no other obvious quarry marked on the map, so maybe stone for these kilns had been brought in by canal, probably from around Newbold as that area was much nearer by canal than Stockton or Long Itchington, about five miles against 15.

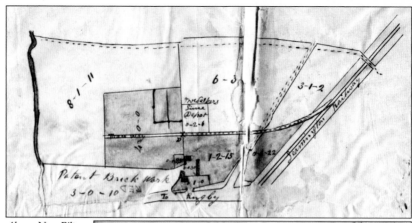

Above: New Bilton, December 1854, showing the 'tramway' serving 'Mr Walkers Lime Depot' and the site of the Victoria Lime Works described as 'Patent Brick Work'.

John Frearson and CEMEX/RPC Archives

Right: New Bilton, December 1865, showing the works and coal wharf.

John Frearson and CEMEX/RPC Archives

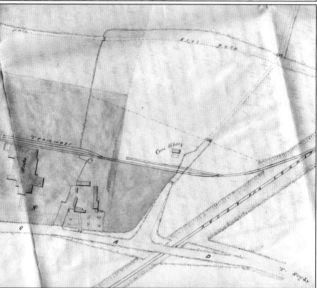

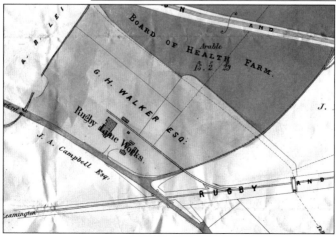

Left: New Bilton, 1872, showing Rugby Lime Works and the extent of Walker's land.

John Frearson and CEMEX/RPC Archives

Chapter Twelve

Rugby (New Bilton) Works

Before 1853	Victoria Lime & Stone Co.
1865	George Walker
1868	Walker Tatham Kaye & Co.
1871	Rugby Portland Cement Co. Ltd
1884	Walker & Hall
1898	Walker Bros
1925	Rugby Portland Cement Co. Ltd
1999	Readymixed Concrete (RMC) Group
2005	Cemex UK

The New Bilton works of the Rugby Portland Cement Co. Ltd are situated on the western outskirts of Rugby (SP 488757), about 1¼ miles from Rugby station, on a site in the fork between the railways to Birmingham (opened 1838) and Leamington Spa (opened 1851). Over the years the quarry extended northwards into the fork between the Birmingham and Trent Valley (Nuneaton, Tamworth and Lichfield) lines (opened 1847). The southern boundary of the site is Lawford Road and the eastern boundary is Parkfield Road, which runs north from New Bilton across the railways to Newbold.

A local landowner, Thomas Walker (1781-1856), erected a works at Newbold, about 1½ miles north-west of Rugby station, and began producing lime in the early 19th century (*see Chapter Eleven*). This was followed in the 1820s by the production of cement, with the 'Crown' trademark, which became the principal product. Although Thomas died in 1856, the business seems to have been passed on to his son George Henry Walker some years before.

The development of the site at New Bilton is shown by reference to a series of surviving maps. One dated December 1852 shows the site of the works as an empty field beside the road, with a building on the main road just outside its eastern boundary. The Victoria Lime & Stone Co.'s premises, occupying the site of the later New Bilton works, are shown on the map accompanying a conveyance dated 18th February, 1853 by a Mr Harris to G.H. Walker Esq. This conveyance was for five fields, totalling about 40 acres north and east of the Victoria Lime Works, most of which in due course became the quarry, and a group of buildings, probably a farm, at the south-east corner, close to the junction of Lawford and Parkfield Roads. The map does not show any details of the Victoria limeworks itself. As the 1853 one inch OS map did not show any limeworks in Rugby, it is likely that the Victoria Lime & Stone Co. had commenced operation a short time before February 1853 but after the OS map had been surveyed, probably in 1852. The site could well have been chosen to take advantage of the nearby railway to Leamington, opened in 1851.

By December 1854 the same field is shown as belonging to a Patent Brick Work [*sic*]. North of it is a 'tramway', really a siding from the 'Leamington Railway', which crosses Parkfield Road, passes 'Mr Walkers Lime Depot' (situated level with the building on the main road) and terminates halfway across the next field. While two areas in this field are marked off there are no buildings, neither are any buildings shown for the 'brick works'. By 1865 a large works (with two sidings) is shown in the field beside the road, the lime depot has disappeared and a coal wharf with a

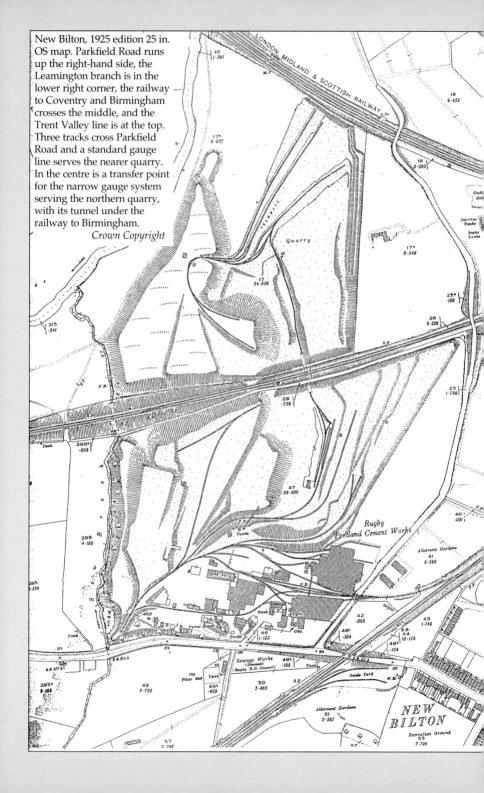

New Bilton, 1925 edition 25 in. OS map. Parkfield Road runs up the right-hand side, the Leamington branch is in the lower right corner, the railway to Coventry and Birmingham crosses the middle, and the Trent Valley line is at the top. Three tracks cross Parkfield Road and a standard gauge line serves the nearer quarry. In the centre is a transfer point for the narrow gauge system serving the northern quarry, with its tunnel under the railway to Birmingham.

Crown Copyright

siding is situated beside Parkfield Road immediately north of Walker's boundary. The New Bilton works of Rugby Portland Cement Co. was opened in 1865, apparently taking over the existing Victoria Lime Works as George Walker changed his company's name from the Newbold Lime & Cement Co. to the Victoria Lime & Stone Co.

By 1872 the siding served 'G.H. Walker Esq Rugby Lime Works', whose land then extended further north, including the site of the coal wharf, which had disappeared. Only a single track is shown but railway detail was probably unimportant as the map appears to relate to the lease or purchase of adjacent land. A plan dated 1880 showed 'Victoria Works' and there was still a 'Lime Depot' nearby, beside the siding.

Trade directories of 1868 and 1872 list the business as Messrs Walker, Tatham, Kaye & Co., who operated works at New Bilton and Newbold, and had offices at 14 & 16 Wharfs, Paddington Basin (south side). Laurence Mallory Tatham was a London lime merchant. Capt. Arthur Lister-Kaye had retired from the army in Australia for health reasons and traded with Tatham in London as Tatham, Kaye & Co. Probably arising from internal difficulties, Walker, Tatham, Kaye & Co. was dissolved in 1868, Walker buying out Tatham and Kaye. However, Walker made a seven-year agreement to supply Tatham, Kaye & Co. with lime and cement, and undertook not to supply any surplus lime or cement to anyone south of Rugby except Tatham Kaye & Co. George Walker died in 1871 so this agreement lasted only three years. In the meantime, Tatham and Kaye took over works at Southam in 1870 (*see Chapter Seven*).

The business at Rugby remained a partnership until George Walker died, when the Rugby Portland Cement Company Limited was formed, with £60,000 capital, to acquire his business interests. A book by Henry Reid (published 1877) says that in 1869 he 'was consulted by the proprietor of this company in order for him to discover the correct method of cement manufacture', which is described below. True Portland cement was first made at Rugby in 1871, which may be the reason why the enterprise appears not to have been very successful until after Walker's death.

Quarrying at that time was seasonal, workers being laid off in winter, and the works ceased production until the spring. The labour force included large numbers of women who sorted the Blue Lias limestone from shale and clay by hand. Limestone and other raw materials were weighed and mixed in their rough condition, then passed through toothed rollers to be ground by millstones. The raw meal was elevated to a storage room, from which it went down a chute, sufficient water being added during its descent to permit the material to be pressed into bricks by a brick making machine. These bricks were stacked in the existing rectangular kilns about 12 ft high, arranged with a layer of gas coke between each course. When the kiln was fired the bricks dried, then burnt to make clinker which was ground to make cement.

By 1880 the rectangular kilns had been replaced by bottle kilns, and the process was steadily improved, for example by replacing the toothed rollers by stone crushers and by drying the shale and clay over heated floors before grinding and mixing. The company employed 280 people and had an annual output of 24,000 tons by 1893. Rotary kilns, producing from 2 to 5 tons per hour, were not introduced until 1910, and were a great advance on bottle kilns (latterly 14 altogether), each of which had produced only 5 tons every few days.

The newly-formed Rugby Portland Cement Co. Ltd did not last long, being dissolved in 1884 on the formation of a new partnership between George's sons

An early view (c.1870?) of New Bilton Works, Rugby, looking north. Lawford Road is in the foreground and Parkfield Road joins at the right-hand side and continues into the distance. Trains are heading towards and away from Rugby on the Birmingham line across the middle of the picture, and in the distance another train is heading north on the Trent Valley line, with its viaduct over the River Avon. Just beyond the viaduct is Newbold Church, and to its left the chimneys of Walker's original Newbold Church Lime Works. Note that the only quarry is west of the works, and is reached through a tunnel in the left foreground. There are fields to the north. Two tracks cross Parkfield Road into the works yard, where a main line locomotive and tender is coupled to eight

Henry Edyvean-Walker and Arthur Caldicott Walker, and Charles Hall, a cement maker who was Managing Partner. Hall died in 1898 and was not replaced. The Walker brothers died in the early 1900s and were succeeded by their sons who continued the business as a partnership until 1925.

The 1908 *Kelly's Directory* stated that 'Rugby Portland Cement have extensive works here, the blue lias lime and Portland cement being of a superior quality'. However, although there were three rotary kilns in operation by this time, the business was generally not very profitable in this period. The Walker brothers seemed unable to afford all the new equipment to keep it up to date.

Rugby Cement became a private limited company in 1925 but still it was not very profitable. (Private limited company: Basically, the advantages of limited liability for the firm's debts and some secrecy in its financial affairs but restricted to a small number of shareholders, which could limit access to additional capital, whereas a public company can sell its shares to the public at large but details of its financial situation are more readily available.) The two works, Newbold and New Bilton, had a combined output of 60,000 tons that year. The works at Newbold (*see Chapter Eleven*) closed around 1925 and henceforth investment was concentrated at New Bilton. The Depression affected the cement industry badly, and fierce competition meant prices were at an unprofitable level. In 1929, one of the Depression's worst years, one of the Directors, Mr Norman Edyvean-Walker, advised consulting his friend, Mr (later Sir) Halford Reddish, a newly qualified accountant, who was invited to join the Board. Following the death of the General Manager, in 1933 Halford Reddish became Managing Director, and Chairman soon afterwards.

The new Chairman decided to expand and modernize the company's production facilities, starting with the works at New Bilton which was rebuilt in the 1930s. Contrary to previous industry tradition, he decided to operate one plant all the year round, thus providing steady employment for all his workers. Following a short layoff in 1933, the workmen were promised that in future there would be no stoppages or layoffs, and this was achieved. The firm had a very good attitude towards its workers and there were never any strikes. Indeed, employees were encouraged to have a stake in their company through the creation of a special class of shares.

Despite the Depression, and the difficulties of selling an increased output, a profit was made at the end of that first year. Further expansion was often by acquisition, Kaye & Co. at Southam being the first, in 1934 (*see Chapter Seven*). RPC became a public limited company in 1935 which facilitated further growth by better access to capital. A number of other cement companies were taken over in the years immediately before and after World War II. In 1991 RPC had works at Rugby, Southam, Rochester (Kent), Barrington (Cambridgeshire), South Ferriby (Lincolnshire), Chinnor (Oxfordshire), and a chalk quarry at Kensworth (Bedfordshire, *see Appendix Three*). There were also works in Perth (Western Australia), and until 1976 in the West Indies. By then, RPC was the third largest cement company in the UK, with 20 per cent of the market.

As stated above, the first rotary kiln was built in 1910 and over the years others followed. Often two or even three kilns were in use at the same time. At the time No. 6 kiln was built in 1969 it was the largest one operated by RPC, having a diameter of 4.5 m. (15 ft) and length of 165 m. (550 ft). It was a wet kiln, using chalk slurry, together with clay and sand to get the chemistry right. Most of the white plume at the top of the tall chimney, visible for miles, was pipeline water, as every 100 tons of slurry input gave 40 tons of steam per hour. Electrostatic precipitators in the flue helped to reduce the problem of dust carried out. Although a wet process used more fuel, at that time

General view of Rugby quarries, *c.*1900. Behind the horse hauling a wagon is an incline to lower levels. On the left, just below the locomotive, is the tunnel under the Birmingham line and beyond it are the first workings in that quarry. In the distance on the left a Trent Valley line train is leaving the viaduct over the Avon, and on the right is the spire of St Andrew's Parish Church, Rugby. *John Frearson and CEMEX/RPC Archives*

Tunnel from quarry and incline up to the works, *c.*1870. Note the double-flanged wheels on the truck in the tunnel and the stub point beyond it. Another truck is on the incline.
Rugby Cement, Bob Darvill Collection

Group of quarrymen pose around a 4 ft (approximately) gauge wagon at Rugby, *c.*1890.
Rugby Cement, Author's Collection

Rugby quarries, with wagons being filled using wheelbarrows - just look at the plank to the right
hand wagon!   *Alan Griffin, Feldon Photographic Archive*

New Bilton Works, 1928. The Leamington branch runs across the bottom of the picture, and serves a small goods yard. The wagons with white contents in the foreground are loaded with full sacks, not chalk, as also are the ones just the other side of the Lawford Road bridge. All the wagons in this area, apart from those loaded with sacks, belong to collieries or local coal merchants. There are numerous loaded and empty chalk wagons beyond the offices, whose tower has now been reduced in height. The bridge over the Birmingham line leads to the 'clay hills'. The mouth of the tunnel under the main line is at the foot of a grassy slope, to the right of the black smoking chimney. Two 'Ship Canal' tipper wagons stand in the quarry on the right, and a rake of five is on the far left, above the battery it was cheaper to operate than installing drying plant. In continuous operation over 24 hours the kiln produced 1,200 tonnes per day, giving an annual capacity of 375,000 tonnes of clinker. In 1971, 96 per cent of cement deliveries were in bulk, by tanker, and only 4 per cent was bagged. Demand for cement peaked in 1972 and then fell steadily, so the older kilns were closed. Reception is now the only part of the original works left. A new kiln, No. 7, the largest in the UK with an annual capacity of 1.8 m. tonnes, was fired for the first time on 15th February, 2000 (and officially commissioned the following August), making 50,000 tonnes of clinker in six weeks. Unfortunately, problems during construction of the new kiln in the late 1990s depressed the RPC share price, and the RMC (Readymix Concrete) Group seized the opportunity to acquire RPC in 2000. The company had long wanted its own source of cement in Britain, as had been the case with its operations in Germany. However, in its turn, RMC was taken over by Cemex UK in 2005. Despite the changes in ownership, the works at New Bilton remains in operation.

Up to 1937 New Bilton works was powered by a Willans & Robinson steam engine, then electric power was introduced, including the installation of standby electricity generators to keep the kilns turning if there was a power failure, otherwise they bent under their own weight.

A brick frieze in North Street, commissioned in 1999, shows 'key elements of Rugby's industrial heritage'. The design shows cement and lime making using beehive kilns to burn the limestone. Other items depicted include a horse-drawn narrow boat on the Oxford Canal (reached Rugby 1773), a London & Birmingham Railway Bury locomotive (opened 1838), the masts of the radio station (opened 1926) and a Meteor (the first British jet fighter 1944, whose engine was developed here).

In common with other local works, for many years the stone quarried was manually separated from the clay and shale excavated with it. The limestone was sent to the works and the waste was dumped in worked-out parts of the quarry. Since the early 1930s, when it became no longer economic to pick out the limestone, chalk was imported by rail from the company's Totternhoe Quarries, near Dunstable, Bedfordshire (*see Appendix Two*). Although some 20 years of reserves remained in the quarries beside the works, by the early 1980s they were not economic to work and from about 1982 clay was brought by lorry from Southam, rail being too expensive.

The original quarry west of the works was Victoria Quarry. Its northern part, towards the Coventry and Birmingham railway, was Jubilee Quarry, presumably because it had been started around Queen Victoria's Golden Jubilee in 1887. Further north, between this railway and the Trent Valley line, were Malpas Quarry towards the west, and Parkfield Quarry towards the east. East of the road was East Quarry.

The quarries were up to 90 ft deep. L. Cumming, Assistant Master at Rugby School, wrote about the Geology of Rugby in *Rugby Past & Present* (Revd W.O. Wait, 1893). A plate shows 'The Victoria Works, New Bilton [from a photograph by E.H. Speight, Rugby]' which was presumably taken in or before 1892. As well as the extensive quarry with access ladders from bench to bench, it shows a rail system with trucks in the foreground, and further rail trucks/tubs on each bench. The geologist, Professor H.B. Woodward, in 1898 described Victoria Quarry as having the finest inland section of the lower lias limestone in the country. In one face there were about 75 bands of limestone with alternating beds of blue shale and clay (*Portland Cement Industry* p.212). The quarrymen had names for the bands 'Big Jumbler, Knotty Rock, Cat Heads etc' (*VCH* Vol. 2 p. 194).

The first quarries were immediately west of the works, and appear to have had tramways to carry the stone from the beginning. An early engraving shows a

Right: Tunnel under Parkfield Road to East Quarry, with dumper passing through, 31st October, 1974.

Author

Below: Steam locomotive shed, 31st October, 1974.

Author

Diesel locomotive shed, 31st October, 1974. *Author*

Level crossing over Parkfield Road, looking west into the works yard. The old coal tippler is on the right, 31st October, 1974. *Author*

An artist's impression of the New Bilton works yard, used for the firm's 1892 calendar, with horses shunting and a LNWR locomotive shunting a rake of wagons.

John Frearson and CEMEX/RPC Archives

Above: Ruston steam excavator abandoned in the quarry. Note it needs a pair of rails on each side, four rails altogether. *C. Flavell, Author's Collection*

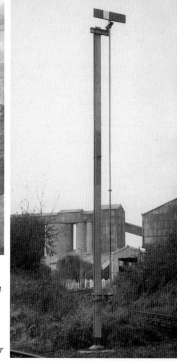

Right: Crossbar signal at the entrance to RPC sidings, with the level crossing just visible in the background and the Leamington branch in the left foreground, 31st October, 1974. *Author*

tramway in the quarry, approximately 3 ft gauge, running through a short tunnel to terminate in a deep (estimated 20-25 ft) cutting on the south side of the works where there was a loop, presumably for full and empty wagons. Horses hauled trains of three or four wagons. Wagons were pushed singly from the loop to an assumed turntable which gave access to the foot of an incline, where they were hauled by rope to a tip above ground level in one of the works' buildings. The wagons had deep wooden bodies - they appear to have been almost cubes - with three fixed sides and one end open, on a wooden frame. Wheels were double flanged and so stub points were used. (Most railways have wheels with a single flange bearing against the inner face of the rail head. Their points have flexible or pivoted blades, made from ordinary rails, with one end tapered to fit against the appropriate fixed stock rails. Stub points for double flanged wheels have a short section of the approach track made to move sideways between the two possible pairs of rails, with a short piece of rail centrally pivoted where a rail of one pair crossed a rail of the other pair.)

By 1887 the quarry extended west of the works as far as the brook, a tributary of the River Avon, and north towards the LNWR line to Birmingham, but no further east than the centre of the works. There was a network of tramways, linking the quarry to both the works and to waste tips. As a deep quarry could cause subsidence of the ground nearby, the LNWR bought the 'Limestone in strip and slope' bordering the south side of the Birmingham line in 1890'. A similar purchase was made along the northern side of the railway in 1895, the two LNWR-owned strips totalling some 10,000 square yards (two acres). The negotiations over the value of the limestone reserves under the railway continued until 1908 when a plan suggests that the railway had bought the rights to the minerals under its track. Around 1895 a tunnel about 70 yards long was driven under the LNWR to give access to the new Malpas Quarry, situated between the Birmingham and Trent Valley lines. A spoil bank had been built in the quarry against the northern side of the railway by 1905.

The LNWR plan and sections of the quarry at this date show four levels of workings, the lowest connecting to a tunnel under LNWR. All four lines joined at the western end of quarry, each with a loop near the junction. A wagon turntable gave access from the quarry to a new tunnel. This tunnel was about 50 yards east of the earlier one, and at a lower level, the original tunnel being isolated half way up the quarry face. There was a loop south of the tunnel and a second loop plus a long siding near works.

Both the LNWR plan c.1905 and the 1913 25 in. OS show two apparently separate quarry tramway systems, one serving the quarries north of the LNWR and going to the north-west corner of the works, and the other serving the eastern end of the quarry near the works. Both systems had inclines up to the works out of the quarry, although by then most of the quarried area near the works was used for spoil banks.

Photographs suggest the quarry systems were about 4 ft gauge. Horses hauled the wagons which had sides made of a single wide plank about 15 in. deep, with the opening end closed by a hinged plank. The wheels were about 18 in. in diameter and had six spokes.

At the top of the works incline from the nearer quarry, the tramway ran round the northern edge of the works, and crossed the other tramway by a bridge to reach the spoil banks. Maybe this system had developed out of the original 'approximately 3 ft gauge' tramway. By the mid-1920s, before this part of the quarry became worked out, the narrow gauge was replaced by a standard gauge line.

The line under the LNWR to Malpas Quarry appears to have been 4 ft gauge, with horses hauling trains of wooden side-tipping wagons built at Rugby. One informant had vague memories of a slab-sided narrow gauge internal combustion locomotive, stored in a shed for a long time and scrapped around 1950, which may have been used in this quarry. It would have been useful as the workings were over 400 yards from the works incline. The stone was dug and the wagons loaded entirely by hand in this quarry. By the mid-1920s the narrow gauge had been cut back to a transhipment dock just south of the tunnel under the LNWR, where standard gauge wagons were filled to take the stone the rest of the way to the works.

An internal standard gauge railway was built to serve the various parts of the works. The layout naturally changed over the years as new plant was built and old plant demolished. From an early date, and probably from the opening of the Victoria limeworks, the works was served by a siding from the Rugby to Leamington line. The junction was 200 yards north of the bridge under Lawford Road, later the A428 from Rugby to Coventry, and was controlled by Bilton Pinfold Sidings signal box. (There was once a small public goods yard immediately south of the road bridge.) The works branch curved in a shallow cutting for 150 yards, divided into two tracks (three by 1913), then crossed Parkfield Road by a level crossing to enter the works yard. Early engravings of the works show the yard with a number of tracks serving various buildings, with loops and at least one wagon turntable. This layout was hardly changed on the 1905 and 1913 25 in. maps.

The 1913 25 in. OS map shows a standard gauge line running round the northern side of the works to the west end. By the mid-1920s this line had been extended to serve three different areas. From west to east, lines ran to the spoil banks, to an interchange siding with the Malpas Quarry narrow gauge system close to the tunnel under the LNWR, and to the east end of the quarry near Parkfield Road. When eventually this was worked out, around 1937, a tunnel about 80 ft long, lined with concrete, was dug under the road to serve the new East Quarry.

The Leamington branch was originally double track. Two trailing crossovers, one north of the RPC branch, the other just south of the Lawford Road bridge, formed a loop about 250 yards long. The works yard had five parallel tracks on the 1971 OS map, and at the far west end trailing connections (passing under the kiln) led to five coal sidings across the end of the old quarry, with a capacity of about 300 wagons. One of these sidings had a branch, crossing the Birmingham line by a bridge, to a tip in old workings of Malpas Quarry. Although tipping on the 'clay hills' had ceased around 1938, due to the threat of slips on to the main line, this bridge remained until the late 1950s, when it was demolished during electrification of the West Coast main line. There were also several tracks behind the works serving the stone grinder plant and chalk tippler, where another 80-90 wagons could be stored. Between the coal and chalk sidings was the former steeply graded line down into East Quarry. Once the chalk trains had been replaced by the pipeline in 1966 (see Appendix Four) the railway was cut back to the main yard.

The original engine shed was situated on a spur near Lawford Road. It was a brick building approximately 100 ft long, with a pit, an asbestos roof and a sliding door, and could hold four locomotives on its single track. Later it became the repair shop for the quarry dumpers. Coal and water supplies were outside the shed.

The internal railway was rationalized in the early 1970s. Following the commissioning of new plant, including the chalk pipeline, the main traffic was coal inwards and cement outwards. By October 1974 the western track of the Leamington branch had been removed, leaving a single track for the coal trains to Southam. At New Bilton the crossovers and loop were left, together with a long section of the former western track to act as a headshunt for access to the works. A 2-lever ground frame controlled the points at each end of the loop, one lever for the points and one for its lock. When rail traffic to Southam ceased in the mid-1980s, the remains of the Leamington branch south of the southern crossover were lifted, leaving just enough track to enable a locomotive to run round a train for New Bilton works.

Latterly the single track from BR split into three before the level crossing, then basically there were three long parallel sidings connected at their western ends to form loops, with three tipplers for coal and a covered loading bay for cement. A new corrugated iron shed, approximately 48 ft long x 25 ft, was built at the west end of the yard for the diesel shunting locomotives. It was semi-circular in section and had a pit, with the fuel oil tank outside. The coal stack for the kiln was nearby.

Horses had been used for shunting until locomotives were introduced in 1919. In 1937 the engines worked three shifts but by 1974 they only worked days. At the peak, three engines, and occasionally all four, were in daily use, one in the quarry and two in the works.

The works used to consume 600 to 700 tons coal per day, mainly obtained from Newdigate Colliery, Bedworth near Nuneaton, hence the 20,000 ton stockpile at the rear. About 20 wagon loads of gypsum were received each week from Kegworth, Leicestershire. From 1919 chalk was brought in by rail from the Dunstable area of Bedfordshire. At first the daily consumption of chalk was 12 to 15 wagons per day, but this later rose to 80 to 90 wagons (see Appendix Five). Incoming chalk was tipped on the stockpile and then reloaded into internal wagons by steam shovel for grinding before use. The company's chalk pipeline caused this rail traffic to cease in 1966.

Latterly stone was dug by two Ruston steam excavators, No. 1 and No. 2, each of which ran on four rails. Water was piped into the quarry for them. The maximum loads for a locomotive working into the quarries was 12 empties, or two full wagons from the West Quarry or four full wagons from the East Quarry.

There were three rail-mounted steam cranes for stockpiling coal, one by T. Smith and two by Grafton of Bedford. One of them was later converted to diesel, and was occasionally used for shunting if neither locomotive was in steam.

Dumpers were introduced in the quarry in the early 1950s to replace the railway. Originally they were 4.5 cubic yard capacity, but by 1974 they were 9.5 cubic yard Aveling Barford vehicles. Dumpers had been used previously to tip overburden in the disused West Quarry. By 1974 the East Quarry was over 100 ft deep and the dumper road spiralled down into it.

For many years main line locomotives used to push trains to the entrance of the works yard, just clear of the level crossing, although the illustration on the firm's 1882 calendar shows a LNWR locomotive well inside the yard. Maybe they used to be allowed further in before RPC had its own shunting locomotives. Following the rationalization of the early 1970s they were allowed right into the yard, as far as a trackside sign by the cement loading bay reading 'NOTICE BR LOCOS STOP HERE'.

The curved cutting made it difficult to control incoming trains, as the shunter could not see the both the locomotive driver (way down the headshunt) and the level crossing at the works entrance. To overcome the problem, in 1974 a crossbar signal was erected near the siding points. It comprised a pair of red semaphore arms bolted horizontally to a rod mounted on a steel girder post, operated by a lever of the type more commonly found on isolating switches for the main line electrification catenary. Instructions for its use are given at the end of Appendix Five.

The last rail traffic was incoming coal, which ceased in August 1991. All the sidings and BR tracks, and the signal, were still in situ in July 1994, although by then out of use for three years.

Manning, Wardle 0-6-0ST (1 or 2) and train of wooden 'Ship Canal' side tipping wagons in quarry. *John Frearson and CEMEX/RPC Archives*

Manning, Wardle 2047 of 1926, 4 (although it did not carry a number), was the last locomotive built by this firm. Note the dumb buffers for working with the quarry wagons, 18th March, 1961. *Ken Cooper, IRS Collection*

Locomotives were introduced on the standard gauge in 1919. Nos. 1 to 4 were similar, all being inside-cylinder 0-6-0ST built by Manning, Wardle, Leeds. The first, Works No. 1972, came in 1919 quickly followed by 1995 in 1920. They were '12 Specials' with cylinders 12 in. x 18 in. Both were later transferred to Totternhoe chalk quarries (see Appendix Two). An older and slightly smaller class 'K' locomotive, No. 1146, with 12 in. x 17 in. cylinders, was bought from Furness Withy Shipbuilding Co. Ltd around March 1924. It had a wooden cab and hand brake, and was scrapped in 1949.

On 17th April, 1926 the company ordered a locomotive from Manning, Wardle, for delivery in eight weeks. In fact it was delivered, after 16 weeks, on 9th August, 1926, and it was the last one built by this firm. No. 2047 was a '14in Special' with cylinders 14 in. x 20 in., copper firebox, brass tubes and a steel boiler. A couple of times it was lent to Southam works. The Warwickshire Industrial Locomotive Preservation Group was formed specifically to preserve this engine, which left Rugby on 21st October, 1967 and arrived the next day on the Severn Valley Railway at Bridgnorth. In 1982, by then named Warwickshire, together with five assorted main line locomotives, it featured on gift wrapping paper designed by Wendy Meadway and produced by Royle Publication Ltd, Gift Wrap, Ref. A5113.

Following the closure of Newbold works in 1925 its locomotive came to New Bilton. This was a Peckett 0-4-0ST, class 'M4' with 10 in. x 15 in. outside cylinders and 2 ft 6 in. diameter wheels. It was much smaller than the others and went to Totternhoe in 1937. It may have been called Avon.

After World War II a new locomotive, No. 5, was ordered from Robert Stephenson & Hawthorns. No. 7387 was delivered from its builder's works in Newcastle in March 1948 and enabled the remaining small locomotives to be disposed of. It had outside cylinders 14 in. x 22 in. and 3 ft 6 in. diameter driving wheels. It was withdrawn in 1964, was seen derelict in January 1966, and had been cut up by March 1966.

All these locomotives had a pair of wooden dumb buffers at each end, for use with the quarry tipping wagons, as well ordinary sprung buffers. No. 5 had a steel bar across the frames close to the rails at each end, so that if it became derailed it should not drop very far and therefore should be easier to re-rail.

In July 1962 a 4-wheel diesel-hydraulic locomotive built by Thomas Hill of Rotherham (trading as Vanguard) came for about six months on trial, and from subsequent events it obviously made a favourable impression. A 100 hp Sentinel steam locomotive, No. 9559 of 1953, was transferred from Totternhoe to New Bilton around October 1964, to replace the withdrawn No. 5. It spent a short time at Southam works between March and May 1966. Presumably the diesel crane was used for shunting in its absence. Soon after the arrival of the new diesel the Sentinel was sold to Thomas Hill, for possible rebuilding into a diesel locomotive - this firm specialized in such conversions.

A new 4-wheel diesel-hydraulic locomotive had been ordered from Thomas Hill in October 1966, and 173V was delivered in April 1967. Following the abandonment of Rugby's railway in 1991, 173V was sold and went to Kent for the Channel Tunnel contract. A similar locomotive, 164V, had been supplied to Southam works. It came to New Bilton in July 1985 when Southam's railway was abandoned, and was soon transferred to the company's works at Chinnor, Oxfordshire.

Two other locomotives remain to be mentioned. Around 1969 a small Strachan & Henshaw road-rail tractor (i.e. it could work both on and off the rails) came for demonstrations, but no purchase resulted. It was probably too small for the work

Manning, Wardle 2047 leaving New Bilton yard for preservation, 21st October, 1967. The large cylinder across the picture is a rotary cement kiln under construction. *P.R. Arnold*

No. 5, Robert Stephenson & Hawthorns 7387 of 1948. Note the dumb buffers, and the transverse girders just above the rails at each end to support the locomotive in the event of derailment. Probably taken soon after delivery in 1948. *Rugby Art Gallery & Museum*

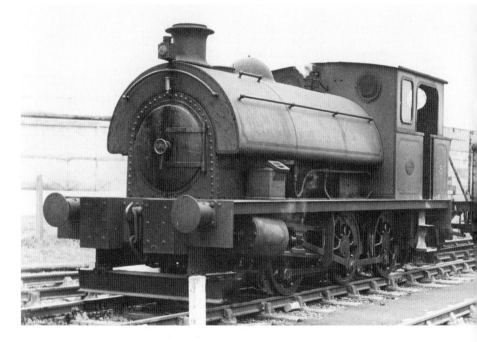

No. 5 at work, 1st August, 1958. *Author*

Thomas Hill 173V of 1966 outside the new coal tippler. The platform inside the building rotated, inverting the wagon which was supported on its side and by the girder above it, 31st October, 1974. *Author*

Above:
Grafton rail crane 2382, formerly steam-powered but rebuilt to diesel, 31st October, 1974.

Author

Right:
T. Smith diesel rail crane No. 75 X50028 transferring coal to a stockpile. Note the buffers and coupling so that it can be used for light shunting, 31st October, 1974.

Author

required. The other was 0-4-0DM *Southam No. 2*, which also came from Southam in July 1985, and soon went to the Leeds Industrial Museum to join its collection of Leeds-built locomotives. Unfortunately, it has not yet been restored and is not on public display.

All the locomotives were painted green with red lining, except for the diesel 173V which was blue. While most of the steam locomotives were allocated numbers, only No. 5 was actually carried, hence Nos. 1-4 are shown (1) to (4) in the table below.

Standard Gauge

(1)	0-6-0ST	IC	MW	1972	1919	New	(1)
(2)	0-6-0ST	IC	MW	1995	1920	New	(2)
(3)	0-6-0ST	IC	MW	1146	1890	(a)	Scr. 1949
(4)	0-6-0ST	IC	MW	2047	1926	New	(3)
5	0-4-0ST	OC	P	947	1903	(b)	(4)
5	0-6-0ST	OC	RSHN	7387	1948	New	Scr. 3.1966
No. 1	4wVBT	VC	S	9559	1953	(c)	(5)
	4wDH		TH	118C#	1962	(d)	(6)
	4wDH	R/R	S&H			(e)	(7)
	4wDH		TH	173V	1966	New	(8)
No. 3	4wDH		TH	164V	1966	(f)	(9)
Southam No. 2	0-4-0DM		HC	D625	1942	(g)	(10)

\#   Built on frame of an unidentified Sentinel steam locomotive

(a)   Ex-Furness Withy Shipbuilding Co. Ltd, Haverton Hill, Co. Durham, *c.*3.1924

(b)   Ex-Newbold-on-Avon works, *c.*1925. May have been named AVON.

(c)   Ex-Totternhoe Quarries, Bedfordshire *c.*10.1964, to Southam works *c.*3.1966 returned *c.*5.1966

(d)   Ex-TH, for demonstrations, received from Roads Reconstruction, Frome, Somerset *c.*27.7.1962

(e)   Ex-S&H, for demonstrations, *c.*1969

(f)   Ex-Southam works, loan 26.6.1982, returned 22.7.1982, ex-Southam works 4.7.1985

(g)   Ex-Southam works 4.7.1985

(1)   To Totternhoe Quarries, 1949

(2)   To Totternhoe Quarries 2.1940, returned 1950, to Totternhoe again *c.*1951

(3)   To Southam works, 1943, loan and returned, to Warwickshire Industrial Locomotive Preservation Group, Severn Valley Railway, Bridgnorth, Shropshire 22.10.1967

(4)   To Totternhoe Quarries, 1937

(5)   To TH 4.1967

(6)   Returned to TH, 1963 thence to NCB Shaw Cross Colliery, Yorkshire 20.3.1963

(7)   To S&H off demonstrations *c.*1969

(8)   Purchased by Yorkshire Engine Co. via Modern Plant Ltd, Rugby. Sent direct to Channel Tunnel contract, Cheriton, Kent, on hire from YEC, 17.6.1992.

(9)   To Chinnor Works, Oxfordshire 29.10.1985

(10) To Leeds Industrial Museum, Armley, Leeds 8.10.1985

Besides the locomotives there were several self-propelled cranes. The pivoted body was carried on a short four-wheel underframe, which had dumb buffers and couplings fitted so wagons could be moved if necessary. The cranes had lattice jibs and were usually fitted with a grab for emptying or loading slack coal or chalk. Latterly the diesel crane was used for light shunting if neither of the locomotives was in steam.

Dumb-buffered wooden quarry wagon being emptied 'Feeding the Ergo Crusher'. For a long time the replacement dumpers emptied their loads here. Note the chains attached to the wheels to prevent the wagon overturning when it tipped. A workman assists the load to discharge with a long crowbar. The top plank of wagon 52 looks as though it has been hit by the excavator bucket.   *John Frearson and CEMEX/RPC Archives*

20-ton steel hopper wagon 206 'for cement raw materials' (probably coal or chalk), built by Hurst, Nelson Ltd, Motherwell, in 1923. The circular plate beside the tare weight shows that the wagon has been registered with the LMS.   *HMRS Collection*

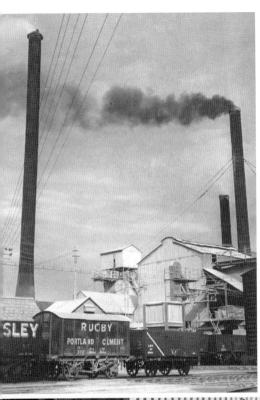

Left: Iron van No. 372 in Rugby works yard, between an LMS wooden mineral wagon with end and bottom doors (note the white markings) and a wagon belonging to Baddesley Collieries, Atherstone, near Nuneaton, Warwickshire. Probably 1930s.

Rugby Cement, Author's Collection

Below: Main line RPC coal wagons at Southam, probably late 1930s. Note the wagons have their lettering arranged differently.

Rugby Cement, Author's Collection

RPC 7-plank end door open wagon No. 73. (Measurements mixture of prototype feet and inches and millimetres for 4mm scale model.)

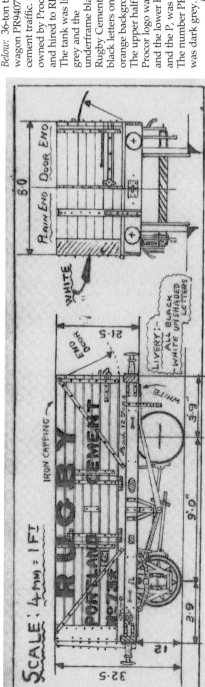

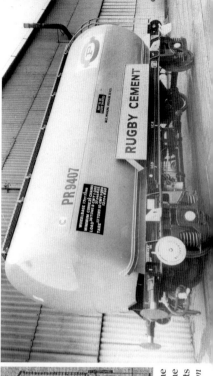

Below: 36-ton tank wagon PR9407 for cement traffic. It was owned by Procor and hired to RPC. The tank was light grey and the underframe black. Rugby Cement was black letters on an orange background. The upper half of the Procor logo was red and the lower half, and the P, was black. The number PR9407 was dark grey.

HMRS

Above: RPC iron van No. 13, apparently a second-hand GWR vehicle of the type known as an 'Iron Mink'. All black with white unshaded lettering. The roof and the rims of the spoked wheels were also white. (Measurements millimetres for 4mm scale.) *Model Railway News,* July 1963, *Author's Collection*

4w steam	Grafton		Scr. by 1974
4w diesel ex-steam	Grafton	2382	Scrapped
4w diesel	T. Smith	No. 75 X50028	Scrapped

Wooden side-tipping 'Ship Canal' wagons were used to carry stone out of the quarry before dumpers were introduced in the 1950s. Some were built by the Cambrian Wagon Co., and some by RPC. As an experiment, a man and boy once built a wagon in 14 days. The home-made wagons used second-hand main line wheelsets, with the outside journals burnt off and new inside bearings turned on the axle. The frame, placed inside the wheels, was 12 in. square oak, pitch pine or elm, and the body was 12 ft long. These inside-framed wagons were the reason why all the locomotives were fitted with a set of dumb buffers inside the normal sprung ones. The typical Ship Canal wagon, with a body 10 ft x 6 ft x 2 ft 9 in. deep, had a capacity of 6 cubic yards, so Rugby's wagons probably held about 7 cubic yards. Tare weight was 2 tons 15 cwt to 3 tons 1cwt. The stone wagons were numbered 1 to 80, in white figures painted at the right-hand end of the frame. Ironwork was black or unpainted. There were four more wagons of slightly different design for locomotive and excavator coal. All these wagons were burnt when the dumpers came.

For internal use to carry coal and clinker there were two batches of former main line open wagons, 'Bostons' numbered 1-6, and others 7-18. They were painted grey.

RPC had its own fleet of main line wagons, maintained by Thomas Hunt, Mill Road, Rugby. There were some 7-plank open wagons for incoming coal. Number 152 was lettered 'RUGBY' (letters two planks high) centrally on the top three planks with 'PORTLAND CEMENT' (letters one and half planks high) on the third and fourth planks up, with 152 (bottom left corner) and 'CO LTD' (central) on the lowest plank. The tare weight 6-0-2 (6 tons, 0 cwt, 2 q.), was in italic below the number, on the edge of the floor plank. Livery appears to have been black with white lettering. Another wagon, No. 8, had 'RUGBY PORTLAND' on the top three planks, with 'R' and 'P' three planks high and the remaining letters slightly smaller, and 'CEMENT WORKS' in letters one plank high on the third plank up, placed either side of the door. Body colour was maybe dark red, with letters white shaded black.

Chalk was originally brought in ordinary mineral or hopper wagons. Hurst, Nelson supplied 20T hopper wagon No 206, registered by the LMS in 1923, for 'cement raw materials', which could mean chalk, coal or gypsum. In the 1950s and 1960s chalk was imported to both Rugby and Southam works in standard BR 27 ton all-steel mineral wagons. Trains of these wagons were a familiar sight on the West Coast main line between Leighton Buzzard and Rugby (see Appendix Five).

RPC owned some iron vans, similar to the GWR type known as 'Iron Mink' (maybe they had been bought second-hand from GWR), for outward traffic in cement. Lettering style varied. No 372 had three lines: (top line, large letters) RUGBY (below and smaller) PORTLAND CEMENT, (below and smaller again) Co. Ltd, in white letters on black and with a white roof, while No. 13 had only two lines: (top, large, central) 'RUGBY' (below, smaller, at each end) 'PORTLAND CEMENT', and was all black with white lettering.

In the 1950s BR introduced 'Presflo' wagons for bulk powders, like cement. They were designed for gravity loading through hatches in the roof, but were unloaded by passing compressed air into the body so that the powder became a fluid and could be pumped out. This technique became common, and was applied to road tankers as well. Procor hired 50 ton capacity Presflo tank wagons to RPC in 1973 (see Appendix Six).

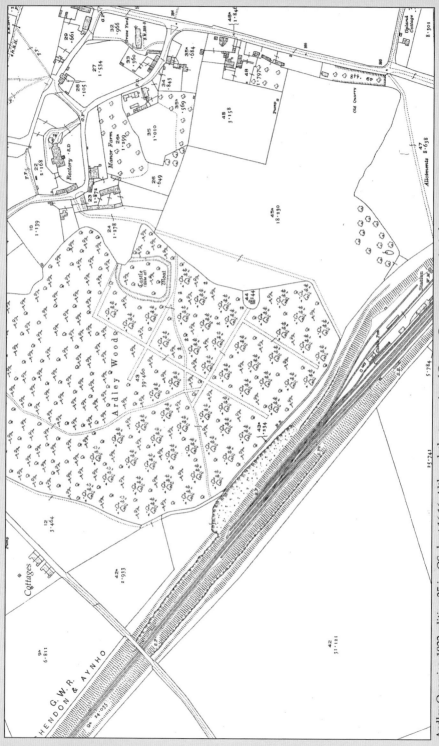

Ardley Quarries, 1922 edition 25 in. OS sheet 16.16. Although the two pairs of Quarry Cottages are marked, there is no sign of any quarry, active or disused, in field 12. The tip for loading main line wagons was probably near the signal post (SP). The later quarries were in Ardley Woods and then east of the main

Appendix One

Ardley Quarries

c.1917	Greaves Bull & Lakin Ltd
1927	Greaves Bull & Lakin (Harbury Works) Ltd
1927	Red Triangle Group
1931	Associated Portland Cement Manufacturers Ltd

Closed *c.*1934

Reopened *c.*1957, operated by Smith & Sons (Bletchington) Ltd

The Oxfordshire village of Ardley is about four miles north-west of Bicester and 13 miles north of Oxford. Although the Great Central Railway's (GCR) London Extension, opened around 1900, shared tracks with the Metropolitan Railway for the section approaching the capital, railway politics made it desirable for the GCR to obtain an alternative route. The result, opening in 1905/6, was the Great Western & Great Central Joint Railway, running from near Greenford through Princes Risborough to Ashendon Junction, where the GCR diverged to the north. The GWR continued north-west from Ashendon Junction through Bicester, to meet its existing route to Birmingham at Aynho Junction, a few miles south of Banbury. This new line opened in 1910, and gave the GWR a competitive fast route to Birmingham, about 20 miles shorter than the existing one through Reading and Oxford. A station to serve Ardley was built on the new railway just south of the village. The entry of Ardley in *Kelly's Directory* states that 'The land about here is principally limestone; subsoil stone brush.'

The trade directory collection at the Oxfordshire History Centre has copies of *Kelly's Directory* for the county at approximately five-yearly intervals. There is no entry for Greaves Bull & Lakin at Ardley in the 1915 edition but there is one in 1920, suggesting that the quarry opened in the later part of World War I or immediately afterwards.

Quarry Cottages, in a lane off Somerton Road, were built by Greaves Bull & Lakin. When one of them, still with many original features, was for sale in 1992 the estate agent described it as 'turn of the century' while the purchaser's property surveyor estimated the building to be 80 years old, built around 1912. The two pairs of brick cottages are marked on the 1922 25 in. OS map.

This could suggest that the quarry had opened around 1912, but in such a small way that GBL did not bother to advertise their presence in Kelly's. However, I think it more likely that the quarry opened in the later part of World War I, possibly to supply limestone for smelting iron. Any workers' houses built at that time could well have used an earlier design. This would explain both the apparent date of construction of the cottages and the date of the company's first entry in Kelly's.

From 1920 to 1935 inclusive *Kelly's Directories* list 'Greaves Bull & Lakin Ltd, Ardley, Bicester' under cement merchants, although there are no entries under lime burners or quarry owners, or in the section about Ardley itself. The entry did not appear in the 1939 edition, nor in Cope's 1934 *Oxfordshire Directory* (an extra volume among the volumes of Kelly's). Neither was there any reference to Associated Portland Cement Manufacturers Ltd instead. The quarry finished in the mid-1930s, probably 1933-34 if Cope's is accurate, the 1935 Kelly's entry then being an oversight by APCM who had taken over GBL.

The quarry (SP 536275) was in the field between the cottages and Ardley Woods, with the main line railway running past the site in a deep cutting. The station and its goods yard were alongside the southern end of the wood. The quarry was subsequently used as a refuse tip and was completely filled. It is now a grassy field. Although the 1922 edition 25 in. OS map marks the two pairs of Quarry Cottages it is curious that there is no indication at all of the quarry, although a later edition does show 'Old Workings'.

215

Some 20 years after the quarry closed, probably around 1957, the southern part of Ardley Woods was quarried by Smith & Sons (Bletchington) Ltd (SP 538272). When this was exhausted the firm opened a new quarry to the south-east (SP 542265), on the east side of the main road (now B430) south of the railway. This quarry later became a tip and recycling centre, operated in 2012 by Viridor, while Smith then had an active quarry a little further south. The quarry in Ardley Woods became a nature reserve in the care of Oxfordshire Wildlife Trust.

A 3 ft gauge tramway served the GBL pits. Although some stone was probably dispatched by road, there was also a tramway from the quarry towards the station where stone was tipped down a chute into main line wagons. As the distance from the southern corner of the field to the nearest part of the station goods yard was about 200 yards, and the edge of the field opposite the cottages was some 150 yards further away, horses were probably used for haulage initially. The main line wagons were probably moved by gravity along the siding under and away from the chute.

The Industrial Railway Society records three petrol locomotives here but with no details. These could well have been former WDLR 40 hp Motor Rail type, available cheap around 1920 from army surplus and regauged from 60 cm to 3 ft. When the quarry closed two of them went to Ufton Quarries (*see Chapter Five*). They appear to have had short lives at Ufton, possibly having stood in the open after the quarry here closed.

3 ft 0 in. gauge

4wPM	MR?	(a)	(1)
4wPM	MR?	(a)	(1)
4wPM	MR?	(a)	(1)

(a)   Ex WDLR *c*.1920 and regauged?
(1)   Two to Ufton Quarries 1934, third s/s by 1934

When the quarries were re-opened around 1957 Smith used 6-wheel Foden dumpers to carry stone to the chute formerly used by the tramway. This chute continued to be used when the new quarry was opened across the main road. However, the dumpers were unable to cross the road when it was foggy, and so a new main line siding with a loading chute was constructed alongside the active quarry. Wagons were probably positioned by the main line locomotive and then run under the chute by gravity as required.

Appendix Two

Totternhoe Limeworks and Quarries

1869	P. De Berenger	
By 1879	A. Gower	
1896	Totternhoe Lime Stone & Cement Co. Ltd	
1915	Totternhoe Lime & Stone Co. Ltd	
		Closed 2009
1936-65	Rugby Portland Cement Co. Ltd owned and operated the quarries but not the limeworks.	

Totternhoe is a long village, stretching about a mile from Lower End up to Church End. It is situated immediately west of Dunstable, Bedfordshire, almost two miles by road from the Watling Street (A5) which runs the length of that town. Stanbridgeford station, on the LNWR Leighton Buzzard to Dunstable branch, opened in 1848, was about 500 yards north of Lower End.

The first quarries at Totternhoe extracted the light grey 'Clunch' stone, which is hard enough for exterior walls of buildings, and was used in a nearby Roman villa. Although initially the stone was worked from the outcrop, from a least the Middle Ages it was obtained from mines beneath the chalk. The bed of stone was 8-17 ft thick, and was worked by a maze of tunnels, typically 8-10 ft high and 6-8 ft wide. The workings extended under parts of the area later quarried for chalk, not least in the area north-east of the workshop. The last recorded exploration of part of the old workings was organized by RPC in 1959. The blocks of quarried stone were brought out either in wheelbarrows or on low trolleys fitted with rollers instead of wheels.

The peak periods for the use of this stone was from the 12th to mid-16th centuries, for churches, abbeys and 'an almost endless succession of royal works at Windsor, Westminster and elsewhere', including St Albans Cathedral and Totternhoe Church. There was then a lull until the mid-18th century, when for about 70 years wealthy local landowners used it to build or rebuild their grand houses, for example at Ashridge and Woburn Abbey. However, demand then virtually ceased, except for small amounts of stone to repair local churches. Joan Curran in *The Story of Totternhoe Quarries* says that, after seven centuries, quarrying ceased in the 1880s, although trade directory entries (*see below*) suggest operation continued (or, at least, quarry owners were prepared to supply the stone) until the 1900s. Much later, in the 1970s, a company opened a small quarry, working opencast, extracting stone to repair Woburn Abbey.

Lime burning started at Totternhoe in 1650, if not before, but remained on a small scale until the end of the 19th century. Locally, lime burning was at a very low ebb, if not moribund, until 1869, when Mr de Berenger leased the property. According to an account in the *Dunstable Borough Gazette* of 11th November, 1931 and quoted by Curran, Philip De Berenger was a builder, or builders' merchant, from London who visited the area, probably in 1869, seeking a source of grey chalk to make lime.

He was waiting at Stanbridgeford Station for the train home, having been unsuccessful in his quest, when he struck up a conversation with the porter and asked about the hills in the distance [Dunstable Downs]. The porter told him about the old quarries and put him in touch with a local man through whom he eventually contacted Lord Brownlow... Convinced that producing lime here was a viable proposition he took out a lease, to run for 60 years from 25 December 1869, for 49 acres of land belonging to Lord Brownlow.

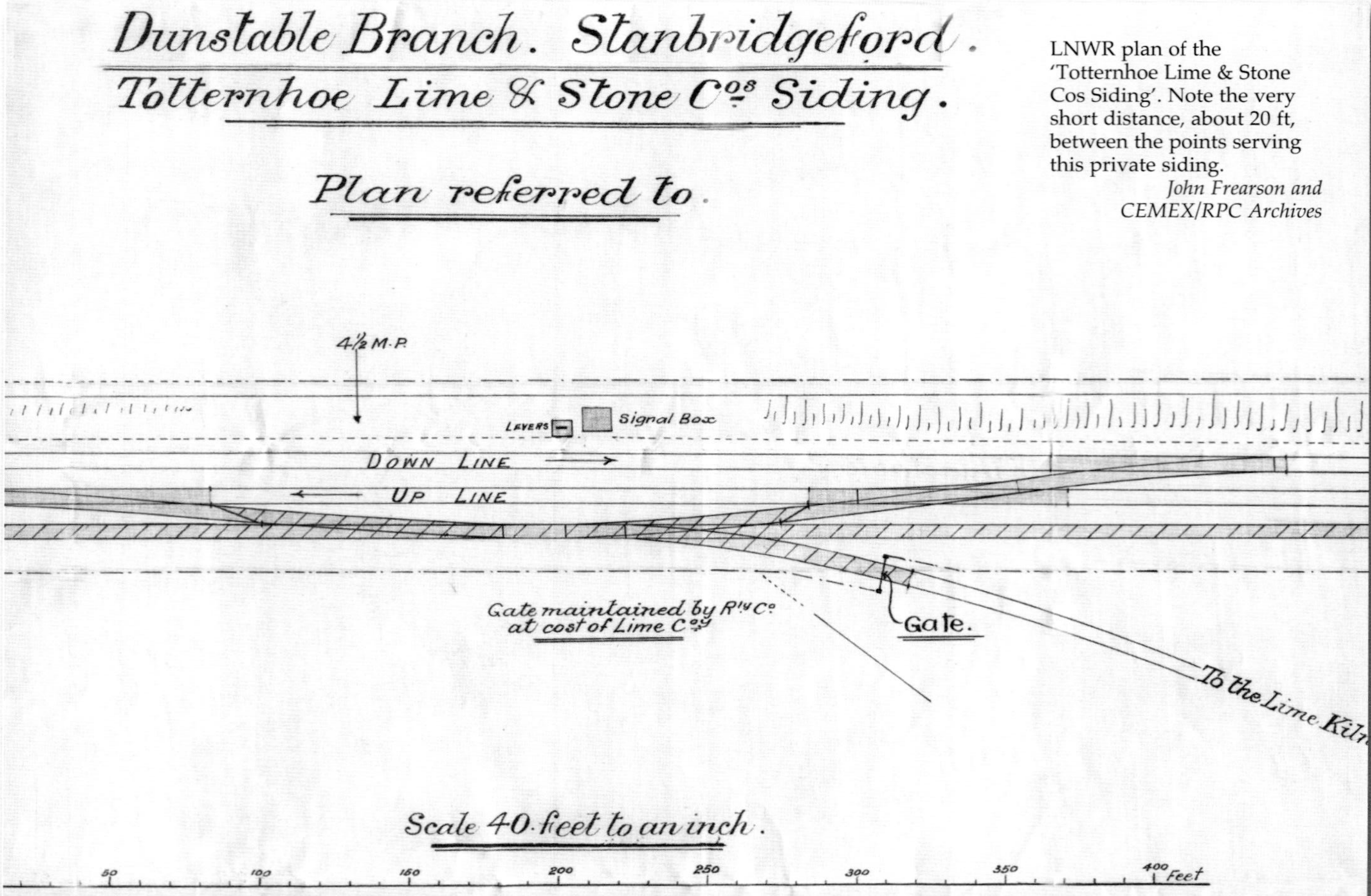

Dunstable Branch. Stanbridgeford.
Totternhoe Lime & Stone Co⁰ˢ Siding.

Plan referred to.

LNWR plan of the
'Totternhoe Lime & Stone
Cos Siding'. Note the very
short distance, about 20 ft,
between the points serving
this private siding.

*John Frearson and
CEMEX/RPC Archives*

4½ M.P.

LEVERS

Signal Box

DOWN LINE

UP LINE

Gate maintained by Rⁱʸ Cᵒ.
at cost of Lime Cᵒ.ᵧ

Gate.

To the Lime Kiln

Scale 40 feet to an inch.

50   100   150   200   250   300   350   400 feet

His lease gave the right to work both chalk and the clunch stone, and to build a railway to Stanbridgeford station. The first reference to de Berenger in a trade directory was in 1876, the entry reading ' The noted free stone quarries and lime works are situated in this parish, about 1 mile from Stanbridge Ford [sic] station, the property of Earl Brownlow.' In addition, it gave De Berenger P & Co, as 'proprietors of stone quarries and lime works'.

Some time before de Berenger died in 1879 he had taken Arthur Gower into partnership. The 1880 edition listed De Berenger & Gower, lime and stone works, and also listed them under Stone & Marble Merchants, presumably working the clunch stone. The first siding agreement with the LNWR had been signed by A.W. Gower on 10th November, 1879. By 1889 it was reported that 18-20 kilns were in use, and according to the *Leighton Buzzard Observer* of 17th September, 1895, the works 'could not make lime quickly enough'. How much cement, if any, was made on site is not known. Gower sold his Totternhoe Lime Works (SP 980224) to the Totternhoe Lime Stone & Cement Co. Ltd in 1896, that firm also having an entry under Stone & Marble Merchants.

The Totternhoe Lime Stone & Cement Co. Ltd was listed under lime burners and Stone & Marble Merchants throughout the 1900s, but the company was in financial difficulties by 1910. A receiver had been appointed in 1908, and operation continued with a skeleton staff. Liquidation proceedings began in 1914 and the assets were acquired by the Totternhoe Lime & Stone Co. Ltd (TLS), registered 9th July, 1915. The manager, Mr Curtis, became the first Managing Director.

By 1900 Totternhoe had 16 flare kilns for making lime. Two still survived in 1996, although they had last been used in the 1930s. Each batch of lime required a wooden arch to be built inside the base of the kiln. This was covered with layers of coal (later coke) and chalk, and then it was lit. The kiln was charged with lumps of chalk, at least 2 in. cube, tipped in about half way up. Lumps were necessary as otherwise there were no voids in the charge and it would not burn. The chalk was screened in the quarry using rakes with only three of four prongs. The fine material was left on the quarry floor, where a 2 ft thick layer can still be found in parts of old workings! It took a day to build the arch and charge the kiln, three days for it to burn and make lime, three days to cool, and then the contents were dug out. Two or three kilns were built and fired each day.

Lord Brownlow (1844-1921), a prominent Conservative politician, decided in 1916 to sell part of his estates in Bedfordshire by auction. Lot 23 listed 64 acres occupied by the Totternhoe Lime Co., with the lease having 13 years to run. As this lot did not reach its reserve price it was withdrawn, and was subsequently sold to the lime company. Another 83 areas of pasture and arable land was sold at the same auction, and by 1925 it was held by Buxton Lime Firms, later part of ICI Lime. Later still this land was bought by RPC and became part of its Totternhoe Quarries.

Before World War II there used to be 17 limeworks in a 20 mile radius of Totternhoe, including several nearby along the former LNWR Dunstable branch. De Berenger's works became the last survivor. Local deliveries of lime were made by horse and cart. The Totternhoe Lime Stone & Cement Co. took out a supplemental railway siding agreement on 17th March, 1897.

As described in earlier chapters, the limestone used by the Warwickshire cement manufacturers occurred in thin layers, separated by beds of clay. The traditional method of operation required most of the calcareous clay to be picked out from the stone by hand, to produce a mixture of the correct chemical composition for cement manufacture. This was both expensive and wasteful. In order to make use of all the rock quarried it was necessary to blend additional material high in calcium carbonate, to counter the surplus clay and make a mixture of the correct chemical composition. The most convenient source for the cement works at Rugby was the Chilterns, about 40 miles away along the West Coast main line. In 1919 Rugby Portland Cement had approached most of the firms along the LNWR branch from Leighton Buzzard to Dunstable (for ease of transport to Rugby) for supplies of small chalk, hitherto left on quarry floor as it was too small to stack in the

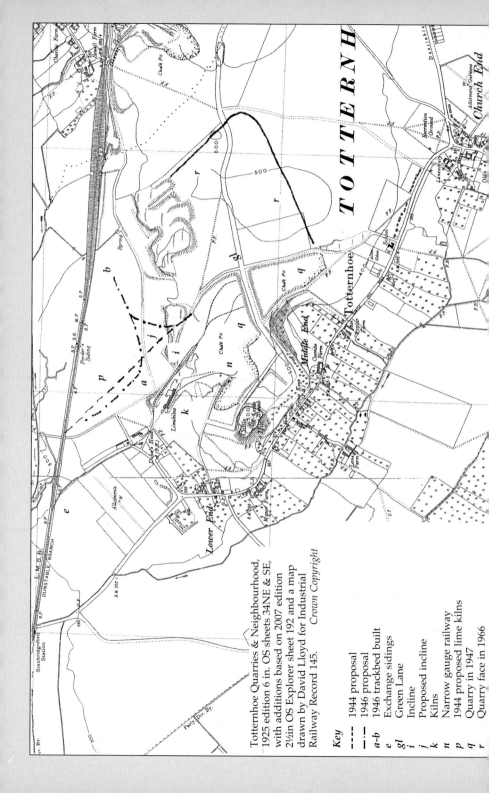

Totternhoe Quarries & Neighbourhood,
1925 edition 6 in. OS sheets 34NE & SE,
with additions based on 2007 edition
2½in OS Explorer sheet 192 and a map
drawn by David Lloyd for Industrial
Railway Record 145.   *Crown Copyright*

Key

- - -	1944 proposal
- · -	1946 proposal
a-b	1946 trackbed built
e	Exchange sidings
gl	Green Lane
i	Incline
j	Proposed incline
k	Kilns
n	Narrow gauge railway
p	1944 proposed lime kilns
q	Quarry in 1947
r	Quarry face in 1966

lime kilns. Kaye, of Southam, followed in 1921 (*see Chapters Twelve and Seven respectively*). TLS supplied both firms, sending about five or six wagons weekly to each company, about 6,000 tons annually in total. With the passage of time the whole operation at Totternhoe became increasingly geared to RPC requirements, with for example the purchase of an additional locomotive in 1924 to handle the increased rail traffic.

Halford Reddish had been appointed to the RPC Board in 1929, becoming Managing Director in 1933 and Chairman soon after. He wanted to guarantee the supply of chalk from Totternhoe (then sold by Totternhoe at 10*d*. per ton - about £1.50 today), as neighbouring sources were being taken over by APCM, who naturally would not supply chalk to RPC, a competitor. Reddish also wanted to mechanize. RPC began quarrying chalk for TLS in 1934, paying 2*d*./ton royalty, using TLS quarry equipment and railways. This led to an agreement with TLS in June 1937, permitting RPC to work the quarries for 44 years. Although RPC assumed responsibility for the railway and locomotives, the limekilns were excluded and continued to be operated by TLS. The father of Mr R.A. Bates, in 1996 the Managing Director, had joined TLS in 1921, later becoming the Company Secretary and, in 1936, MD. He had opposed the link with RPC but had been over-ruled. Quarrying was now governed by RPC needs, not by Totternhoe's kilns.

Arising from the new agreement, RPC made plans to open a large new quarry east of the kilns, on a much larger scale than the existing one. TLS retained ownership of a few acres of the quarry, to safeguard its own supplies, extending as far south as Castle Hill (Motte & Bailey). In 1960 there was an area about 100 yards square (about two acres) remaining untouched behind the Cross Keys in Middle End.

A new agreement with TLS dated 30th June, 1948 gave RPC much more control. It took over the siding from Totternhoe, and agreed to provide a locomotive which would shunt up to 36 wagons a week for the limeworks. It seems that TLS was now paying RPC for each ton of chalk produced. The rate was 1*s*. (£1.25) per ton in 1948, rising to 3*s*. 6*d*. (£2.70) by 1960. There had been a surcharge of 5¼*d*. (40p) per ton from October 1955 to cover various works, including removal of the 'Tunnel', laying rails and land restoration.

After RPC ceased to use Totternhoe quarry the shunting agreement was terminated in 1966, because '… for many years past the Totternhoe Company has not required the Rugby Company to provide services under the shunting agreement …' and as 'The Rugby Company has no longer any use for the sidings ….and the Totternhoe Company … no longer wishes to retain the right to have its works connected to the main line railway…'

At first, RPC used two Ruston Bycyrus 32RB 1 cubic yard (bucket capacity) excavators and one 37RB 1.5 cu. yd excavator. Shortly after, two 43RB 1.75 cu. yd excavators were obtained. Later, a Lima 802 2 cu. yd excavator was 'acquired through the government supply system'. When RPC operations finished in 1965 three excavators, one 43RB, and two larger 54RB, were in use.

Only a few years' supply of chalk was left at Totternhoe by the early 1960s. There was still chalk in the area towards Sewell, particularly on the east side of Drovers Way, but as that was owned by Blue Circle Industries (successors to APCM) it was unavailable to RPC. Instead, RPC decided to move to Kensworth before Totternhoe was completely worked out (*see Appendix Three*). The anticipated gradual changeover to the new quarry was of quite short duration, and Totternhoe Quarries closed on Maundy Thursday 15th April, 1965. Subsequently arrangements had to be made for assorted unlicensed quarry vehicles to be driven to Kensworth: three dump trucks, two Fordson tractors with air compressors, one Aveling Barford loading shovel, one fuel bowser, and one trailer. The three excavators were also transferred there, by low loader.

Totternhoe chalk is grey and gives grey lime. It used to be considered as good as white lime, but since World War II demand for grey lime steadily dropped, and eventually production was no longer viable. In 1948 production was 14,000 tons pa, in 1976 it was still 12,000 tons, but in 1992 it was only 2,000 tons, and so production ceased. Some lime was slaked to make quicklime in a hydrating plant, purchased from RPC Chinnor works, Oxfordshire, in 1987. It had four stacks, and was responsible for the plumes of steam

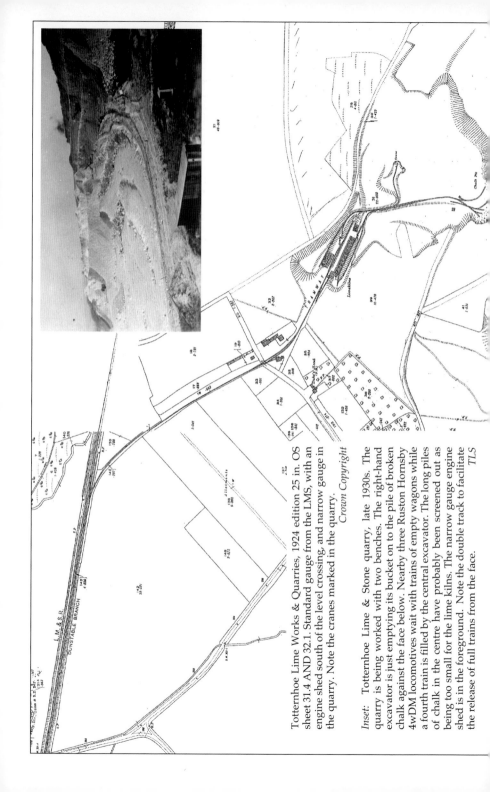

Totternhoe Lime Works & Quarries, 1924 edition 25 in. OS sheet 31.4 AND 32.1. Standard gauge from the LMS, with an engine shed south of the level crossing, and narrow gauge in the quarry. Note the cranes marked in the quarry.

Crown Copyright

Inset: Totternhoe Lime & Stone quarry, late 1930s. The quarry is being worked with two benches. The right-hand excavator is just emptying its bucket on to the pile of broken chalk against the face below. Nearby three Ruston Hornsby 4wDM locomotives wait with trains of empty wagons while a fourth train is filled by the central excavator. The long piles of chalk in the centre have probably been screened out as being too small for the lime kilns. The narrow gauge engine shed is in the foreground. Note the double track to facilitate the release of full trains from the face.

TLS

which identified the site from a distance. After lime ceased to be made at Totternhoe in 1992, TLS bought it from manufacturers in the Buxton, Grassington (Yorkshire Dales) and Humberside areas. The lime was brought in by road, often as 'return hauls', it was hydrated at Totternhoe, and was then sold on, much going to the south of England.

After RPC operations closed in 1965 TLS recommenced working their original quarry area for some chalk. This was ground and sold in a 30 mile radius as 'aglime', although in reality it was agricultural chalk. From 1984/5 it was mainly sold to spreading contractors, rather than direct to the farmers themselves. TLS eventually closed in September 2009. The site was bought by J.G.E. Commercials, a firm selling contractors' plant and heavy goods vehicles. The new owners moved in at the end of February 2010. Some of the old kilns were then still standing.

The old quarry is now the home of two rare butterflies. One is the small brown fritillary 'Duke of Burgundy' which can be found on the eastern side in May. It lays its eggs on the underside of primrose and cowslip leaves, which form the food for its young. The other is the 'Little (or Small) Blue', one of Britain's smallest butterflies. There are several colonies at Totternhoe on the west side behind the limeworks, along an east-facing slope. They emerge in May and June, to lay their eggs on vetch, and have been recorded here since 1977.

The quarry floor was some 60 ft above the limeworks, just above the hard clunch stone. TLS had worked southwards, and later RPC worked eastwards. Originally the quarry was worked by 'getters' with pick and shovel. They stood halfway up the face digging chalk, which they threw down for screening and it was then loaded into small railway wagons for transport to the kilns.

Chalk is naturally very moist which makes it 'dead', meaning that when the bottom of a pile is removed the material at the top will not then flow down the sides, unlike gravel or stone chippings. It is therefore dangerous to use an excavator on a high pile of loose chalk. As the excavator steadily undercut the pile it would eventually collapse, probably burying the excavator and killing its driver. To overcome this problem, when excavators were introduced into the quarry the face was worked as a series of 'benches', each about 30ft high. The excavator on the highest bench dug chalk and dropped it on to the bench below. The excavator there dug this chalk, and also chalk from its own face, and dropped it to the quarry floor, where a third excavator loaded chalk dropped from above, plus material from its own face, into railway wagons. Blasting was introduced in the early 1950s to loosen the chalk. A Fordson tractor with an air compressor was used to drill 2 in. diameter shot holes in the lowest face. Enough explosive was used to loosen the chalk, and so facilitate digging, but not to blow it down, due to the danger when digging out a pile of broken chalk.

For many years chalk was transported from the quarry to the kilns by a 2 ft 6 in. gauge railway. The 1901 OS map shows a single track running north from the face near Castle Mound, then dividing in two after about 300 yards. One branch turned west to run on the south side of the main battery of kilns. The other passed the end of the standard gauge siding before turning west to pass north of the smaller battery of kilns. There was also a high level siding, parallel to the standard gauge headshunt, presumably for loading raw chalk into main line wagons. By the 1924 edition a small quarry had been opened east of the main line to the quarry. A long loop had been built beside the main kilns, and the map marks a 'Crane' at the end of the (assumed) chalk transfer siding. (Another crane is marked in the small quarry.) Perhaps this was to load chalk tipped on a stockpile into standard gauge wagons, as by then the agreement to supply RPC was in force. Later, probably in the 1930s, TLS extended the quarry railway to run down a gradient on to a gantry to load main line wagons. The narrow gauge continued in use to supply chalk to the lime kilns, but as the use of lime was diminishing three of the locomotives were sent to RPC at Rochester, Kent, in 1950. Changes at the screening plant in 1952 meant the narrow gauge became redundant and its equipment was scrapped. A locomotive shed had been built in the quarry by 1924, and was still standing in the early 1960s, although by then its only occupant was a wagon frame.

Totternhoe lime kilns, with a narrow gauge track running alongside each battery of kilns. A wagon stands towards the left-hand end of the nearer track. The loading point for standard gauge wagons was below and behind the battery of four kilns. The function of the building with the chimney is not known. *TLS*

The only known photograph of one of the 'Crewe Tractors', seen in front of the kilns. Note the sprockets for the transmission. *TLS*

Gantry built by RPC for loading chalk into standard gauge wagons. One of the Ruston diesels waits while its train is emptied, and a second one is spare *c.*1935. Again note the double track, with a catch point near the foot of the left hand track to derail any loaded train which got out of control on the gradient. The line serving the battery of four kilns is at a higher level above the cutting. The later standard gauge incline ran along the edge of the field.

Ruston & Hornsby Ltd, Andrew Neale Collection

Undated, but probably pre-1914, photograph of two locomotives at Totternhoe, a geared 2-2-0WT and 0-4-0ST. See text for analysis and comment. The Totternhoe wagon (the name is just visible on the original print) has no roof but relies on a tarpaulin to keep the contents dry. A strut joining the high ends of the wagon prevents hollows forming in the tarpaulin, where water could collect and slowly seep through.

F. Jones, TLS Collection

Aveling & Porter 3730. Note the two different sized cylinders as it was a compound. The casing behind the wheels contained a large gear wheel to transmit the drive from the crankshaft in the cab to the wheels - the 'coupling rod' served to keep the axles parallel and the gear teeth in mesh.

F. Jones Collection

RPC locomotive No. 4 shunting in the TLS yard.   *TLS*

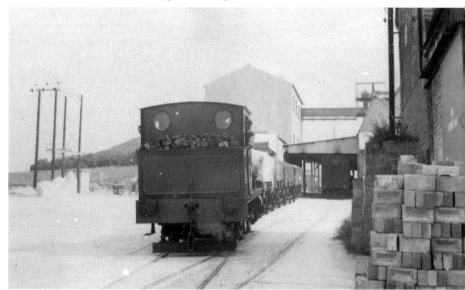

A tractor shunting in the TLS yard.

TLS

Totternhoe Lime Co. Ltd open wagons, Nos. 115 and 117. On the left is a lorry loaded with sacks.

TLS

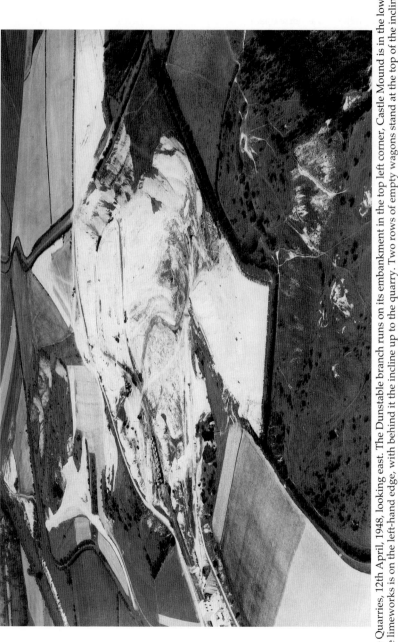

Totternhoe Quarries, 12th April, 1948, looking east. The Dunstable branch runs on its embankment in the top left corner, Castle Mound is in the lower right corner. The limeworks is on the left-hand edge, with behind it the incline up to the quarry. Two rows of empty wagons stand at the top of the incline. Two trains are being loaded in the quarry. Although at this time the railway serving the quarry forms a loop, trains go each way alternately - the two locomotives would be buffer to buffer if they were closer. The quarry has worked close to the two rights of way, and working has commenced beyond both of them. Just to the right of the nearer train is the mouth of the tunnel under Drovers Way, serving a new quarry. To the left of the further train is a girder bridge carrying Wheelbarrow Highway over the access to another new quarry. The shed in the lower right corner of the quarry housed the narrow gauge diesel locomotives, one of which is hauling a train of five skips about halfway between the shed and kilns. Several empty skips stand near the kilns.

Originally the railway was horse operated, but in 1919 or 1920 two locomotives driven by Model 'T' Ford engines were bought, possibly to handle the increased traffic following the RPC agreement. Unfortunately the only known photograph is a rear view, but it seems probable that these were two 'Crewe Tractors', designed by the LNWR and built for use on lightly laid front line railways in World War I. They were scrapped around 1931 after the purchase of two German Orenstein & Koppel locomotives.

One of the Orenstein & Koppel locomotives, No. 4547, had been built around 1931 at the firm's Montania works, Nordhausen, and was powered by a single cylinder gasoline engine, probably 8½ hp. It is likely that it was started on petrol and then, after the engine had warmed up, switched to paraffin for more economical running. It may have come via the dealer J.C. Oliver & Co. of Leeds. The other Orenstein & Koppel locomotive, 4621, was dispatched from the Montania works on 22nd October, 1931. It was a type 'RL1a' locomotive, powered by a single cylinder 4-stroke diesel engine producing 11 hp at 1300 rpm. The drive was through a two-speed cone clutch and chain drive to the leading axle, with a second chain to couple the axles. It may have been supplied by Wm Jones, the British agent for Orenstein & Koppel. Jones probably regauged it to 2 ft 6 in., as the gauge as built was 605mm - almost 2 ft. It weighed 3 tons and had a maximum speed of 5.4 mph. During 1941 both of these three ton locomotives were transferred to RPC Halling, Kent.

Following the 1934 agreement, with its need for a greatly increased output, it is hardly surprising that TLS bought a fleet of four 10 hp diesel locomotives from Ruston & Hornsby, of Lincoln, in 1935. RPC bought a fifth locomotive, similar but 12 hp, in 1937. Early orders for spares were bought by RPC, but once the standard gauge line into the quarry had been built in 1938 the narrow gauge was used only by TLS, who bought the necessary spares for the locomotives.

The last locomotive, bought by RPC, 183427, weighed 2½ tons. It had a 10/12 hp '2JP' engine, developing 10 hp at 600 rpm. Nominal haulage capacity on level track was: 1st gear 52 tons at 2½ mph, 2nd gear 30 tons at 4 mph, and 3rd gear 20 tons at 6 mph. IRS records allege it to have been lent to RPC Southam works in the summer of 1938, although staff I met at both Southam and Totternhoe thought this unlikely, particularly as the Southam system was 2 ft gauge so the locomotive would have needed to be regauged. All of the Rustons had standard cabs, and all disappeared in the 1950s when the narrow gauge fell out of use.

TLS locomotives, survivors taken over by RPC with site in 1936
2 ft 6 in gauge

4wPM	Crewe			(a)	Scrapped c./1930
4wPM	Crewe			(a)	Scrapped c./1930
4wPM	OK	4547	c.1931	(b)	(1) (2)
4wDM	OK	4621	1931	(c)	(1) (2)
4wDM	RH	172334	1935	New	(1) (2)
4wDM	RH	172336	1935	New	(1) (3)
4wDM	RH	172337	1935	New	(1) (3)
4wDM	RH	172342	1935	New	(1) (4)
4wDM	RH	183427	1937	New	(5)

(a) Origins uncertain; here by 1919. Ford engined units, believed to have been examples of the well-known 'Crewe Tractors', built by the LNWR at Crewe around Model 'T' Ford motor cars for use on front line tramways in World War I.

(b) Possibly ex-J.C. Oliver & Co., dealers, Leeds

(c) Possibly ex-Wm Jones Ltd, dealer, Greenwich, London

(1) Bought by TLS, taken over by RPC Co. Ltd with site, 1936

(2) To RPC Rochester works, Halling, Kent, after 24.3.1941 by 21.11.1941, where regauged to 2 ft 0 in.

(3) To Draper Bros, scrap merchants, Leighton Buzzard, 1957, then to F.D. O'Dell & Son Ltd Shefford until at least 6.1959, then s/s

(4) To RH, Lincoln, for overhaul, 29.12.1937, returned 1.1938, to RPC Rochester works, Halling, Kent, by 7.1950

(5) Alleged short loan to RPC Southam works summer 1938, and returned. s/s after 3.1953

General view of the quarry in 1957 showing four benches, each with an excavator feeding chalk to the one below. The Avonside takes a rake of empties to the bottom excavator. Note the colour light signals controlling trains leaving the face, and the signal box in the right foreground. The signals and hut are on wooden frames for ease of movement as the track layout frequently changed to follow the face. *Rugby Cement*

Quarrying in a confined space between the two rights of way. The girders of the bridge are visible in the right foreground. *Rugby Cement*

0-6-0ST No. 4 shunting near the main line connection on 27th June, 1961. The concrete hut is the weigh house. The white buildings of Stanbridgeford station are just visible left of the locomotive's tank. *Author*

Testing the accuracy of the weighbridge with known weights.
Rugby Cement

No. 4 outside the lower engine shed, with a Manning, Wardle inside. *Rugby Cement*

Totternhoe 2 ft 6 in. gauge tipping wagon, (derelict) 26th June 1965.   *Author*

Totternhoe 2 ft 6 in. gauge end tipping wagon.   *Author*

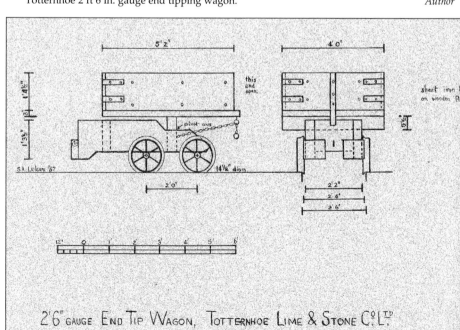

Rolling stock was wooden end tipping wagons, later replaced by steel V-skip side tippers. By the early 1960s a number of mouldering remains of wooden trucks lay near the engine shed, whilst just one reasonably preserved vehicle, a wooden end-tipping wagon formerly used when the line was horse operated, stood near the siding to the kilns. The open end of the body overhung the frame so it could tip further, and thereby obscured the coupling chain. To facilitate coupling, a length of chain was attached to an eye bolt fitted to the frame's front end stretcher. The chain was taken through a ring screwed under the floor at the open end, and the free end terminated in a large ring, hanging free. This ring could be easily reached and dropped over a hook on the rear end of the next wagon's frame, and so couple the wagons together.

The original standard gauge siding agreement had been signed on 10th November, 1879, but (not surprisingly) no siding is shown on the 1880 25 in. OS map. At this time there was a small lime kiln about 300 yards from the road, about the end of the later battery of kilns, and further lime kilns about 200 yards further, in the quarry area later worked by RPC. This map shows the kilns and their quarries occupying a single parcel of land, and they must have been those originally used by de Berenger. These kilns were later pulled down and new ones built at a lower level, slightly nearer the road and LNWR. The works siding climbed only about 10 ft from the LNWR to the later kilns, a distance of about ¼ mile. It was originally horse worked. The 1902 OS map shows an engine shed, so it is likely that locomotives were introduced following the 1897 supplemental siding agreement, if not before. The junction with the LNWR was controlled by 'De Berenger and Gowers Siding Ground Frame', situated 500 yards on the Dunstable (east) side of Stanbridgeford station.

In 1909, the double track Dunstable branch had a very short loop on its south side (an LNWR plan showed a distance of only 20 feet between the two sets of points, confirmed by scaling from the 25 in. OS map). The western end of the loop was extended for about 70 yards (say 10 wagons) as a headshunt, and had access by a trailing crossover to the westbound track. A trailing connection from the eastbound track crossed the westbound line with a single slip (to form a trailing crossover) and terminated at the eastern end of the loop with a 3-way point. The central track served a siding about 70 yards long beside the LNWR, and the right-hand track ran south-east through a gate to the limeworks. It would have been easy enough for a train in either direction to collect or leave a few wagons, but it would have been very difficult with this layout for a train of more than about 10 empties from Leighton Buzzard to be exchanged for a similar train of loaded wagons. Maybe empties were normally left by a train going to Dunstable, and then loaded wagons were collected as it returned to Leighton Buzzard. By the time chalk was being sent to Rugby by the trainload the main line siding layout must have been altered.

About 350 yards from the LNWR, just before crossing a lane (now called Knolls View), were the points for a loop, which was about 80 yards long, most of it being south of the lane. The western loop track threw off a short siding to a single-road engine shed. Scaled from the 1902 25 in. OS map, it was about 40 ft long by 24 ft wide, and by the 1924 edition it had been extended by about 16 ft. It was on the opposite side of the railway from the later RPC shed. Another 140 yards beyond the end of the loop was another loop running the length of the kilns, with a short headshunt beyond.

Once RPC took over quarrying in the mid-1930s, a number of long loops and sidings were laid on the lime works side of the siding gate, for storage of full and empty wagons, and a weighbridge was constructed. A siding was laid at the back of the kilns, close to the route of the later incline, to facilitate the transfer of chalk from the narrow gauge quarry trains into main line wagons for transport to Rugby. The LMS (successors to the LNWR) supplied assorted mineral wagons for the chalk traffic.

There is little definite information about the first locomotives at Totternhoe. A Peckett catalogue illustrates four classes of small standard gauge 4-coupled tank engine, each having a length over buffers between 15 ft and 19 ft 6 in. Therefore it can be reasonably assumed that the engine shed, approximately 40 ft long, was built to house two locomotives. For the shed to have been marked on the 1902 edition of the OS map, it must have been built before the area was surveyed, which implies that in 1901 (at the latest) TLS either owned two locomotives, or it was confident that it soon would have two. While this suggests a fair amount of rail traffic, it is hardly excessive provision, as the second locomotive would provide backup when the first was undergoing routine maintenance, as well as covering peak traffic. The second one could well have been obtained around 1897, when the siding agreement was changed, if not before. There is an undated but possibly pre-1914 photograph of two locomotives in use (*see page 225*).

An advertisement in the *Contract Journal*, 29th November, 1911, stated 'Wanted immediately; standard gauge, two speed geared locomotive, 10/12hp, Totternhoe Lime Co Ltd.' Some sources say that a 'new' locomotive was acquired in 1912, so either one of the existing ones was needing heavy repair at the end of 1911 or, if there had been an upsurge of traffic, a third locomotive was necessary, with maybe two in daily use and the third spare. It would account for the extension to the shed, although as this was approximately 16 ft it would imply that the new occupant was quite small. On the other hand, if rail traffic urgently needed an extra locomotive, why was the company shortly to go into liquidation?

The use of Aveling & Porter geared locomotives (*see later purchases below*) suggests that the Totternhoe Lime Stone & Cement Co. had links with the Kent cement industry, at least through the trade press if not by more direct contact. Aveling & Porter supplied about 40 geared locomotives to firms in Kent between 1876 and 1926.

One of the locomotives in the early photograph was a 2-2-0, basically a traction engine on rails. Although this sounds an improbable design, the fact remains that Aveling & Porter built a lot of these 2-2-0s for use in the Kent cement industry. The Totternhoe locomotive had a single cylinder mounted on top of the boiler and a simple canopy over the driver. A very curious feature was the position of the flywheel, on the right-hand side, as the majority of road locomotives and their railway derivatives (and in particular Aveling & Porter 'traction engine' types) had it on the left. This seems to rule out suggestions that it was based on the early 1870s Aveling & Porter 'Steam Sapper' design. However, at that time all manner of firms, large and small, built, rebuilt and repaired steam engines of all kinds, and sometimes these firms built small locomotives for their own use or even occasionally for sale, so it is possible that Totternhoe's 2-2-0 was the product of a small engineering company. Maybe it had even been rebuilt from a suitable traction engine. According to Mr Bates, after the new locomotive was bought in 1912 the old one was used to drive a mill to crush lime, which could be done easily with a belt from the flywheel. It was finally scrapped in 1934.

The other locomotive in the early photograph is an outside cylinder 0-4-0ST, with its cab open above the waist except for the front sheet. It carried a short name (unreadable on the photograph) on a straight plate on its tank. It has been suggested that this locomotive has strong Falcon or Brush characteristics. According to *The Cement Railways of Kent* (B.D. Stoyel & R.W. Kidner, Oakwood Press, 2nd edition 1990, p. 62), the London Portland Cement Co., Northfleet, Kent had a Falcon 0-4-0ST named *Vulcan* (built 1884) which disappeared after a boiler explosion in 1895. Assuming Totternhoe's link with Kent, it could have been rebuilt by a suitable engineering firm then sold to Totternhoe in 1895 or 1896. Alternatively, it has been suggested that this locomotive 'bears all the characteristics in design of one of a batch of locos known to have been built by Thomas Spittle, Cambrian Iron Foundry, Newport, Gwent between 1877 & 1879'. T. King, Engineer, of Maidstone, had an advertisement in *Machinery Market*, 15th November, 1912, which stated 'for sale [3] four-wheeled saddle tanks standard gauge … 'Spittle' 10½ x 15 in.' This also could have been the source of the 'new' Totternhoe locomotive in 1912. Whatever the origins of this 0-4-0ST, it was probably scrapped when a new Aveling & Porter came in 1924.

Whether the 0-4-0ST came around 1895 or 1912, a third locomotive is still required for the period pre-World War I. If the 0-4-0ST came in 1895, then what was the 'new' locomotive in 1912? If the 0-4-0ST came in 1912, then what was the second occupant of the pre-1902 engine shed? Bearing in mind the 1911 advertisement for a 'two speed geared locomotive, 10/12hp', and Mr Bates' statement to me that 'A Fowler engine was purchased in 1912', I think the 0-4-0ST had been bought around 1895 and the missing locomotive was an Aveling & Porter 2-2-0 (although Mr Bates described it as a Fowler), probably obtained from Kent, and it was scrapped in 1930. (Both Fowler and Aveling & Porter constructed large numbers of road engines, but only Aveling & Porter built railway locomotives as well.)

Sometime in the early 1920s another Aveling & Porter locomotive, No. 3730 of 1896, was bought second-hand from Fraser & Chalmers Ltd, Erith, Kent (Kent again!). It was a compound, with two cylinders $7\frac{1}{2}$ in. and $11\frac{1}{2}$ in. diameter by 12 in. stroke, giving a nominal 10 hp. (Compound: Steam from the boiler was used in the smaller cylinder, and was then exhausted into the larger cylinder to expand further and power a second stroke, before being exhausted to the atmosphere. Compounding economized on fuel and water, at the expense of increased complexity.) The four 4 ft diameter wheels were driven by gears from the crankshaft. As Fraser & Chalmers appear to have managed with only a single locomotive for many years until 1945, their Aveling & Porter could well have been sold to Totternhoe soon after their new Andrew Barclay 0-4-0ST was delivered in 1919. No. 3730 was not taken over by RPC but was scrapped in the late 1930s.

TLS bought a new locomotive in April 1924, another 4-wheel geared Aveling & Porter, 11087. It had cylinders 7 in. and $11\frac{1}{2}$ in diameter by 12 in. stroke and 4 ft diameter wheels. It survived to be taken over by RPC, was withdrawn around 1940, and was eventually scrapped around 1943.

If correct, this account would require the engine shed to hold three small locomotives by the early 1920s, and would also give TLS adequate motive power for the increasing demands of RPC chalk traffic.

Although RPC took responsibility for handling any TLS rail traffic, a locomotive was not always available when required, so after 1940 TLS sometimes used a shunting tractor fitted with a steel plate buffer plank across its front to move wagons. A Chaseside loading shovel and a farm tractor were both used in this way.

TLS locomotives
Standard Gauge

2-2-0WT	G	?			(a)	(1)
0-4-0ST	OC	?			(b)	s/s c.1924
2-2-0WT	G	AP?			(c)	scr c.1930
4wWT	G	AP	3730	1896	(d)	scr 1937-40
4wWT	G	AP	11087	1924	New	(2)

(a)   Origin and details unknown
(b)   Ex? Possibly FE of 1884, originally VULCAN at London Portland Cement Co., Northfleet, Kent c1895/96?
(c)   Ex? Probably from Kent, 1912
(d)   Ex-Fraser & Chalmers Ltd, Erith, Kent, probably 1919/20, by 1924
(1)   Scrapped on site by Drapers, of Leighton Buzzard, 1935, having been used to drive a grinding mill since c.1912
(2)   Taken over by RPC, 1936

TLS owned 13 main line open wagons and leased many more. Photographs suggest they were painted red, with white lettering shaded black.

The annual quarry output was about 150,000 tons when RPC took over quarrying in 1934, by which time TLS is believed to have been using one or two Ruston Buycyrus 32RB 1 cu. yd excavators. In 1936 RPC purchased the bulk of reserves owned by TLS, and it also obtained extensive adjoining lands from Buxton Lime Firms. Although the existing narrow

Right: View looking up the incline. The ascending empty wagon near the summit had gone over the scissors crossover, just as the descending full one is doing. The next pair of wagons, though, will need not use the crossover, as the full one will come down on the far track, going into the full siding, while the empty will go straight up the nearer track, 28th June, 1961.

Author

Below: View down the incline as a full wagon begins its descent. The full siding can be seen on the right at the bottom, with empties on the left. The line of wagons beyond the full ones is probably the site of the former narrow gauge transfer point. The hedge in the middle distance marks the route of the connection to the main line, and above the hedge is a train of empties.

Rugby Cement

gauge railway in the quarry had been improved, transport still limited production. A major difficulty was the height of the quarry floor above the level of the main line siding, approximately 70 ft. The quarry could not be worked any lower because the chalk lay on the Totternhoe clunch stone, which could not be used for either lime or cement manufacture. RPC decided to build an incline to overcome the difference in levels. It was constructed in 1938 by Thos Ward, who also laid the initial standard gauge lines in the quarry and did alterations to the main line sidings. Some of the additional track was on the site of an old kiln which RPC was permitted to demolish. In the future the quarry would spread both east and south, with its face eventually about half a mile from the incline head.

During the changes in 1934-38 the narrow gauge quarry railway continued to serve the kilns and also the new standard gauge transfer point. This was reached by extending the narrow gauge down a steep gradient along the edge of the field behind the kilns, roughly parallel to the future incline, to terminate on an elevated wooden platform about 80 ft long. While there was only a single track on the wooden platform, it had a double track connection to the quarry, to facilitate intensive operation. There were three, or maybe four, narrow gauge trains in operation, each with three or four V-skips. It seems that all the improvements to the narrow gauge were seen as only an interim measure until the standard gauge was brought into the quarry.

The incline was brought into use in 1938, and RPC began to work its new quarry towards the south-east. By now annual output had risen to 200,000 tons (i.e. 650-750 tons per day). RPC began to supply chalk to TLS, which was carried in three, later six, standard gauge hopper wagons purchased by TLS in 1939. Maybe RPC 12-ton hoppers had been used previously. The wagons for TLS were hauled to a point above the kilns and emptied on the stockpile. The chalk was then reloaded into narrow gauge wagons, latterly by 10RB excavator, for the last few yards to the kilns. This system continued to the early 1950s. TLS also continued intermittent operation of the narrow gauge in their part of the quarry for a few years. Closure of the narrow gauge had been deferred in the period 1947-50 due to problems with chalk quality, and it had been completely reopened to serve TLS remaining quarry area, its last burst of activity.

In 1950 TLS bought a rake of standard gauge side-tipping wagons to replace the 1939 hoppers, and RPC continued haulage to the stockpile. However, the track was altered in 1952 so that the standard gauge wagons could tip direct into the screening plant for the kilns. The narrow gauge was then no longer required and the remnant was closed. Small chalk, amounting to about one wagon per day, was screened out of the TLS chalk and sold back to RPC, who hauled it to the exchange sidings whence it was sent to Warwickshire with the rest.

Relations between RPC and TLS became strained in 1944 and came to a head in 1947. Most of the chalk in the former TLS area of the quarry was exhausted, and while TLS still had a couple of acres available, it considered the 1934 wayleave agreement no longer applied as RPC was no longer working TLS chalk. RPC therefore drew up plans to safeguard its access, and even contemplated an alternative limeworks. Plans were drawn up in 1944 by 'Honorary Surveyor' F. Oliver (Chief Engineer of Luton Borough Council, and therefore presumably prohibited from taking paid outside work). They show a new siding connection with the LMS, a new branch to the quarry, and a rope-worked incline. Planning consent was obtained for a new siding in May 1947, very similar to the proposals made in 1944, except that a 1 in 38 gradient replaced the incline. The scheme was drawn up by engineers Parry & Elmquist of Scunthorpe, dated 26th November, 1946. It included additional siding accommodation for 60 full and 70 empty wagons, partly on the site of Forder's siding. Forder's siding, whose agreement was dated 5th August, 1885, was about 800 yards beyond the existing TLS siding, and Forder's Sewell Limeworks had closed around 1940. Part of the 1946 branch was built but nothing more, as the disagreement had been settled. TLS gave further acreage to RPC, and RPC supplied chalk to TLS at a modest price. It could be that the whole project was merely a negotiating ploy.

By the late 1940s the north-west quarter of the quarrying area had been worked as far as two rights of way, which had to be kept passable and unobstructed. The first one

Breakaway on the incline (1) - the loaded steel and empty wooden wagons after the collision.
Rugby Cement

Breakaway (2) - the broken screw coupling, still attached to the incline cable. Note the hook and chain at the end of the cable.
Rugby Cement

Breakaway (3) - the part of the screw coupling left attached to the wagon.
Rugby Cement

encountered was the Green Lane called Drovers Way, from Dunstable going west to Totternhoe Knolls. A brick-lined tunnel, in line with the future face nearest the Knolls, was constructed under Drovers Way. The tunnel continued a short distance into the site of the new quarry, where it met a vertical shaft dug from the surface. At the foot of the shaft was a pan feeder, a strongly made metal conveyor able to withstand the impact of chalk falling on it. The pan feeder passed the chalk to a crusher near the inner end of the tunnel.

When the new quarry was first brought into use, the chalk was taken by 3 cu. yard dumpers and tipped down the shaft, where the chalk was crushed and loaded by conveyor into a train of about four wagons which had been pushed into the tunnel. Once sufficient space had been excavated at the level of the quarry floor, the tunnel was broken out into the new quarry, the track was extended, and henceforth trains were loaded direct at the face. This was the only time that quarried chalk was crushed at Totternhoe. The feeder and conveyor were removed when they were no longer required. The tunnel was about 150-200 yards from the engine shed loop (*see below*), and was in use by 1947. As the new quarry developed the face curved to follow the boundary, but it left a corner of the quarry untouched as the railway track could not reach it. This corner was then dug out and the chalk bulldozed to the excavator loading the railway trucks.

The other right of way was known as Wheelbarrow Highway, and ran from Totternhoe Church End north to Tilsworth. A Bailey Bridge was constructed on the ground above the planned route of the railway, and a cutting for the railway was then dug through the chalk beneath it. About 1953 authority was received to divert the two rights of way, which were then marked by fences across the quarry floor. The chalk formerly beneath them was excavated, and this then permitted one long face to be worked. Until about 1955 the quarry had been worked so that the floor had a slight slope from north to south but thereafter it was worked to leave a level quarry floor. Two 54RB 2 cu. yd excavators were received around 1954 and the Lima 802 disposed of.

The main line sidings were realigned and extra ones were laid in the early 1950s, including a new track behind the weighbridge to give extra capacity. Periodically the weighbridge was tested with known weights. By the early 1960s there were four sidings close to the main line connection. Numbered from west to east, loaded wagons normally used numbers 1 & 2, while empties used numbers 3 & 4. Sidings numbers 1 & 3 were 'straight through roads'. There were two tracks from the southern end of these sidings. The one which passed over the weighbridge was used by all empty and loaded wagons. The other track, the continuation of No. 3 siding, threw off a siding for cripple wagons, and a few yards further on a trailing point gave access to the brick shed for the locomotive working the main line connection.

Just before an ungated crossing over the lane the tracks curved left and included a single slip. One line continued up into the lime works yard, terminating in a loop in front of the kilns. A nearby trailing siding might have been used to load lorries. The other track threw off a set of three sidings and then divided into two tracks which served the foot of the incline, which had also been modernized in the early 1950s. RPC had substantially developed Totternhoe, whose annual output was now about 950,000 tons (3,000-3,500 tons per day).

RPC bought Kensworth Quarry in 1956 as the eventual replacement for Totternhoe (*see Appendix Three*). Although dumpers for Kensworth were tested at Totternhoe they were never regularly used here. The chalk pipeline (*see Appendix Four*) crossed the floor of the quarry, alongside Wheelbarrow Highway. The ground here was too hard for the trenching machine so the trench had to be dug by hand. Chalk extraction ceased on 17th April, 1965, Maundy Thursday, despite sufficient reserves remaining for several years' production, and all Totternhoe staff transferred to Kensworth.

Following the closure, the locomotives were scrapped or transferred away. The exchange sidings were left full of tippler wagons, and later BR found them very difficult to move due to weeds. The internal railway was removed in 1967-9. BR offered the Dunstable branch to RPC as a single track access route to Totternhoe, but the offer was

Top of the incline, looking towards the quarry. Note the two tracks of empties in the middle, flanked on either side by full wagons on raised track. In the right distance is the mouth of the tunnel into the quarry beyond the green lane, Drovers Way. In the left distance are the quarry engine shed and workshops.   *Rugby Cement*

One of the Sentinels, No. 6 (9564 of 1954), hauls a rake of TLS Hudson steel side tippers to the quarry, 27th June, 1961.   *Author*

declined, and so it was lifted in 1970 (the last passenger train had run in 1962). Although much of the route of the branch line was used for a new road, the site of the junction for Totternhoe sidings can be made out just east of the road junction for Totternhoe and Eaton Bray. The RPC quarries were restored for agriculture, but TLS continued to extract chalk for some years.

The decision by RPC to extend the standard gauge system into the quarries required the construction of a double track incline, 620 ft long, with a ruling gradient of 1 in 7.95, which lifted the line 78 ft to the level of the quarry floor. The incline was laid with 75 lb./yard flat bottomed rails. The incline was reached by two tracks which branched off the original lime works siding near the level crossing, and sloped gently down towards the incline foot. Looking towards the incline, empties were on the right and full wagons on the left. On the double track incline, quite close to its foot, was a scissors crossover, so that both tracks had easy access to both the empty and full roads. Slightly uphill from the crossover each track had a catch point in case of breakaways. The control cabin was latterly in a large gantry across the top of the incline, constructed in the early 1950s.

The incline needed no external power, as the descending loaded wagon pulled up the empty one. Single wagons were connected to the opposite ends of the haulage cable, which ran round a horizontal brake wheel at the summit. At full stretch the incline could handle 30 wagons per hour. When locomotives had to be taken up or down they were balanced as follows: a descending locomotive by two empties, an ascending one by three full wagons, with the engine in steam to assist.

One day in the 1950s a loaded 16-ton steel bodied wagon was descending the incline when its coupling broke. The cable had been hooked to the lower link of a screw coupling, and the screw had been pulled out of the nut which attached it to the upper link and the drawbar. Although the full wagon ran away and hit a wooden empty standing at the bottom there was surprisingly little damage.

Each of the incline tracks divided into two at the summit. The outer tracks, sloping gently towards the top of the incline, were for the full wagons. A lever-operated block across the rails prevented runaways. The inner pair of tracks was for the incoming empties. These tracks were about 4 ft lower than the full tracks, and sloped away from the incline head, so once over the brow and released from the cable the wagons could run along the track by gravity.

The layout beyond the top of the incline, after the four tracks had joined into one, obviously changed as the quarry developed, but it always permitted two trains to be loaded at once. In 1948 the face included a right angle bend, so the track was laid as a figure 6 in plan, with the stalk at the incline and the loop beside the face. However, trains did not run right round the loop, but only as far as 'their' excavator. Later a long single track, with passing loops, was laid from the incline into the quarrying area, splitting into two lines near the face.

The description of the quarry layout which follows is based on the situation existing in the 1960s, as seen travelling from the incline to the face. Near the top of the incline was a trailing siding on the right which had formerly extended to the kilns and had included a weighbridge, but latterly had been reduced to a sand drag. A short distance further was a loop, from which a trailing siding on the left served the workshops. The track in the workshop building was off centre and had a long pit, no track being laid on the other side of the workshop as it was for general maintenance work. Old stone workings had been discovered when digging the inspection pit here. At the further end of the loop another trailing siding on the left served the two-road locomotive shed, with coal and water facilities. Nearby was a short siding for crippled wagons, where the frame and other parts of a Manning, Wardle locomotive lay on the ballast in May 1964. The main line then ran straight across the featureless quarry floor towards the face.

As the face receded so one, and later two, intermediate passing loops were laid. Beyond the last loop there was a signal box and the line divided to serve two excavators at

Above: Signalling system (1) - Depression bar in track and trip lever beside it.

Right: Signalling system (2) - Bar on locomotive engaging with trip lever.

Below: Signalling system (3) - Loaded train going through the straight side of a loop, passing a colour light signal. Depression bar and trip lever visible for the other loop track.   *(All) Rugby Cement*

different parts of the face. The points here were manually operated for convenience, because the junction was frequently being moved as the face receded. Most other points in the quarry were sprung, set so that loaded trains took the straight route through loops. When the locomotive was leading it was up to the driver to check that the points were correctly set, but he could not do this when pushing the loaded wagons. To give an indication to the driver that it was safe to proceed, all the spring controlled points had a 4-contact switch attached to the tie bar linking the blades, which was adjusted to operate a clear signal light only if the blade was fully home against the stock rail.

Colour light signalling was installed on the quarry floor once the distance from the incline had become too great for simple operation and delays began to occur. The signalling system was effective, controlling the intensive operation of up to four locomotives serving the two excavators, and ensured reliable safe operation of the continuous heavy traffic in all weather and lighting conditions, including fog. The signalling system was probably part of the improvements installed in the early 1950s.

The main signal box - a hut - was situated by the junction where the main line divided to serve the two sections of the face then being worked, with a smaller box (another hut) at the incline summit, near the quarry end of the multiple tracks. On the exit track at each intermediate loop was a pivoted bar 15 ft long which was depressed by the wheels of a train standing on it, thus causing the appropriate red lights (two lights for safety) to illuminate on the panel in the signal box, thus showing the presence of a train. A similar but shorter bar was laid at each end of the single track section between two loops. Being shorter, each wheel depressed it in turn, so that the light on the panel flashed as the train moved over it.

Every exit from the loops was guarded by a signal which could show red or green. All the signals were operated from the box in the quarry, except the one controlling the exit of loaded trains from the workshop loop towards the incline. This one was worked from the box near the incline, the operator there being able to see both the loop and the top of the incline.

The loop nearest the face had three tracks, the central track for empties and the other two for loaded trains. The empties track had a double aspect signal controlling entry to the two loading points. Spring points prevented loaded trains from entering the empties track in error. Similarly, at the incline end of the loop, spring points caused empties trains to take the central track.

The points controlling the sidings to the engine shed and workshops were operated by ground levers, and an indicator showed which way they were set. Normally it was for the main line and the lever was locked.

Locomotives hauled empties to the face and pushed the full wagons back to the incline. Typical trains were five wagons long, although the Avonside was limited to only four. The incline required five men to operate it: two handlers at the top, two at the bottom, and one man controlling the brake. One man controlled the flow of full trucks into each of the top tracks, depending on the space currently available, and operated the signal at the workshop loop to call the loaded train forward. After the engine had uncoupled from the full wagons, it ran to one of the middle tracks and coupled on to five empties from one of the centre tracks (unless it held less than five wagons, in which case the balance would be taken from the other track) and returned towards the quarry, trailing through the sand drag points and into the curved track of the workshop loop, where the driver waited at a red signal until called forward by the quarry signalman.

A loaded train leaving the face stopped at a signal just short of the quarry signal box. When the line was clear throughout the driver was given the green signal, taking the straight line through the loops to the loop by the workshops, where the driver waited to be called on by one of the incline shunters. A depression bar in the loop illuminated a white lamp in the shunters' hut to indicate that a loaded train was waiting. When the shunter was ready he gave the green signal, so the train started for the incline.

Assuming his train was under control, the driver pressed a foot pedal in the cab, which caused a horizontal rod to protrude from the derailing beam, a transverse girder mounted a few inches above track level at each end of the locomotive. The rod hit a trip, which caused a BTH hydraulic thruster to change the sand drag points, so the train could proceed to the track selected by the shunter who had called it up. When the locomotive had cleared the points a second trip reset them for the drag. After the engine had uncoupled it collected five empties and returned towards the quarry, trailing through the sand drag points and into the curved track of the workshop loop. Meanwhile the incline shunter uncoupled the waiting full wagons in readiness for passing the incline, and coupled empties into rakes of five.

In addition to the five men operating the incline, on the quarry level there were five excavator drivers and two mates, two shot firers, one signalman, probably two each in the workshops and on track maintenance, and one each in the office and stores.

The engine based in the main line sidings hauled full wagons away from the incline to the middle of the three tracks near the engine shed. It then ran round and pushed them over the weighbridge, finally leaving them in one of three sidings ready for collection. Often the loaded wagons were let down from the weighbridge into the sidings by gravity by the shunter, using the brakes on the wagons to keep them under control. The engine then collected a rake of 8/10 empties which were taken over the weighbridge and weighed 'on the roll'. The painted tare weights were not always reliable as sometimes (particularly in frosty weather) the wagons still had some chalk left in them. The empties were then propelled to the foot of the incline. Since the incline was round a curve, out of sight of most of the sidings, a green light was situated near the entrance of the empties siding, with a repeater near the level crossing, to inform the driver when another set of loaded wagons was waiting. To avoid confusing road traffic going to TLS, the signals had a notice reading 'light signals for rail traffic only'. Operation of these sidings changed little over the years, although track in the area around the weighbridge was altered in 1955 to improve the working. Four men were employed in the sidings: a driver and shunter on the locomotive, one at the weighbridge, and a shunter marshalling trains. The RPC locomotive also shunted wagons to and from TLS premises as required.

In the early 1950s BR allocated 16-ton steel mineral wagons, running on a closed circuit, which were replaced in the later 1950s by 27-ton tippler wagons, originally designed for iron ore but labelled 'CHALK TIPPLER'. These were robust steel wagons without any doors so they had to be emptied by inversion in a suitable tippler.

BR delivered three trains of about 70 empty 16 ton wagons from the Leighton Buzzard direction each day in the early 1950s, and took away four trains, each about 55 wagons carrying some 900 tons, back towards Leighton Buzzard and the main line. In order for the main line locomotive to shunt the empties into the RPC sidings, it needed to be able to run-round its train. Seventy wagons, each 19 ft 6 in. over buffers, occupy 455 yards. Adding the brake van and an allowance for some buffers not touching, meant that the loop had to be about 480 yards long. As the distance from Stanbridgeford station level crossing and the line to the quarry was about 520 yards, it is probable that the former headshunt was extended almost to the level crossing and a new connection installed there. Incoming trains of empties stopped beyond the eastern entrance to the sidings, and reversed into the - assumed extended - loop on the south side of main line. The locomotive uncoupled, ran forward a few yards, and then used the single slip to run back to the level crossing. It then reversed into the loop and coupled to its brake van. The empties could then be pushed into the appropriate sidings. After leaving the brake van in a convenient siding, a rake of loaded wagons could be hauled out, coupled to the brake van, and in due course depart from the loop.

Chalk was always sent from Totternhoe by rail, except during strikes when lorries, often coal lorries returning empty to the Midlands, were used. Although the pipeline crossed the floor of the quarry it was never used for Totternhoe chalk.

In its last years of operation, working a 9-hour day, five days a week, the quarry dispatched 950,000 tons pa (about 3,500 tons daily), in trains of up to 42 27-ton wagons (1,100 tons nominal load).

The first quarry locomotive was Peckett No. 947 of 1903, class 'M4' with 10 in. x 14 in. cylinders and 2 ft 6 in. diameter wheels. It came from RPC New Bilton works at Rugby in 1937, having originally been at RPC Newbold Works (*see Chapters Twelve and Eleven respectively*). It was withdrawn and scrapped on site, probably in the second half of 1952.

It was soon joined by an Avonside 0-4-0ST, 1875 of 1921, with 12 in. x 18 in. cylinders. This was one of a batch of eight locomotives, Nos. 1874-81, delivered to the Bombay Harbour Improvement Trust and subsequently bought by T.W. Ward Ltd. No. 1875 was sold to RPC Totternhoe in 1938, and two others were also sold to the cement industry, 1874 to APCM Crown & Quarry works, Frindsbury, Kent, and 1877 to Tunnel Cement, Grays, Essex. It seems likely that Ward had used three locomotives on the contract to build the incline and to lay the initial standard gauge quarry railway, so it would not be surprising if one was sold to RPC at the end of the contract. There was a need, the engine was on site, it had been seen in operation, and no doubt the price was right. It was fitted with dumb buffers and normally worked in the quarry, where it was limited to four wagons. Apparently this engine once had a tendency for its axleboxes to run hot, but this was miraculously cured one day following a derailment! For a time, around 1950, it had an ugly stovepipe chimney, but this was later replaced with a more elegant design. Latterly its livery was dark green with red frames, motion and buffer beams, and a yellow/black dazzle front. Following closure, it went to RPC's Barrington works (Eastwoods Cement Ltd until 1962) and finally to the Stour Valley Railway Preservation Society.

Manning, Wardle No. 1995 of 1920 (No. 3, formerly 2) was an 'L' class 0-6-0ST with 12 in. x 18 in. cylinders and 3 ft 0 in. diameter wheels, transferred from Rugby in 1940. It returned briefly to Rugby in 1950/1, and last worked at Totternhoe in October 1960. By April 1962 it had been dismantled and was scrapped on site in the spring of 1965. A similar locomotive, 1972 (No. 5), came from Rugby in 1949 and was withdrawn in 1952, being gradually dismantled over the following 10 years.

Robert Stephenson & Hawthorns supplied a new 0-6-0ST, No. 7413, in July 1948 (No. 4), identical to one supplied to Rugby works a few months before. With 14 in. x 22 in. cylinders and 3 ft 6 in. wheels it was the most powerful locomotive to date, being able to pull eight loaded wagons. Unfortunately it suffered from trouble with its boiler tubes, and spent a lot of time on blocks in the shed. In September 1961 it was sold to the NCB, East Midlands Division, No. 7 Area, Cadley Hill Colliery near Swadlincote, Leicestershire.

A Sentinel 100 hp locomotive was demonstrated in the quarry in early 1953, and made a considerable impact. The first was ordered 15th July, 1953, and No. 9559 which had been built for stock was delivered to Totternhoe on 24th July. The vertical boiler in the cab supplied superheated steam to a vertical 2-cylinder double-acting poppet valve engine having cylinders $6\frac{3}{4}$ in. x 9 in. The crankshaft drove a 2-speed gear box, although changing gear had to be done when the locomotive was stationary. A chain from the gearbox drove the front axle, and a second chain coupled the two axles. The wheels were 2 ft 6 in. diameter. The water tank was inside the casing, immediately in front of the cab and behind the engine which was right at the front. When used in the main line sidings, it was found that a Sentinel could do the same work as the 14 in. 0-6-0ST. On one occasion, in low gear, the siding Sentinel had moved a full train of loaded wagons which had run too far and fouled the points to BR. Normal loads were five wagons in the quarry or eight wagons in the sidings. Following closure it went to Rugby works.

A second similar locomotive was ordered in April 1954. In June a number of modifications were ordered, including alterations to the brake gear and water gauges, and adjustments to the ballast weights to give more even axle loadings. No. 9564 had been built for stock, and was delivered new to Totternhoe on 1st July, 1954. The modifications in fact continued after its arrival.

Three more 100 hp Sentinels came second-hand in the early 1960s. No. 9627 came from the Whitehead Iron & Steel Co. Ltd, Newport, Monmouthshire, in December 1960 where

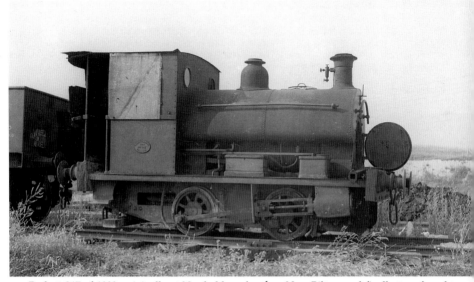

Peckett 947 of 1903, originally at Newbold works, then New Bilton, and finally transferred to Totternhoe.   *F. Jones*

No. 2, Avonside 1875 of 1921.   *K. Lane Collection*

No. 2 when fitted with a stovepipe chimney.   *F. Jones*

No. 3, Manning, Wardle 1995 of 1920, transferred from Rugby works.   *K. Lane Collection*

No. 4, Robert Stephenson & Hawthorns 7413 of 1948, seen brand new at Darlington in transit from Newcastle to Totternhoe, June 1948. Note that the motion rods have been removed to facilitate towing in a goods train (standard practice over the main lines).　　*Aiden Fuller/IRS*

No. 5, Manning, Wardle 1972 of 1919, transferred from Rugby works, seen dumped near the shed after withdrawal on 2nd May, 1959. No. 3 was at this spot in similar condition a few years later.　　*P.J. Kelley*

it was named *Courtybella*. It continued to carry this name for some months at Totternhoe, but had lost its name by June 1963. After closure it went to RPC Rochester works, and around November 1969 it left there, going to R.B. Tennant Ltd, Whifflet, on the outskirts of Coatbridge. It was one of the last steam locomotives to work in industry, and is now preserved by the Scottish Railway Preservation Society at Bo'ness, near Edinburgh.

No. 9565 came from Willington power station, beside the River Trent near Derby, around October 1961. The last 100 hp Sentinel, 9556, was bought from Craven Bros (Manchester) Ltd, Reddish, Lancashire around December 1962. It retained its name, *Craven*, at Totternhoe. Thomas Hill (Rotherham) Ltd arranged both of these sales.

Three of the Sentinels, Nos. 9564, 9565 and 9556, went to RPC Barrington works after closure, and soon after went to Thomas Hill (Rotherham) Ltd. While this may not have been the fate of the Totternhoe locomotives, at that time Thomas Hill rebuilt many Sentinel steam locomotives with diesel engines, which it sold under the Vanguard label.

The original livery of the locomotives seems to have been dark green. By 1961 No. 4 had yellow and black diagonal stripes painted on the ends. In the later years the Avonside was painted medium green, again with warning stripes on the ends, with red frames and motion. Wheels and cylinders were green and the boiler mountings black. The livery of all the Sentinels was green, latterly with black and yellow diagonal stripes at the front and rear, and black frames below the running plate. They were kept in beautiful condition and were regarded with much affection.

RPC locomotives
Standard Gauge

	4wWT	G	AP	11087	1924	(a)	(1)
5	0-4-0ST	OC	P	947	1903	(b)	(2)
No. 2 (ex-*Isobel*)	0-4-0ST	OC	AE	1875	1921	(c)	(3)
No. 3 (ex-2)	0-6-0ST	IC	MW	1995	1920	(d)	(4)
No. 4	0-6-0ST	OC	RSHN	7413	1948	New	(5)
No. 5	0-6-0ST	IC	MW	1972	1919	(e)	(6)
No. 1	4wVBT	VCG	S	9559	1953	New	(7)
No. 6	4wVBT	VCG	S	9564	1954	New	(8)
No. 7 (*Courtybella*)	4wVBT	VCG	S	9627	1957	(f)	(9)
No. 8	4wVBT	VCG	S	9565	1954	(g)	(8)
No. 9 *Craven*	4wVBT	VCG	S	9556	1953	(h)	(10)

(a) Taken over from Totternhoe Lime & Stone Co. Ltd, Stanbridgeford, with site, 1936
(b) Ex-RPC Rugby works, 1937
(c) Ex-Thos W. Ward Ltd, Charlton works, Sheffield, 12.1.1938; orig Bombay Harbour Improvements Trust No 10; to unknown location, after 7.5.1948, by 7.1949; returned by 8/1950
(d) Ex-RPC Rugby works, 2.1940; to Rugby works after 7.1949, by 27.8.1949; returned here after 8.1951, by 5.1952
(e) Ex-RPC Rugby works, 1949 (by 7.1949)
(f) Ex-Whitehead Iron & Steel Co. Ltd, Courtybella works, Newport, Gwent per TH, after 2.1.1961, by 26.1.1961
(g) Ex-Central Electricity Generating Board, Willington, Derbyshire, per TH, c.10.1961 (after 29.9.1961)
(h) Ex-Craven Bros (Manchester) Ltd, Reddish, Manchester, per TH c.12.1962 (after 6.12.1962)
(1) Withdrawn by 10.11.1940, scrapped on site c.1943-44
(2) Scrapped on site, after 5.1952, by 3.1953
(3) To RPC, Barrington works, Cambs, 2.1965
(4) Withdrawn 10.1960, dismantled by 4.1962 and scrapped on site after 3.3.1965, by 30.5.1965
(5) To NCB, East Midlands Division, No. 7 Area, Cadley Hill Colliery, South Derbyshire, 9.1961
(6) Withdrawn 1952, derelict by 3.1958 and scrapped on site 1960
(7) To RPC New Bilton works, Rugby, 9.1964
(8) To RPC, Barrington works, Cambs, 4.1965
(9) To RPC Rochester works, Kent, after 7.1965, by 9.1965
(10) To RPC, Barrington works, Cambs, after 7.1965, by 12.1965

Sentinel locomotive on trial - the maker's name is on the bonnet side - probably early 1953. Beyond is a bridge formerly used to carry a right of way over the railway, although it is now being quarried away. *Rugby Cement*

View under the bonnet of a Sentinel. The vertical cylinders are in front of the water tank, supplied by steam from the boiler in the cab by the long lagged pipe. The gearbox is below the cylinders, and the final drive is by chains to the axles. *Rugby Cement*

No. 1, Sentinel 9559 of 1953, at the face. Nearby is the ex-LMS brake van used for carrying staff, mess room etc., 27th June, 1961. *Author*

When Sentinel 9627 of 1957 arrived it carried the name *Courtybella*, as seen here on 27th June, 1961. The third and fifth wagons from the locomotive are branded 'IRON ORE TIPPLER', not 'CHALK TIPPLER'. *Author*

However, *Courtybella* did not retain its name for long, and became plain number 7! The diagonal strut immediately in front of each axlebox permits the driving chains to be adjusted as they stretch in use.   *F. Jones*

No. 9, Sentinel 9556 of 1953, *did* retain its name *Craven*.   *F. Jones*

Two Hudson standard gauge side tipping wagons owned by TLS to bring chalk to its kilns, 26th
June, 1965.   *Author*

Weed killing trolley.   *Rugby Cement*

Examination of the locomotive stock changes recorded by the IRS suggests the following usage. Initially the surviving TLS Aveling & Porter was used on the main line sidings until 1940, when it was replaced by Manning, Wardle 1995 from Rugby works. The quarry system was operated until around 1950 by the two second-hand 0-4-0ST, the Avonside and Peckett. In 1948 a new 0-6-0ST was purchased from Robert Stephenson & Hawthorns for the main line sidings, and the Manning, Wardle was transferred to the quarry, although around 1950 it returned to Rugby for a time, its place in the quarry being taken by a sister, 1972, from Rugby. Also around 1949/50, the Avonside 'disappeared' for about 18 months, possibly for major overhaul, delayed by post-war shortages. The quarry itself had two or three locomotives at this time.

By the early 1950s, the motive power position in the quarry was not good. Although both the Avonside and Manning, Wardle 1995 had returned, the Peckett and Manning, Wardle 1972 were both life expired. At just the right time a Sentinel salesman visited and demonstrated his 100 hp geared locomotive. Two were bought new, in 1953 and 1954. Three more, second-hand, followed in 1961 and 1962. As the surviving Manning, Wardle had been withdrawn in 1960, and the Robert Stephenson & Hawthorns 0-6-0ST had been sold to the National Coal Board in September 1961, this left a fleet of five Sentinels with the little Avonside as spare. Following closure of the system all the locomotives were transferred away. Two of them, the Avonside and a Sentinel, were eventually preserved.

As previously stated, chalk was transported to Rugby and Southam in ordinary main line wagons, loaded at the face. After RPC had taken over quarrying, in 1939 TLS bought three hopper wagons for its supply of chalk, later purchasing three more. After World War II these wagons were replaced by six 10-ton steel side-tipping wagons built by Robert Hudson of Leeds. These side tippers had inside bearings, spoked wheels and were fitted with brakes operated by a handwheel on either side at one end. They were painted dull red. When the railway closed the tippers were brought down the incline and sold to NCB Doncaster Area. They were dispatched on Monday 19th July, 1965, loaded on well wagons as their flanges were too deep for BR.

RPC bought a former LMS 20-ton brake van in the mid-1950s. After removing 13 tons of ballast weights, the van was used as passenger transport, to enable the quarry workers to get to the face without facing a long trudge over completely exposed, and in winter, very mucky, ground. During working hours it was kept in a siding near the face. The van was also used as a canteen/mess room, and to hold track laying tools. The remaining rail vehicle was a light trolley carrying a petrol-driven pump to spray weed killer. It was pushed by hand all over the system.

One of the Manning, Wardles hauling a train in the quarry.   *Rugby Cement*

Appendix Three

Kensworth Quarries

RPC bought Kensworth Quarry in 1956, against the time when Totternhoe Quarries would be exhausted. It was virtually a green field site when purchased, with an old small whitening (low grade agricultural lime) works located towards Kensworth village (TL 020195). The site of the quarry is about one and a half miles south of Dunstable and three miles south-east of Totternhoe , not far from Whipsnade. Unfortunately there was no rail access and the local roads were (and are) mainly narrow lanes. It was bought before any decision was made about chalk transport.

One informant said that initially RPC toyed with idea of buying land near Milton Keynes (at that time still just a small village) and conveying chalk by canal to Southam. I assume large boats would have been used, probably based on the 12 ft 6 in. wide, 66 ton capacity, prototype, constructed for the Grand Union Canal Co. in the early 1930s. It is not clear how the chalk would have travelled from the quarry about 20 miles to the canal wharf, but it was probably by lorry along the A5. Lorries would probably have been used between wharf and works at Rugby.

Using the 1957 edition of the 1 in. OS map, to show the then limits of the built-up area around Dunstable, and the 1998 edition of the 2½ in. OS map, with contours every 5 metres, the rail route described below would appear to have been feasible. Note that there is no suggestion that RPC ever considered rail access, or that it would have used this route had it been required.

The obvious point for connection with the main line, the former Great Northern Railway branch from Welwyn to Luton and Dunstable (where it joined the LNWR branch from Leighton Buzzard), was at the foot of Blow's Down (TL 035218, contour height 150 m.), about ½ mile east of Dunstable Town station. In 1957 the direct route from here to the Watling Street (A5) was virtually the edge of the built up area. Such building as existed could have been avoided by an S-bend to the south, to cross the Watling Street at TL 027210, contour height 160 m. A climb of 10 m., plus 6 m. to give adequate road clearance under the necessary bridge, in a distance of about 1,200 m., gives an average gradient of 1 in 75. (At that time a colliery near Atherstone, Warwickshire, still used an ungated level crossing over a three-lane section of the A5, but I doubt whether a new level crossing would have been permitted at Dunstable!) Continuing in a straight line, the line would reach the downhill edge of the quarry site, height 200 m., after another 1,100 m., giving an average gradient of 1 in 32. This would have been steep, but a northwards deviation along the sides of a valley near Downs Farm would have increased the distance to about 1,700 m., giving an average gradient of 1 in 50, or say 1 in 45 allowing for an easier gradient on the sharp curves at the head of the valley. This would have been quite feasible; Hanging Houghton ironstone quarry a few miles north of Northampton had been reached by a line climbing up the side of the valley on a gradient of 1 in 44. Breakaways could have been prevented by always having the locomotive at the downhill end of its train. Care would have been necessary to keep loaded descending trains under control, pinning down a significant proportion of brakes on the wagons before leaving the quarry. If and when the BR wagons used had been fitted with continuous brakes, control would have been less of a problem. Rail access to this quarry would have ensured the retention for freight of either the Leighton Buzzard to Dunstable Town line, or the Dunstable Town to Luton and the Bedford to Northampton lines, either of which would give an easy route to Rugby. However, this is fantasy; chalk never left Kensworth by road, let alone rail, but always by pipeline (*see Appendix Four*). It would have needed some powerful locomotives, and would have been a grand line to have watched in operation!

Kensworth Quarry began operations around 1962. Other staff and equipment were transferred from Totternhoe following its closure on 15th April, 1965.

A contractor is employed to remove the overburden, top soil and subsoil, which have a total depth of about 2 m. (6 ft 7 in.). It is later replaced to return the land to agriculture. In 1996 three or four benches were worked, each 10 m. to 15 m. (33-49 ft) high, but planning permission permitting the quarry to double its depth had been obtained so seven or eight benches were likely in the future. Each bench was worked in two stages.

When first opened the quarry used three or four rope-driven face shovels, but by 1996 all the rope shovels had been replaced by hydraulic equipment. There were two hydraulic face shovels with 5.5 cubic metres (about 7 cubic yard) buckets (each dug an average of 750 tonnes per hour, although 1,000 tonnes per hour was possible), and a smaller back-actor hydraulic shovel. Chalk was transported from the face by three Aveling Barford RD55 50 tonne and two Caterpillar 769 40 tonne rigid dumpers. The Caterpillar shovels and the Aveling Barford dumpers together dug and transported 75 per cent of the output, topped up by the other excavator and dumpers. The dumpers had previously been tested at Totternhoe.

While articulated dumpers have good traction, it is at the expense of payload and increased complexity, so the rigid type is preferred for fast hauls over good roads. A grader was used to maintain the roads within the quarry. A layer of flint was put down for the wearing surface, and later (when that portion of road was quarried away) it was screened out in the washmill and reused. The upper beds of chalk at Kensworth are 3-5 per cent flint, then there is 1 m. of very hard chalk, below which the flint content is less than 1 per cent. In 1996, annual output averaged 1.25 million tonnes, increasing to 2 million tonnes once the new plant opened at Rugby in 1998. The quarry had reserves for 30 to 40 years.

The quarry developed first north-west from the offices towards Dunstable, then south-east towards Kensworth, then south-west and parallel to the lane, but a field width away so hedges shielded it from view. A noise bund containing 100,000 cubic metres of dirt was constructed near Kensworth church.

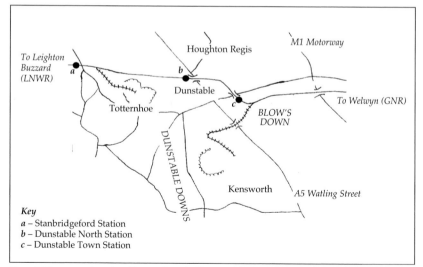

Dunstable area, showing Totternhoe & Kensworth Quarries, and route of possible rail access to Kensworth Quarries (*see text*).

Appendix Four

Chalk Pipeline

Totternhoe Quarries were approaching exhaustion by the late 1950s so RPC bought a quarry at Kensworth. Blue Circle had once operated a small limeworks on the site. The quarry had no rail link, and road access was poor, along narrow lanes (*see Appendix Three*).

The RPC Chief Engineer, John Walker, had experimented for a number of years and eventually suggested the possibility of pumping chalk slurry along a pipeline to Rugby. This would mean that there would be no need for the quarry to be served by either a railway or heavy road vehicles. At the time there was no known chalk slurry pipeline, although some coal pipelines were known to exist. RPC was pioneering the idea.

The Pipelines Act 1962 greatly facilitated the proposal. Previously companies needed to obtain private acts of Parliament for their pipelines. Pipelines proposed by the gas board and RPC were the first cross-country pipelines to be authorized by the Minister of Power under the new act.

The July 1963 issue of *Cement & Lime Manufacture* reported that RPC had commenced construction of a chalk slurry pipeline. When the gas main from Canvey Island (in the Thames Estuary) to Liverpool was being constructed, RPC took the opportunity to lay the chalk pipeline at the same time, sharing the same easement between Dunstable and Crick (five miles south-east of Rugby) and so taking advantage of the same wayleaves. The chalk pipeline has its own easement at each end of the route. The first section of pipeline, from Newport Pagnell to Rugby (36 miles), was built by Taylor Woodrow Construction.

The route of the pipeline is Kensworth, Houghton Regis (Dunstable), M1, then beside the gas grid from Luton to Crick. There the chalk pipeline passes north of Rugby and curves west to Rugby works. The distance from Kensworth to Rugby is about 57 miles. A second pipeline ran south from Rugby works, under the A45, past Draycote Water, to Southam works, a distance of about 12 miles.

The steel pipes were laid on the ground, the joints welded, and then checked for soundness by X-rays. The pipe was lagged, the trench dug by machine (usually), and then the pipe was snaked in. A thruster was used to bore under roads without interrupting traffic. The pipeline was opened in 1965. No longer was chalk brought in by the trainload to Rugby and Southam works, and a once-familiar sight to travellers on the West Coast main line between Leighton Buzzard and Rugby became a memory.

The original intention seems to have been to phase Totternhoe out gradually, until its reserves were exhausted, and steadily increase production at Kensworth, but the construction of the gas pipeline forced the pace, as it was desirable to construct both pipelines at the same time to minimize construction costs.

Natural chalk, as quarried, contains 22-24 per cent moisture, which is why it feels slimy. If chalk is merely ground and mixed with water to form slurry it needs 60 per cent moisture content. However, by using suitable additives (about 1 kg per tonne) to control dispersion and viscosity, the moisture content required for a stable slurry could be reduced to 42 per cent or less. The additional water used is clean effluent from Houghton Regis sewage works at Thorn, where RPC made a long term agreement to take water at nominal cost. The water pipe and slurry pipe share the same easement between Kensworth and the A5 at Thorn. Steam from the slurry water accounted for much of the white plume emitted by the cement works' chimney at Rugby. Every 1 per cent reduction in the moisture content of the slurry saved £100,000 on fuel consumption at Rugby in 1996.

In 1996, slurry was pumped 6 am Monday to 6 am Saturday, and took about 22 hours to reach Rugby. Seven-day pumping was expected when the new plant opened at Rugby. The longest break in pumping since opening has been four days, and the slurry had remained liquid.

Excavating the pipeline trench at Totternhoe. The Avonside is in steam in the left distance and a Sentinel waits with a rake of full wagons in the workshops loop. *Rugby Cement*

Laying the pipe into the trench. *Rugby Cement*

The pipe needs negligible maintenance. It is necessary to exclude air from the slurry to prevent problems, as differential aeration causes pumping difficulties, and air collecting along the top of the pipe causes pitting and internal corrosion. In the early days, some pipe replacement was necessary near Kensworth following bursts, the first five miles having the highest pressures. The pipes were renewed in 1990-92. The gas company inspectors who cover the whole route also watch the chalk pipeline.

The pipe from Kensworth to Rugby is 10 in. internal diameter, and the three pumps required (two in use, one standby) are all at Kensworth, making it the longest solids pipeline without intermediate pumping stations. The extension from Rugby to Southam, and the water supply from Houghton Regis to Kensworth, are both 8 in. internal diameter. The Southam section was pumped from Rugby, and RPC has its own pumps at Houghton Regis for pumping water.

The thick-walled pipe was double wrapped in bitumen for protection, and cathodic protection was also provided. Provision was made for automatic shutdown if necessary, and shear relief valves were fitted in case the internal pressure exceeded a specified limit. The pipe was continuously welded, and the minimum radius curve was 16 m. (about 53 ft).

The excavated chalk is crushed to a maximum size of 200 mm (8 in.). This is fed to a washmill where the chalk is ground to 6 mm (¼ in), being screened at the exit point. Flint accumulates in the washmill and is periodically cleared through bottom doors. The washmills are basically octagonal in plan. Each washmill has four rotating harrows, each with seven or eight steel prongs, which grind up the lumps of chalk. Viscosity additives and water are added at the washmill. The coarse chalk slurry is screened under pressure (maximum size permitted 0.5 mm, 0.02 in.), with rejects being returned to the washmill. The pumpable slurry passes to a surge basin and then it is pumped to Rugby.

In 1996, Rugby typically received 400 gallons/min. of slurry, the equivalent of 110 tons of dry chalk per hour (2,640 tons per day). The slurry tanks there received the chalk, holding about 6 weeks' requirements, and thickened it. They were 240 ft in diameter with a total depth of 30 ft, (15 ft above and 15 ft below the ground). Moisture content had dropped to 39 per cent by time the slurry entered the kiln. Southam had two chalk thickener basins but Rugby had only one. At that time, the pipeline carried 1.25 million tons annually, half to Rugby, half to Southam, at a cost of 1.25p per ton, against 35p per ton by rail in 1965. The pipeline paid for itself in 18 months.

Pipeline data	Dunstable-Rugby	Rugby-Southam
Approx length	57 miles/99 km	9 miles/16 km
Nominal bore	10 in./254 mm	8 in./200 mm
Average volume delivered	780 gall./min.	630 gall./min.
Equivalent dry chalk	207 tonnes/hr	168 tonnes/hr
Average slurry velocity	4 ft/sec. / 4.7 km/hr	5 ft/sec. / 5.9 km/hr
Maximum working pressure	1,800 psi	850 psi
Test pressure (24 hour)	3,000 psi	3,000 psi
Pipe wall thickness	0.365 in./9.27 mm	0.344 in./8.7 mm
Pipe steel grade	A.P.I.5L X52	A.P.I.5L X52

Note: A metric 'tonne' is about 40 lb. lighter than an imperial 'ton', reducing the dry chalk figures in the table above to 203 and 165 tons respectively.

Appendix Five

Main Line Aspects and Chalk Train Operation

The chalk trains finished running in 1965. Since then, many features of British railways have changed, and none more so than freight train operation. In view of this, the basics of traditional British practice will be described before dealing with the chalk trains themselves. Traditional British freight train operation was built around the characteristics of the typical British wagon and the steam locomotive that hauled it.

Until the 1960s, if not later, the British railway wagon had changed very little from the trucks shown in illustrations of the Liverpool & Manchester Railway drawn in the early 1830s, and even from the tramroad vehicles which preceded them. In these early wagons, the body was carried on four wheels and extensions of the underframe formed dumb (unsprung) buffers at each end. Wagons were coupled together to form a train by a hook and chain mounted centrally at each end. The body came in a variety of types, open and closed, depending on the load to be carried, with the majority being little more than an open box with side doors.

Over the years, wagons became larger, with nominal loads increasing from 6 tons to 10 or 12 tons, or more in the case of steel wagons. Construction was mainly wood with iron fittings, with steel underframes often being used from the 1920s, although iron or steel wagons (particularly hopper wagons for minerals) were common before then. However, ordinary wagons made of iron, and wooden wagons with iron frames, had been built even in the early days. For example, Rowland Brotherhood at Chippenham, had built iron box vans for the Bristol & Exeter Railway in 1849 and wooden box vans with iron frames for the GWR in 1861 (*Brotherhoods, Engineers*, S.A. Leleux, David & Charles, 1965).

The main line railways soon found that dumb buffers were a liability and sprung buffers were preferable, although wagons with dumb buffers continued to be built for many years. It was not until the early 1900s that dumb-buffered rolling stock was formally prohibited from British public railways, but it lasted on both standard and narrow gauge wagons in quarries for another 50 years or so.

Eventually most wagons were fitted with a brake, usually operated by a long lever. On early wagons the brake often acted on only one pair of wheels. Typically, the lever was pivoted at the centre of the wagon, and the free end moved between a pair of vertical perforated guides. A pin, fastened to a short length of light chain to prevent it getting lost, was passed through a suitable pair of holes to hold the brake lever down, and so apply the brakes through levers attached to the pivot rod. A shunter's pole was often used to obtain more leverage when holding the brake lever down before inserting the pin. When the brake was off, the lever rested in a bracket near the top of the perforated guides.

The brake worked, but could not be applied (or released) while the train was in motion, and that was the problem. From the beginning of the 20th century a small but growing proportion of wagons, mainly vans, had been 'fitted' with continuous brake, or sometimes merely 'piped' (although the brakes on any piped wagons were not capable of remote operation). These fitted and piped wagons had a flexible pipe at each end, for connection to the next vehicle, so the brake pipe was continuous throughout the train and the brakes on every fitted vehicle were then under the control of the driver. Fitted wagons could also be attached to passenger and parcel trains, and were specially maintained to be suitable for operation at higher speeds. In British Railways' days, fitted wagons were painted dark brown (often with the letters 'XP' painted near the wagon number) and unfitted wagons were painted medium grey.

The lack of continuous brakes on most freight trains meant that the only brakes available while the train was in motion were on the engine and its tender, and on the brake van at the rear of the train. With such limited brake power speeds were inevitably low - 20 mph was a good average for a 'loose coupled' goods or mineral train. (Fully fitted trains, or trains with a number of fitted wagons at the front with their brakes connected to the locomotive, could run much faster, but in the early 1960s mineral wagons were only just being fitted with continuous brakes.)

Another consequence of low speeds was the frequent need to shunt slow freight trains out of the way so that faster passenger trains could overtake. This could be done by reversing into a dead end siding, being routed into a goods loop, or, on heavily used lines, by laying four tracks, one pair for fast trains and one for slow trains, particularly freight. One of the aims of the 1955 Modernisation Plan was to fit every goods wagon with continuous brakes, and thereby raise speeds. However, the chalk trains ceased running before their wagons were so fitted.

This lack of continuous brakes probably arose due to the railways' desire to keep down the costs of their vast wagon fleets, and the fact that until World War II around half the wagons were privately owned anyway (*see below*). The British wagon fleet altogether comprised about 1.25 million vehicles in 1939.

From the 1920s, wagons with end doors often had a diagonal white stripe painted on their sides, with the top of the stripe at the hinge of the end door, so that it was easy to check that wagons were the right way round for discharge in some types of tippler or coal hoist. In BR days some mineral wagons had bottom doors as well, which were indicated by a pair of white lines - almost a V - at floor level in the centre of the wagon side.

The law considered the first railways to be simply specialized highways, which anyone could use with a suitable vehicle on payment of the appropriate tolls, just like a canal or turnpike. However, experience soon showed that for efficient operation, a railway's traffic had to be directly controlled by the railway company. In the vast majority of cases the company also provided haulage, although there were a number of places, even in the 1960s, where private locomotives hauled their own trains over British Railways' track for distances of up to 10 miles. Although private haulage generally soon disappeared, it was replaced by traders wagons, later known as privately owned (PO), wagons.

Traders wagons are first mentioned in the mid-1840s, and soon became very common. By the outbreak of World War II there were about 600,000 PO wagons, belonging to some 4,000 different owners, and comprising almost half of the total wagon fleet. Although the vast majority were 4-wheel mineral wagons belonging to mines, quarries and coal merchants, there were also tank wagons for liquids (e.g. oil, tar) and vans for goods that had to be kept dry, such as food - and lime and cement.

For the trader, a major advantage in having a fleet of wagons was that there was no penalty in keeping his wagons under load. They could provide storage or warehousing, and enabled urgent orders to be met quickly. The railway companies permitted a trader only a couple of days to load or unload a wagon, and if this period was exceeded they charged 'demurrage' as the wagon was not available to earn money elsewhere. Like modern lorries, PO wagons also provided a means of advertising. Of course, if a trader had more goods to transport than could be carried in his own wagons he used the railway company's own vehicles as well. A disadvantage to the trader was the capital cost of his wagons. This was overcome by the formation of finance companies which enabled wagons to be bought on hire purchase. Indeed, many companies later providing domestic finance had 'wagon' in their title reflecting their railway origins.

PO wagons were a very mixed blessing for the railway companies. While they meant that the companies' own wagon fleets could be smaller, so tying up less money, every PO wagon had to be returned empty to its owner's sidings. This entailed a lot of empty wagon mileage and extensive shunting. It also meant that as the PO fleets were largely outside the railways' control it was difficult to encourage users to buy larger, more economic, wagons, let alone make them fit expensive devices like continuous brakes. It was also difficult to ensure that PO wagons were well maintained.

The financial aspects of PO wagon operation, including the division of the charge between the companies concerned if two or more railways had been involved in the wagon's journey, was done by the Railway Clearing House (RCH). Some PO wagons had a yellow plate with the letters 'CC' in black at the bottom left corner of the wagon near the wagon number. This showed that the trader was a member of the scheme, introduced in 1926, which allowed the trader to pay one shilling (5p - £1.50) per wagon per year to cover any siding or shunting charges which should occur if the wagon became crippled en route. Another scheme, introduced by the RCH in 1933, charged the trader an annual fee to cover all his empty wagon movements. This was indicated by a yellow 5-pointed star, 6 in. in diameter, painted near the wagon number. The RCH also developed standard designs for the 10 ton and 12 ton wooden wagons which comprised the bulk of the PO fleet.

There were two operational reasons for favouring 'loose coupled' trains, although whether this really countered the effect of low speeds due to lack of effective brakes is a good question! The first was that wagons with ordinary 3-link couplings could be easily coupled and uncoupled, even when slowly moving, by a shunter walking alongside using his shunter's pole with its special curved hook at one end. Taut, an ordinary 3-link coupling gave a gap of about eight inches between the buffers, so when the wagons' buffers were touching there was sufficient slack for the shunter to manipulate the coupling with ease. This slack accounted for the term loose coupled. The other reason was the ease of starting a heavy train, see below.

However, experience showed that dangerous longitudinal surging could occur when the brakes were applied in a loose-coupled train fitted with continuous brakes, so means had to be found to take out the slack from of the couplings. There were two common methods. The best one, and the only type used on passenger coaches, was the screw coupling, where the centre coupling link was replaced by a long heavy screw. The coupling had to be unscrewed to lengthen it before uncoupling was possible, and then after coupling the screw had to be tightened so that the buffer faces were touching. This took considerably more time than just using a shunter's pole, and also required both vehicles to be stationary so that the shunter could go between them to couple up (or uncouple). The coupling was also heavier.

The alternative was the 'instanter' coupling which was a modified 3-link coupling. The centre link was T-shaped, and had a pair of lugs at the plain end of this link. When the plain end and one of the T-ends rested in the neighbouring links the coupling was slack and was as easy to manage as an ordinary 3-link coupling. However, if the shunter used the lugs to turn the special link vertical, so that both of the T-ends were used, the effective length of the link was reduced and the wagons were brought closer together. Unlike a screw coupling, an instanter coupling did not permit fine adjustment, but it did enable a lot of the slack in the coupling to be removed without sacrificing many of the advantages of an ordinary 3-link coupling.

The steam engine and its tender had power operated brakes, usually steam on the engine and vacuum on the tender. When diesel locomotives began replacing steam ones in earnest from the early 1960s, it was discovered that the change brought its own problems to freight train operating. Diesel locomotives were usually lighter than the steam locomotive and tender of equivalent power that they had replaced, which meant that there was even less brake power available to control the train! In some areas special brake tenders were even used to give more brake power.

The higher speeds and longer runs that dieselisation helped to make possible showed up other defects in the basic design of traditional wagons, particularly in the suspension and riding qualities. Minor variations in track conditions could cause traditional wagons having a wheelbase of 10 ft or less and receiving 'average' maintenance to derail at speed even on plain track (i.e. not at points). The number of freight train derailments rose alarmingly in the early 1960s and speed limits down to 45 mph were imposed until modern long wheelbase 4-wheeled and bogie stock replaced the majority of traditional wagons.

Freight trains had a crew of three men, guard, driver and fireman. The guard was in charge of the train. Before it set off he noted the number and weight of every wagon so that he could give the totals to the driver. (Nowadays a computer printout is available and the guard just checks the details against the wagons in the train.) The guard gave the driver the signal to start, by showing a green flag or a green light. He rode in a brake van at the rear of the train, several hundred yards from the locomotive - possibly even quarter of a mile away in the case of a long train. The brake van was usually a long wheelbase (for good riding) 4-wheeled vehicle. The body, which might or might not extend the full length of the underframe, had a veranda at one or both ends and was usually fitted with duckets (bulges on either side of the body, with tall narrow windows fitted front and rear) so that the guard could look along the length of his train. The most vital fitting was the brake column, by means of which the guard could apply and release the brakes on his van. Sand boxes were often fitted, like on the locomotive, to improve adhesion when braking in slippery conditions. As goods trains became heavier over the years so the weight of brake vans steadily increased. By 1960 a typical brake van was ballasted with slabs of iron or concrete so that it had a weight of 20 or even 25 tons.

One particular aspect of the guard's role with loose-coupled freight trains was setting wagon brakes at the top of long or steep gradients. Typically a board was placed beside the track just before the top of such a gradient, reading 'Goods trains to stop and fasten brakes'. Sometimes it even detailed the proportion of wagons to be braked. The guard would apply the hand brakes on the leading wagons, pinning down the brake lever to hold the brakes on. In theory enough brakes would be applied to keep the speed of the train in check, leaving the brakes on the engine and brake van for fine control. The driver then pulled the train against the brakes to the top of the gradient and gingerly descended. At night the wheels of the braked wagons appeared as rings of fire due to the sparks from the brake blocks. When the train reached the bottom of the gradient it had to stop to release the wagon brakes, making yet more delay.

Failure to apply sufficient brakes, or to jerk a train so that a coupling or drawbar broke, would cause a runaway. On double track lines runaway catch points were often provided at intervals along ascending sections. One of the rails was normally held open by means of a spring or weight, and was closed by every pair of wheels passing over it in the proper direction, but anything running back would meet the open tongue and be derailed towards the side of the line. Drastic, but effective. If a train ran away out of control downhill it was hoped that the signalmen could keep other trains out of the way, and perhaps deflect the runaway into a siding.

The driver controlled his locomotive, obeying signals from the guard and the fixed lineside signals observed during the journey. When he received the guard's green flag he put his engine into forward gear and gently opened the regulator, admitting steam to the cylinders. Ideally the train would be 'buffered up' behind him - all the buffers would be touching and the couplings slack. The engine and tender began to move slowly and took the slack out of the first coupling. When it was taut the first wagon would be jerked into motion, and then the second coupling would then tighten in its turn. The driver was thus able to progressively get his train into motion, gradually opening up the regulator as the load increased. As the starting resistance of wagons was more than the rolling resistance it meant that it was easier to start a loose coupled train than a screw coupled one of the same weight, which only moved as a single unit.

The sound of couplings tightening and drawbar springs flexing as a loose coupled train started was very distinctive. The guard listened to the sound as it approached his van, and at the appropriate time released his brake in readiness. He then firmly grasped the brake wheel, or some other part of his van, so that he was not thrown off his feet as his van, in its turn, was jerked into motion, as by then the engine and train could be moving at a brisk walking pace.

Running on level track caused few problems, but most lines had gradients and successful operation required all of the driver's skill. Uphill was not too difficult. On a downhill section the train often coasted and the trucks buffered up. As the train approached the foot of the grade the driver gradually applied steam so that the locomotive would gradually tighten the couplings throughout the train, ready for the following level or uphill section. At all costs sudden jerks had to be avoided, as these could break couplings (or even a wagon drawbar) and cause the train to divide. The problem of driving a train over an undulating track, particularly if the changes of gradient were frequent so that some parts of the train were going uphill while other parts of the same train were going down, can be imagined.

When the train stopped the driver aimed to make the wagons buffer up, to facilitate restarting. The clash of buffers as they came together, progressively moving back along the train, was another very distinctive noise associated with loose-coupled freight trains.

The second person on the footplate of the locomotive was the fireman. His chief responsibility was to manage the boiler so that the driver had steam when required. In addition, he helped the driver observe signals, particularly if curvature of the track or some other reason made them easier to see from his side of the cab. In the absence of a shunter, the fireman also coupled the engine to its train, including connecting the flexible pipes for the continuous brakes (and steam heating on passenger trains).

Managing the boiler required skill, balancing the demand for high pressure steam with keeping sufficient water in the boiler - although for limited periods the boiler feed water supply could be stopped as an aid to maintaining steam pressure. While early locomotives used feed water pumps, the usual method of delivering water to the boiler used an injector, effectively a pump with no moving parts. Within the injector a jet of steam mixed with the boiler feed water, causing the steam to condense and give up its considerable pressure and latent heat energy, which was then given to the water as kinetic energy. The water now moved fast enough and with sufficient force to overcome the boiler pressure, and passed through the clack valves into the boiler. In operation an injector emitted a 'happy hum'.

The obvious part of the fireman's work was to feed coal on to the fire, which required skill. The fire grate for a British freight locomotive was typically between 20 and 30 sq. ft in area. The width of the grate was up to 40 inches (so that the firebox would fit between the frames) and its length between 5 ft and 8 ft 6 in. In the longer fireboxes the furthest 3 ft or so of the grate sloped down towards the front. Some fireboxes were designed to have a shallow fire and others a thick fire, but in both cases the fireman had to ensure that the fire bed was never allowed to burn through, allowing cold air to come into the firebox.

Not only did the fireman have to feed the fire carefully he also had to anticipate his driver's needs. A finite time elapsed before an increased firing rate produced more steam; most certainly it was not an instantaneous response. Similarly, when less steam was required, the firing rate could be reduced some time before and the engine could run on the reserve of heat held in the boiler. The fireman had to 'know the road' just as much as the driver.

This is all written from the point of view of the main line train operation. The industrial locomotive crew had much the same responsibilities and problems, even if their runs were generally far shorter. Guards were very rare. The driver was usually responsible for firing as well, as the second man was mainly a shunter. The shunter coupled and uncoupled wagons, applied their brakes and changed points. Many internal wagons, particularly on the narrow gauge, did not have brakes so they were 'spragged' instead. A sprag was a piece of wood, or sometimes a steel bar, thrust through the spokes of a wheel to stop it turning.

While distances might be shorter, industrial drivers often had a selection of additional hazards not usually encountered by their main line counterparts, such as indifferently maintained track, very sharp curves, steep gradients, limited visibility due to curves or industrial plant, obstructions including road vehicles, and (in ironworks) hauling wagons containing red hot liquid metal or slag.

Chalk was originally carried in ordinary mineral or hopper wagons. Hurst, Nelson supplied 20-ton hopper wagon No. 206, registered by the LMS in 1923, for 'cement raw materials', which could mean chalk, coal or gypsum. From 1936 the LMS supplied assorted wagons, probably its own designs of 12-ton wooden mineral wagon, for the Totternhoe chalk traffic. In the early 1950s, BR allocated 16-ton steel mineral wagons, working on a closed circuit to Rugby or Southam. These were replaced in the later 1950s by tippler wagons.

The 27-ton tipplers had been designed originally for iron ore, but some were branded 'CHALK TIPPLER'. These were of similar size to the standard 16-ton mineral wagons but of more robust construction, particularly in the suspension for the wheels. The body was an open box, 16 ft 6 in. long by 8 ft 7 in. wide (length and width measured over framing) by 5 ft deep. Two stiffening members were fitted on each side and end, and around the top of the body. The sturdy underframe was carried on 3-hole disc wheels, 3 ft 1½ in. in diameter on a wheelbase of 9 ft. The axles ran in British Timken roller bearing axleboxes. No doors were fitted; emptying required a tippler, a device which inverted the whole wagon over a suitable hopper. Traditional three-link couplings, spring buffers and lever-operated handbrakes were fitted. The wagons had a tare (empty) weight of about 7½ tons. Livery was grey with black underframe and wheels. Lettering was white on a black background, with load and running number in the bottom left corner of the body, tare weight on the bottom right. A large panel central on the body was lettered 'CHALK TIPPLER'. Occasionally a wagon labelled for iron ore would appear in the rake of chalk wagons. By 1967 some iron ore tipplers had been fitted (or built) with continuous vacuum brakes, screw couplings and stronger buffers, and the body colour was changed to the 'fitted' colour bauxite (brown). It is unlikely that this change was made to any chalk tipplers as the traffic had ceased by then. Trains of these wagons were a familiar sight on the West Coast main line between Leighton Buzzard and Rugby. I estimate that well over 350 wagons, and probably nearer 500, were allocated to this traffic.

The traditional method of dispatching lime and cement was in casks (wooden barrels), later replaced by paper sacks. Both were loaded into vans to keep them dry. Many early PO wagons for lime and cement traffic had ridged roofs, like a house. After the discovery of techniques which enabled powders, like cement, to be 'fluidised' by passing compressed air through them, in the 1950s BR introduced vacuum braked 'Presflo' wagons (*see Appendix Six*). These were basically covered hopper wagons with reinforced sides and roof. About 20 tons of cement could be loaded by gravity through the roof. Pipes were provided for compressed air inlet and cement outlet, so that the wagon could be simply pumped out to empty it. Later designs of cement wagon, built for the various cement companies, had cylindrical tanks (to prevent cement accumulating in the corners) made of aluminium (to reduce the tare weight). At first they had vacuum brakes, and then from 1966 air braked wagons were built. The design favoured by APCM had a tank which sloped down towards the middle from each end. A number of bogie wagons were built as well in 1969, each with a pair of these 'bent' tanks. Known details of the cement companies' PO wagons are given in the section about the appropriate works.

The LNWR Dunstable branch was double track, 'down' to Dunstable and 'up' to Leighton Buzzard. Near the 4½ mile post was the signal box controlling De Berenger & Gower's Siding. It was a simple single-storey shed, with windows (or the glass panelled door) filling three sides. The walls were vertical planks. It housed a frame with seven levers:

No. 1	Up distant
No. 2	Up home
No. 3	Crossover down to up line
No. 4	Loop points (east end)
No. 5	Loop points (west end)
No. 6	Down home
No. 7	Down distant

There were no ground signals, all instructions being by hand, and hand lamp after dark. All the points on the main line were trailing for normal traffic. Stanbridgeford station closed to passengers 2nd July, 1962, to goods 1st June, 1964, and the last chalk train ran 15th April, 1965, Maundy Thursday.

BRITISH RAIL

27-TON ALL-STEEL MINERAL WAGONS

by Ken Werrett

Welded body on riveted and welded underframe. Provided for discharge by wagon tippler.

Colour: Grey Body.

White markings and letters as shown. Underframes, axle boxes, buffers: Black. Number plate: Black base. White letters and border.

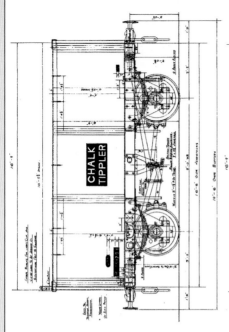

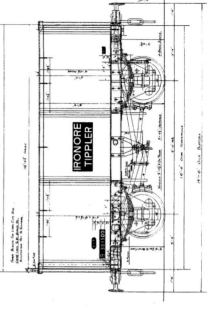

Drawing full size for 7 mm./ft. scale.

For non-commercial purposes it may be photostatted at any scale.

CHALK TIPPLER (upper)
IRON ORE TIPPLER (lower)

Photographs and information by courtesy of F.P.O., BR, L.M.R.

Model Railway News, February 1967, Author's Collection

British Railways 27T chalk tippler wagon.

The chalk trains were hauled by ex-LNWR 'Super D' 0-8-0s, replaced in the last years by ex-LMS '8F' class 2-8-0s. I never witnessed operation in the main line sidings, and the two descriptions I have read differ slightly. One method of working the siding was to bring a down train of empties from Leighton Buzzard and reverse it on to the up line. The engine could then run round its train, using the loop. It then pushed the train back on to the down line. The locomotive was coupled on to the brake van which it left on the up track, so that it could go into the sidings and collect a rake of loaded wagons, which were coupled to the van. The locomotive then returned to its empties, which were collected and pushed into the chalk sidings. Finally, it rejoined its train, coupled on, and proceeded to Leighton Buzzard, once the Stanbridgeford home signal by the level crossing cleared.

The other method was for the train of empties to proceed in the Dunstable direction until it cleared the crossover, and it then set back on to the up line. The locomotive returned to the crossover and ran via the loop line to the rear of its train. The wagons were then hauled in the Leighton Buzzard direction until the loop points had been cleared, when the train could be set back direct into the quarry sidings. The brake van was then shunted to one side, and a rake of loaded wagons brought out of the sidings and coupled to it, ready for the run to Leighton Buzzard and thence to Rugby or Southam.

Both methods required the loop to be longer than the train - see comments about this in the Totternhoe section (*Appendix Two*). The first method required the up home signal to be a train length away from the points by the signal box. The second method required the train to go over the level crossing at Stanbridgeford station before it could reverse into the loop.

In 1964, there were four trains per day, each comprising up to 42 loaded wagons, leaving Totternhoe every weekday, Monday to Friday. The first, at 10.45 am, ran direct to Rugby, and those at 12.55, 3.15 and 5.00 pm went to the sidings at Leighton Buzzard, to continue their journeys later.

The Dunstable branch was not an easy line to work. It left Leighton Buzzard station by a long curve on a falling gradient of 1 in 80, passing over Wing and Ledburn Road level crossings. There was then a short climb at 1 in 220 to cross the Grand Junction (later Grand Union) Canal, followed by a short fall at 1 in 220 after the bridge to mile post 1. Then there were almost two miles uphill at about 1 in 210, followed by a mile downhill at 1 in 264, and Gowers Siding was reached after a further mile at 1 in 528 down. At least the chalk trains did not have to go any further, as the line beyond climbed Sewell bank, well over a mile of 1 in 40, before a short downhill stretch brought it to Dunstable station. This bank was the reason why all locomotives working the branch faced towards Dunstable, to ensure that the firebox crown was always well covered with water.

The problem for up trains was the little hump over the canal bridge followed by the long curve uphill. Reminiscences from a number of men who worked the chalk trains were published in *The Dunstable Branch* by Bill Simpson (Lamplight Publications, 1998). The guard would gently apply his brakes at Billington Crossing, about a mile before the bridge, so that the couplings were taut by the time he reached the hump and so avoiding any snatches. If there was a breakaway on the climb up to the station, the guard would blow his whistle loudly to warn the crossing keepers to open the gates.

If a chalk train had the misfortune to be brought to a stand at Grovebury Crossing, just before the bridge, then the restart would rattle windows across Leighton and Linslade (basically, that part of Leighton then in Buckinghamshire)! If a train stalled on the gradient it was divided and worked up to the station in two parts.

A local enthusiast, Ken Scanes, remembers the chalk trains well. A mile away, at Leighton Buzzard station,

… we could hear the chalk train cross the canal bridge, and based on sound could judge (or thought we could) whether it would make it up into the station, or stall and have to set back down to the crossings and split the train. The crossing nearer the station was under orders not to open the traffic to road users until the chalk train was reported as safely in the station. Those orders, of course, only came in after a chalk train had stalled and slid backwards down from the station and smashed the gates.

Although some chalk trains ran straight through Leighton Buzzard, most of them, both full wagons and empties, were held for a time in Wing yard, a collection of sidings south of the station in the angle between the main line and the Dunstable branch. The engine shed here had two roads, and was situated in a restricted site at the top of the branch incline, level with the entrance to Wing yard. In the late 1940s it had an allocation of 10 ex-LNWR 'Super D' 0-8-0s, not least for chalk traffic, and an ex-LNWR 2-4-2T or 'Coal Tank' 0-6-2T for the branch push and pull passenger train. This was replaced by a modern Ivatt 2-6-2T around 1950. The shed closed officially on 5th November, 1962, and the workings were transferred to Bletchley, about eight miles further north along the main line.

Traffic for Rugby could go along the main line all the way, or could travel via the Northampton loop. Traffic for Southam used the main line to Weedon and then took the Daventry and Leamington branch. Empty chalk wagons were often seen in the sidings at Blisworth, one of the junctions for Northampton and a few miles south of Weedon. After the closure of the branch through Daventry, the remaining rail traffic for Southam, mainly coal, was worked via Rugby and the remains of the Leamington branch.

By the time rail traffic to the works at Rugby and Southam had reduced to little more than coal, both were worked to their final destination by Rugby crews. Traffic from the local yards to New Bilton sidings was worked by a BR class '08' 0-6-0DE shunter.

The BR (London Midland Region) Southern Section operating appendix dated April 1991 had a paragraph dealing with the New Bilton branch.

Rugby Portland Cement Company's Private Siding, Bilton. A crossbar shunting signal, at right angles to the siding, is situated at the entrance to the Rugby Portland Cement Co.'s Siding. Immediately on arrival at the siding the Person in charge of the train must check that the crossbar signal is in the 'DANGER' position. He must then obtain the permission from the Person in charge, Portland Cement Company's Siding for the movement to commence and obtain an assurance that the level-crossing gates are closed to road traffic and the points within the sidings are correctly set. He must then set the hand points from the [shunting] neck towards the cement sidings and operate the crossbar signal to the 'OFF' position. This will indicate to the Driver that he may commence the set-back movement into the cement sidings, but the Driver must still be prepared to observe any hand signals given by the Person in charge of the train.

The crossbar signal must be operated each time it is necessary to make a setting-back movement into the cement sidings. On completion of shunting the Person in charge of the train must ensure that the signal is left in the 'DANGER' position and the operating lever secured by padlock.

In the final years, traffic to Southam was hauled by class '25' diesel-electric locomotives until mid-1986, then class '31s' were used, and finally '08' shunters made occasional trips from Rugby. Trains were pulled in both directions between Rugby and Marton Junction, about 10 miles. There was a loop at the junction and a short cripple siding. Trains from Rugby were then pushed from the junction about three miles to Southam cement works sidings. Trains from Southam were hauled to the junction, where the locomotive ran round and hauled the train to Rugby.

Appendix Six

Bulk Carriage of Cement

Lime and cement obviously need to be kept dry in transit. Barrels were used for a long time, and then sturdy paper sacks for the standard 1 cwt (50 kg) bag of cement. The bags were carried in vans for protection. The earliest vans were wooden with ridged roofs, like a house, although later vehicles had ordinary curved roofs. There was often a door in the roof, probably to give light and headroom as the side height was quite low, and it would have been easier to make a flat door watertight than a curved one.

Following World War II, large quantities of cement were required for reconstruction. British Railways' first attempt at providing a method of bulk transport was the introduction of L-type containers. They were almost cubes, with a tare weight of 12 cwt each, and held 4 tons of cement. Three were carried on a 4-wheel vacuum braked Conflat 'L' flat wagon weighing 6 tons 17 cwt. The wagons had holes in their floors so that the containers could be emptied without unloading. Unfortunately the 12 ton load required a tare weight of 8 ton 13 cwt, so that the load was only 58 per cent of the total weight.

A major step forward came with the introduction of Pressure Discharge Bulk Powder wagons (Presflos). The prototype was ordered in January 1954, and as No. B888000 it was delivered from BR Shildon works (Co. Durham) that June. It could carry 20 (later 22) tons for a tare weight of about 13 tons (load 61 per cent of total). From 1955 to 1961 almost 2,000 Presflos were built for British Railways by a variety of firms, while APCM itself bought over 200 in 1960-63. They were not just used for cement but were used to carry a variety of substances, from flour to slate powder.

'Presflo' wagons were all-steel construction, with a heavily ribbed body to withstand the internal air pressure used for unloading. They had four wheels with roller bearing axleboxes, hydraulic buffers, screw couplings and vacuum brakes, so that they were suitable for high speed running. Loading the powder was by gravity using doors in the roof.

In the bottom of the body was a perforated plate which could be connected to a compressed air supply. As the gas forced its way through the powder the aerodynamic drag made the powder expand a little. Increasing the gas flow caused the powder to expand more until eventually a critical state was reached when the upward aerodynamic drag on each powder particle equalled the weight of the particle, which was then freely suspended within the system. At this point the mass of powder was said to have become fluidised, and it behaved like a fluid. In particular, the suspended powder could be pumped along a pipe. The emerging stream of cement looked just like milk! While the phenomenon had been known since the 1920s, if not before, successful commercial applications did not develop until after World War II.

Instructions for unloading Presflo wagons were painted on the body:

Discharge to be operated with compressed air at 20 psi. Rate of air flow 200 cu. ft per minute. Air pressure in hopper to be built up to 20 psi by opening hopper air valve before opening ejector valve followed by opening cement discharge valve. After discharging operation is completed care to be taken to close valves in correct order (1) hopper air valve (2) discharge valve (3) ejector valve. Then replace cap on air inlet pipe and discharge pipe. To release pressure in hopper open depressurising valve.

Although the 'Presflos' marked a considerable improvement in cement handling, experience showed that the square corners of the hopper caused solids to collect and so full discharge was impaired. New types of cement wagon with compressed air discharge were designed to overcome this drawback. Cement has a steep 'angle of repose' (the sides of a pile do not readily flatten under gravity but are still stable even when steeply inclined), and also the powder would not drop out of a shallow-sided hopper unaided. In addition, the cement powder settled during transit and it often did not settle uniformly. This caused uneven loading on the individual wheels, to the extent that occasionally some of the wheels merely glided along the top of the rail, with the wagon held in position by the tension in the couplings. The high centre of gravity of bulk cement wagons could cause them to roll or hunt (yaw from side to side) at speed. The abrasive nature of cement dust had an adverse effect on a wagon's suspension. All these factors aggravated the risk of derailment, particularly if there were minor irregularities in the track. A combination of them caused the derailment of a train of APCM 4-wheel 26 ton capacity 'Cemflo' tank wagons at Thirsk on 31st July, 1967 while travelling at 45 mph. Despite the quick reactions of its driver, an express hauled by the prototype diesel-electric locomotive No. DP2 was too close to stop before running into the wreckage, killing seven passengers and seriously injuring 45 more. The locomotive was not repaired.

Even now, not all cement is carried as bulk powder. APCM bought 96 modern vans with wide sliding doors in the mid-1960s, which enabled fork lift trucks to load and unload pallets of the traditional paper cement bags with ease.

(Based on: http://glostransporthistory.visit-gloucestershire.co.uk/grcwandcement.htm and http://en.wikipedia.org/wiki/fluidization)

Appendix Seven

Charles Nelson's Canal Boats

In view of the size of Charles Nelson's fleet of canal boats, and the availability of information about them, it is appropriate to summarize it here. Much of this information was obtained from boat registration records.

Following public concern about overcrowding and cleanliness on family-operated canal boats, the Canal Boats Act 1877 (and subsequent revisions) required all rural and urban district councils having a canal or navigable river within their area to appoint a canal boat inspector to ensure compliance with the acts. In addition, some of these authorities were empowered to register canal boats and keep appropriate records. Over the years some new registration authorities were appointed and others ceased registration. After the first Act was passed in 1877 a few authorities began registration late in 1878, but most began in January 1879. If a boat had major work done to its cabin it was re-registered, and often when it was sold. Registration details - place and boat number, plus the word 'Registered' - had to be painted on the side of the cabin in white letters at least two inches high on a black background.

The canal companies kept Gauging Registers, probably from the very early days, as these were necessary to calculate tolls. When a new boat was completed it was loaded with a succession of known weights. For each weight, its freeboard was measured in four specified places, on each side near each end. These sets of measurements formed the boat's gauging register, and were distributed to toll offices. When a laden boat reached a toll office the official there measured the freeboard at the specified places. Comparison with the boat's gauging register enabled the load to be determined and thus the toll due could be calculated.

It is worth adding that the canal companies never formed an organization comparable to the Railway Clearing House, to allocate freight charges when a consignment began on one canal and finished on another, maybe passing over other canals en route.

This list, produced by Christopher M. Jones and Alan Faulkner, was first published in *Narrow Boat* magazine, Spring 2011 and is reproduced by permission.

Name	Entered Fleet	Registration Place	Reg. No.	Date registered	Remarks
Acheron	*5.1855	Warwick	71	13.5.1879	
Alexandra	7.1902	Daventry	190	9.7.1902	New: William Nurser & Sons
Arab	*1.1854	Not registered			
Captain Cuttle	7.1922	Daventry	346	25.7.1922	New: William Nurser & Sons
		Daventry	422	16.6.1931	To T. & S. Element Ltd, 11.1941
Centaur	*1.1860	Not registered			
Centaur	3.1887	Paddington	170	6.4.1887	To William Nurser & Sons, 9.1912
Cerberus	*11.1854	Warwick	45	4.1879	
		Warwick	45	26.9.1885	
Challenger	10.1894	Paddington	174	7.11.1894	To Marshall Ashby & Co., 10.1897
Charles	*3.1862	Warwick	81	13.5.1879	
Charles	4.1898	Towcester	114	4.1898	
Charybdis	*3.1857	Not registered			
Charybdis	*7.1885	Warwick	101	8.7.1885	To A. Woodward, 7.1912
Cyclops	*8.1885				
Cyclops	*3.1877	Warwick	59	4.1879	To Joseph Coles, 6.1908
Edward VII	4.1901	Daventry	169	17.4.1901	New: William Nurser & Sons
					To John Brooks Jnr, 11.1923
Fairy	*6.1854	Warwick	10	11.3.1879	To John Garner, 4.1903
Frederick	9.1853	Warwick	49	4.1879	

Name	Entered Fleet	Registration Place	Reg. No.	Date registered	Remarks
Frederick	2.1898	Port of London	324	10.3.1898	Ex-Griffin & Co. (John)
					To Bushell Bros, Tring, 3.1918
The Game	5.1923	Daventry	355	29.5.1923	New: William Nurser & Sons
Cock (m)					To Samuel Barlow Coal Co. Ltd, 8.1935
Geneva	10.1924	Daventry	366	11.11.1924	New: William Nurser & Sons
					To James Hambridge
George	*3.1861	Warwick	66	13.5.1879	Ex-J. Cramp, Warwick
					To William Nurser & Sons, 8.1903
Henry & Emma	5.1879	Warwick	62	13.5.1879	
Hermit	*8.1867	Not registered			To James Bricknell, Stockton, 12.1894
Janus (s)	6.1885	Warwick	102	11.7.1885	To Jees Hartshill Granite Co., 10.1908
Jason (s)	9.1884	Warwick	104	14.7.1885	To L.B. Faulkner, 6.1912
Jason II (m)	10.1924	Daventry	365	14.10.1924	New: William Nurser & Sons
					To Samuel Barlow Coal Co. Ltd, 10.1935
John	1.1898	Daventry	130	16.6.1897	†Renamed Frederick, 1898
Juno	*2.1866	Not registered			
Juno	4.1889	Paddington	173	7.5.1889	
Jupiter (s)	10.1881	Warwick	99	10.1881	New
		Warwick	99	13.6.1882	Alterations
		Warwick	103	14.7.1885	To Jees Hartshill Granite Co., 10.1908
May	1.1936	Tamworth	116	15.10.1932	Ex-Fellows Morton & Clayton (Violet)
					via Lees & Atkins
Montague	*8.1851	Not registered			To James Bricknell, Stockton, 12.1894
Montague	10.1900	Paddington	206	16.10.1900	To William Nurser & Sons, 11.1922
Natal	4.1903	Daventry	201	13.5.1903	New: William Nurser & Sons
					To A.S. Kendall, 3.1921
Orangia	4.1903	Daventry	199	15.4.1903	New: William Nurser & Sons
					Converted to motor, 10.1920
Orangia (m)	10.1920	Daventry	335	19.10.1920	Ex-horse boat
Pegasus	*5.1857	Not registered			
Pegasus	4.1880	Warwick	91	12.3.1881	
		Warwick	127	14.1.1902	
Phlegethon	*4.1855	Warwick	61	5.1879	
Phlegethon	9.1903	Warwick	130	13.10.1903	New: William Nurser & Sons
					To John Wilson, 1.1921
Princess Mary	3.1922	Daventry	344	4.4.1922	New: William Nurser & Sons
		Daventry	373	7.12.1926	To T. & S. Element Ltd, 11.1941
Queen	*1.1860	Not registered			
Rattler	*12.1853	Not registered			
Rhodesia	11.1921	Daventry	342	13.12.1921	New: William Nurser & Sons
					To A. Harvey-Taylor, 4.1937
Sheik	*3.1854				
Sheik	*12.1866	Not registered			
Sheik	5.1890	Towcester	32	15.7.1890	To F.W. & A. Sephton, 8.1923
Sphynx	*9.1854	Not registered			
Sphynx	2.1880	Warwick	90	21.3.1881	
William	*5.1868	Not registered			To H. Simpson, 5.1891
William	6.1891	Warwick	115		12.1.1892

Notes

The Warwick Canal Boat Register was begun in 1879 but is incomplete. A reconstruction has been attempted, based partly on the entries in a receipt book copied by the late Philip Weaver and partly on additional research in various inspection registers by Christopher M. Jones. The names of over a dozen of the earliest boats have not been found and in view of this lack of detail they have not been included.

Key

* The early boats in this list would not have been registered - so they have been sourced from various gauging registers, the entry date being marked by an asterisk.

All boats are horse drawn or unpowered 'butties', unless otherwise stated. (m) Motor boat i.e. internal combustion engine. (s) Steamer.

† The registration relates to the previous owner.

Appendix Eight

Napton Brickworks

1878	Mason & Watson	
1901	Watson Nelson	
1934	Allied Brick & Tile Co. Ltd	Closed 1970s

Napton is a village ½ mile south of the main road (A425) from Southam (3 miles) to Daventry (7 miles). Most of the village is built on the southern and eastern slopes of Napton Hill (500 ft) with the church and windmill at the east and west ends of the summit respectively. The Oxford Canal skirts the north, west and south sides of Napton Hill on the 330 ft (approx) contour.

Napton Brick & Tile Works was situated on the south bank of the Oxford Canal ½ mile north-west of the village (SP 454615). This 40 acre site on the side of the canal gave good access going south to the Thames and London, and to the Birmingham & Warwick Canal and Grand Junction (later Grand Union) Canal for northbound traffic. The quarry was some 120 ft above the works, near the top of Napton Hill (SP 457612), immediately below the windmill.

William Watson started Napton brickyard in 1878, trading as Mason & Watson. He had been born in 1812, and was noted locally as a church builder and architect (he restored Napton, Southam and Stockton churches in the 1860s and built a church in Long Itchington in 1873). William Watson died in 1879, and his son Charles took over. Mason was listed as a farmer in 1866, and appears to have retired soon after 1888. Mason & Watson are given as brickmakers in the 1888 trade directory. Charles Watson's eldest son, Charles Henry Watson, who had been born in Napton, was works manager by 1900, and also 'assessor of taxes'(!), two positions he retained in the 1912 edition.

Initially only bricks were made, many being used on the canal, but later roof tiles and floor tiles were made as well. The works was described in the November 1903 issue of the *British Clayworker*. One of Wm Watson's first contracts was for the LNWR, and a recent one (in 1903) had been to supply 15,000,000 bricks to the Great Central Railway - presumably for its extension to London, constructed 1894-98. C.Watson had a patent tile which enabled a roof to be 'covered at slating pitch'. Production in 1903 was 'speciality roofing tiles and fittings, and finials, also common bricks, a few facings [bricks], and a large quantity of agricultural pipes'.

All the works' machinery was driven by an 80 hp engine by Ernest Wilkes, Pelsall Foundry, Walsall of 1905 (which appears to have replaced an earlier engine by the same manufacturer) with a Lancashire boiler by Isca Foundry, Newport and a Cornish boiler by J. & G. Joicey, Newcastle-upon-Tyne. (Two common types of large diameter horizontal boilers were the Cornish, with a single flue along its lenth, and the Lancashire, with a pair of flues. In both cases the fire grate was at one end of the flue(s), and the draught was provided by a tall chimney.) Brick drying sheds were 150 x 40 ft, with ¼ in. steel plate floor, heated by exhaust steam. 'The brick kiln is a continuous one by Sercombe, containing fourteen chambers with a stack 105 ft high, each chamber holding about 10,000 [bricks]. The cost of burning is roughly 4 cwt [coal] per thousand, and Messrs Watson Nelson have no reason to be dissatisfied with the quality of the bricks.'

In 1901 the firm was converted to a limited company, Watson Nelson Ltd, in conjunction with Charles Nelson & Co. 'the well-known lime and cement firm' whose works at Stockton were about two miles away. Nelson ceased making yellow bricks at Stockton in the early 1900s, which probably reflects his interest in the Napton firm. By 1916 the firm had a telephone, Southam 19. Watson Nelson Ltd sold out to Allied Brick & Tile Works Ltd in 1934.

In its heyday over 100 men were employed altogether, making six million tiles per annum. The works used some 90 tons coal per week, brought by boat. Before World War I three men were paid 6s. (£15) for emptying a 30 ton load. In 1903 there were three sheds to dry tiles before firing, two holding 350,000 tiles each and one holding 500,000. When

273

Napton Brickworks and Church Leyes Farm (CLF), 1886 6 in. OS sheet 41NW.   *Crown Copyright*

the tiles had been burnt in the kiln they came out 'Brilliant red from top to bottom, with a metallic ring which told its own tale of weather-resting properties'. Brick making was then 16,000 per day, using beehive kilns.

Production ceased on the outbreak of war in 1939, completed goods being fired over a period of three months. Sales from stock continued throughout the war, although reduced to a very small quota. Only three men were employed during the war period. The works was taken over by the Ministry of Aircraft Production in November 1940, and was immediately occupied by Messrs Cornercrofts of Coventry who had been bombed out. As the accommodation was inadequate, Cornercroft moved out at end of 1941 and GEC, Witton, moved in, remaining for the rest of the war.

The location of the works on the bank of a major canal initially gave it excellent transport facilities. However, times and customers' needs change, and after 1895 bricks or tiles for dispatch by rail could to be carted two miles to Napton & Stockton station. Before then they would have had to go seven miles to Daventry. The works itself never had rail access.

Once Charles Nelson & Co. became involved the output for dispatch by rail was loaded on to one of the Napton's two steel canal boats and hauled by horse about three miles to Nelson's Stockton cement works. The route was about a mile along the Oxford Canal to Napton Junction, then along the Warwick & Napton, through the three Calcutt locks, to the works. Here the boats were emptied and the products transferred to railway wagons. The 1903 article stated that 'In the case of tiles, [transhipment] is simplified by specially made crates, with holding capacity of 1,000 each, which are filled and loaded into barges, and lifted direct into trucks with a steam crane.' The output then required about three boat loads per week, a boat carrying 6 tons of bricks or 6,700 tiles. The boatman was usually up at 5 am for a 6 am start. Later the boats went about three-quarters of a mile, and one lock, further on, to Griffin's former limeworks, and transhipment to rail was done there until about 1934 (*see Chapter Nine*). Eventually the output was loaded directly on lorries at Napton, a change probably hastened by the change of ownership.

British Waterways' Archives show that Watson Nelson Ltd bought a canal boat *Evelyn* in October 1933, and their boat *Harry* was repaired at this time.

The advent of cheap machine-made bricks and roof tiles made many of the firm's products uneconomic, so in 1947 it concentrated on the manufacture of floor tiles. The back of Napton tiles had a trademark depicting four symbolic windmill sails, radiating from the centre to each corner. A new oil-fired kiln, on the site of the old beehive ones, was opened in 1952 by John Profumo MP and halved fuel costs (oil was cheap then). The kiln was of Dutch design, the longest in Europe when it was built, with a 90 ft chimney, and it operated continuously. The works was maintained by its own staff, who often had to make their own spares because parts of the plant were so old.

The potential output of tiles was 200,000 per week but as it was hard to sell that number attempts were made to develop an export trade. This was hampered by numerous dock strikes, which meant that often lorry drivers had to bring back their loads. One driver was so angry that he unloaded his tiles across the door of the dockers' canteen in Bristol, and they were dispatched alright! Tile manufacture ceased in the early 1960s.

An expensive plant to make very hard engineering bricks was installed in 1966. The brick making machine extruded clay like toothpaste, and a wire frame cut off 11 bricks at a time. When 55 bricks had been cut they were lifted on to a trolley by a set of 55 vacuum pads for drying, 24 hours in warm moist air and then 42 hours in warmer drier air. Unfortunately this project was not success as the kilns were too narrow, having been made for tiles, and although it cut the labour force from 100 to less than 30, in 1968 a receiver had to be appointed. The works finally closed in the late 1970s, although its last entry in the telephone directory was 1986. It had 'tried all sorts of things to keep going. Glazed tiles, many shapes and sizes of skirting, five different colours, even selling 3 tons a fortnight of ground clay to a face powder firm. (If only women knew what they put on their faces!)'. By 1994 the site was the Windmill Business Park and the quarry had become a conservation area. (Another

Napton Quarry, 1908, with the return wheel for the chain haulage in the foreground. The only wagon visible is in the drying shed. The troughs down the quarry face were probably to convey clay dug higher up down to the level of the railway.   *J.N. Cain*

Scene in the clay pit below Napton windmill. Note the narrow ledges up the face where the quarrymen stood to work and the flat wagon, 27th July, 1961.   *Author*

sign of the times: in the mid-1960s the arch of the hump back canal bridge by the works was reinforced with concrete, to take the shock of speeding road vehicles.)

The bed of clay in the hilltop quarry was said to be 120 ft deep, and comprised several layers. The top layer in 1903 was stiff plastic yellow-brown clay which burnt a brilliant red, and was used mainly for Windmill brand tiles. Below this was blue shale, used for making very strong metallic bricks, equal to many 'blue bricks'. Later workings nearer the top of the hill comprised layers of clay with beds of sand, and occasionally rock, between them. In the 1920s, and no doubt since the works opened, clay was dug with clay picks, barrowed to the edge of the face and tipped down a chute to the narrow gauge tubs which conveyed it to the works. Even in 1961 the quarrymen cut ledges at intervals up the face, so they could stand to dig out the clay with a pick, letting it fall down a gully to the quarry floor for subsequent loading into the tubs. The *British Clayworker* noted that 'In very wet or showery weather some clay was given a preliminary drying in a shed to assist the grinding of that obtained fresh from the bank.'

Tile manufacture was discontinued in the early 1960s, and by 1965 production was only bricks. As brick manufacture could use clay mixed with some sand it was possible to use mechanical excavation, and so each year the firm hired a scraper to replenish the clay dump at the works. The railway was lifted and the old workings were landscaped.

As previously stated, the clay pit was about 120 ft above the works, just below Napton windmill. A 16 in. gauge railway served the clay pit and connected it with the works below. The line is shown on the 1887 OS map, and in view of the difference in levels, it was probably laid from the commencement of the works in 1878. In 1955 or 1956 a small dumper truck was substituted for the main line down the hill but the railway was retained in the quarry for another 10 years.

At the back of the works, beside the tip serving the clay mill, was the 80 hp stationary steam engine which powered the continuous chain haulage system on the incline to the clay pit, as well as all the plant in the works itself. A double track line ran up the hillside from the tip. After crossing a works road it was mostly in a cutting. At one point a bridge carried a path over the line. At the head of the incline, which had lifted the railway some 70 ft in 300 yards (1 in 12 average) was a large horizontal return wheel for the haulage chain. An illustration in the 1903 article shows that this wheel was then situated on the quarry floor, near a large shed, presumably the one used to dry clay in wet weather. The 1887 25 in. OS map shows a siding about 70 yards from the works, serving another building, and having connections to both of the main tracks. Presumably at this time two tips were in use, probably one for bricks and one for tiles.

At some date, no doubt because the working face had receded and was now higher up the hill, much closer to the windmill, a balanced incline was constructed near the end of the chain haulage. Just before the return wheel the double track levelled, turned eastwards, became single and then branched in two. This section was hand operated, and led to a double track incline with a gradient of about 1 in 1 which lifted the wagons the remaining 30 ft to the quarry floor. A pair of 16½ in. gauge cradles ran on this incline, having one pair of wheels much lower than the other so that the floor was level. Capacity was one tub per cradle. A brake wheel at the incline head controlled the cradles which were operated by gravity, the descending full tub raising an empty one. Hand-operated lines ran from the incline brake drum to the working face.

In the final years track in the quarry was some 20 ft above the level of the brake drum and it was entirely self-contained. Temporary tracks served all the working faces, with permanent track to the dumper loading point and the waste sand tip.

Following the closure of the main line, the cutting rapidly became overgrown and wet, and the waste tip encroached over the bottom of the balanced incline. The two cradles disappeared. The brake house and incline rails survived for some years, and a few horn fitted wagons were dumped by the works, the remainder being broken up except for the ones needed in the quarry. The substitute dumper truck needed eight wagons to fill it, and it made about 14 journeys daily down the hill to the works.

Downhill, so ride while you can! The tip for loading the dumper which had replaced the chain haulage is opposite the hut, and the line continues past it to the tip, 27th July, 1961.   *Author*

A 16 inch gauge end-door wagon in the clay pit below Napton windmill on 27th July, 1961.
             Author

Very light rail weighing about 11 or 14 lb./yd was used, laid on wooden sleepers 3 ft x 6 in. x 3 in., often widely spaced. Points were prefabricated on steel sleepers, but with wooden sleepers placed underneath to maintain a uniform height. They were operated by a kick. The track was extended as the face receded by the addition of an assembly comprising two rails, 5 ft or 6 ft long, and one sleeper. The very ends of the rails were spiked down halfway across the sleeper. Two more pairs of spikes were driven into the other half of the sleeper, opposite each rail end. The assembly was installed by carrying it to the existing railhead, and inserting the free ends of the rails into the spare sets of spikes on the existing last sleeper. The more permanent tracks were more robustly laid and had joints with fishplates.

In the final years of operation the clay occurred in layers, with sand and stone between them. The waste, some 40 per cent of the total excavated, was tipped on the edge of the pit. All excavation was done by hand, with six men employed in 1960, some digging waste rock and some clay. The higher beds of sand and clay were reached by climbing up the face. The quarryman dislodged about a wagon load of material, shovelling it over the edge of his level, then he climbed down to load the wagon and push it to the appropriate tip, even riding perched on the end of the wagon if the gradient was in his favour. If necessary, stone was blasted to dislodge it or break up the lumps into manageable size. Wagons were scotched, at the tip and elsewhere, by throwing a light chain across the rails under the wheels.

Only end-door wagons had been used on the main line to the works, running with the open end facing the works for ease of tipping. Loaded wagons descended on the western incline track and the empties ascended on the eastern one. Pulleys and rollers were laid between the rails to support the haulage chain. Normally there were about 14 or 15 wagons on the incline at any given time, about 40 yards apart. The incline was halted if a vehicle on the works road needed to cross the railway.

In 1961, at the end of the day, wagons were often filled and then deliberately derailed at key points to prevent unauthorised use after hours, which otherwise often saw one or more wagons run off the end of the tip.

About two dozen wagons were required when the inclines were in use, but latterly only about 10 remained. Most were end-door open wagons, but a few had side doors and there were two flat wagons. In both types the doors were not hinged but simply lifted out.

A 4 ft length of 2 x 3 in. wood was provided to enable the quarryman to lift the closed end of his wagon for emptying. The piece of wood was slid under the floor above the axles until a wooden block 6 in. long, mounted 15 in. from one end, pushed against the axle. With the wood in position the quarryman had sufficient leverage to lift the wagon. The wooden lifting bar was carried under the wagon, resting on the axles, and was used as a footrest cum brake when the men rode on the downhill sections. On the level and uphill sections men pushed the wagons.

The wagons were all made at the works by the carpenter, who also made other items, like 50 wheelbarrows soon after World War II. Typically, the body of both end and side door wagons was 42 in. long, 17 in. high and having ends which tapered from 22 in. wide at the bottom to 26 in. at the top. The sides, ends, and door, were each a single piece of elm, $1\frac{1}{2}$ in. thick. A handhold was cut in the top of the door. The frame was oak, outside the wheels, and was extended at each end beyond the body to form dumb buffers. The wheels were $7\frac{1}{2}$ in. in diameter at $20\frac{1}{2}$ in. wheelbase, and had five curved spokes, although the thick deposit of clay which covered them gave the appearance of disc wheels! The axles ran in plain bearings bolted to the frames. There were no springs or couplings. On early wagons the end doors were held in position by wooden slides nailed to the body planks. Later, both side and end doors were made to overlap the fixed body ends or sides. An iron bracket on the floor held each end of the door, and an iron catch pivoted inside the side or end secured its top to the body. The major components were held together by simple iron strapping. Wagons carried $\frac{1}{3}$ cu. yd, about 8 cwt, and had a tare weight of about 56 lb.

The end-door wagons which had been used on the main line were fitted with a vertical horn bolted firmly to the closed end of the body. The horn was a strip of iron, about 8 in. high, with a vee cut in the end to hold the chain. A vertical link of the chain fitted in the

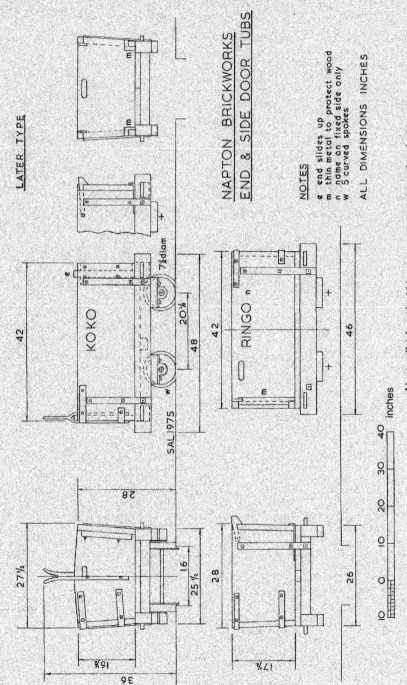

LATER TYPE

NAPTON BRICKWORKS
END & SIDE DOOR TUBS

NOTES

e end slides up
m thin metal to protect wood
c name on fixed side only
w 5 curved spokes

ALL DIMENSIONS INCHES

KOKO

7½ diam

20½

48

42

SAL.1975

RINGO n

42

46

28

26

16½

36

28

27½

16

25½

17½

inches

40

30

20

10

0

10

Napton Brickworks 16 in. gauge wagons. Note that the horn was fitted only to wagons going down to the works, and by 1960 none the wagons in use had a horn.

Author

Wagon *Koko* abandoned after the haulage system ceased. Note the horn on the end which gripped the chain in its slot, and the painted name, 27th July, 1961.   *Author*

Wagons, rails and sleepers dumped in the quarry after the railway closed. Note the side door wagon in the foreground, while *Dobbin* has an end door, 30th May, 1966.   *Author*

cut and the horizontal links either side of the horn held the wagon and hauled it along. At each end of the chain haulage the return wheels were raised so the chain lifted out of the horn, freeing the wagon.

The flat wagons, 'bogies', were used to carry large lumps of stone too big or heavy to load into the ordinary wagons. The body was 42 in. x 25 in., and the length of the frame was 45 in.

Many of the wagons had names painted on the sides in black. They could be the workman's name or nickname, or just something that took the carpenter's fancy. Examples noted at various times were: *Arthur, Barrie, Carla, Harry, ER* (with a crude crown beneath), *BR* (with a crude lion and wheel between the letters), *Koko, Muffin, The Lady?, Dobbin* and *Ringo*.

I obtained one wagon, *Koko*, for private preservation, and collected it in the boot of a friend's estate car. It moved with me when I married, and accompanied me on several subsequent moves, but in 1975 as I could no longer take it with me I gave it to a friend in the Potteries. It has since been broken up, having become too rotten.

By May 1966 the line had been lifted and surviving equipment was dumped in a heap on a level below the main quarry. In addition to the track materials there were two side-door wagons (*Carla, Ringo*), seven end-door wagons (*Dobbin, BR*), and a single flat bogie. Seven wagons remained here in July 1973, five end-door and one each side-door and flat.

The oil-fired tunnel kiln opened in 1952 was served by a 31 in. gauge railway. The rail system consisted basically of three parallel tracks, linked by a traverser at each end. One outer track ran through the kiln and the other two alongside. The kiln burnt continuously.

This railway had 92 all-steel flat wagons, 7 ft long, 4 ft 8 in. wide, with a 4 ft wheelbase. The floor of the wagon was a layer of fondu concrete, with low towers of firebrick built on it. Tiles on the top of the towers supported the load of unfired tiles. The result was that the floor of the wagon looked something like a Roman hypocaust, and permitted the hot gases to reach the inner tiles to achieve even firing.

Tiles were stacked on a wagon which was pushed by hand under a loading gauge to the entrance of the kiln, which was sealed by doors at each end to retain the heat. When the doors were opened a hydraulic ram pushed the wagon into the kiln, moving along all the other wagons within, and one was expelled from the far end. The kiln held 54 wagons when full, and a new one was introduced every 2½ to 3½ hours, depending on production. By the time a wagon had passed the length of the kiln the tiles were fired.

31 inch gauge flat wagons used in the tunnel kiln, 15th June, 1962.   *Author*

Appendix Nine

R.T. Crick, Church Leyes Farm, Napton

After 20 years and a lot of negotiating, Mr R.T. (Bob) Crick obtained the remains of the railway from Napton brickworks (*see Appendix Eight*). He intended to relay it in his garden at Church Leyes Farm, some 350 yards east of the windmill on the top of Napton Hill (SP 461613). His aims were to preserve part of old Napton, a folly to recreate the atmosphere of the pre-preservation Welsh narrow gauge lines (as a child he had seen the Talyllyn Railway), and for possible domestic use - to carry firewood to the house, grass cuttings etc. The railway had been laid by 1990. Rolling stock seen in the main station in 2007 comprised: wagon *Dobbin*, four underframes, and two other wagons, one having slatted sides apparently built on a Napton flat wagon. The rails were a mixture of 11 and 14 lb./yd flat-bottomed, and 14 lb./yd bridge (in section like an inverted lower case 'v'), many lengths having been recovered from use as fence posts at the quarry. Assorted available timber was used for sleepers, including old fence posts and even fence slats. The rails were spiked with 3 inch nails bent over. Mr Crick used to open his farm to visitors and would push children along in the trucks. However, child visitors ceased after a foot & mouth outbreak and the imposition of stringent Health & Safety regulations.

The layout of the system, laid through a patch of woodland, was basically a figure '6'. Close to the house was a small wooden shed whose sloping roof projected over the low platform. This was Howcombe Halt (Howcombe is the name of this part of Napton). After 100 ft the line divided. The right-hand track continued straight ahead through the trees for 125 ft to the main station Hafod Y Fach - Welsh for 'summer dwelling' (where sheep grazed on the mountains). The left-hand track curved sharply left for 80 ft, when it crossed the drive. There was then a long right-hand curve, with a direct connection from the main station trailing in on the right after 120 ft, eventually reaching the main station after a further 200 ft. The main station was a wooden shed with ridged roof and waiting room. The through track had a low platform made of bricks laid on the ground edged with a length of wood. Outside the station were points leading to the long curve (80 ft away), with a trailing siding back into the station. Nearby were two level crossings over the drive, one on each route. Most of the rolling stock was stored under cover at this station.

By 2007 the railway looked as though it had not been used for some time, and a few lengths of rail were missing. However, of all the railways covered in this book, this is the only one to survive at the time of writing - just!

A wagon with new body constructed on an underframe from the brickworks. Note the brick platform edge and seat, 27th June, 1994. *Author*

Church Leyes Farm, Napton. Hafod y Fach station and assorted wagons. Note the thin fence slats used as sleepers, 2nd August, 2007.
Author

All-Works Locomotive List

Loco ID	Maker	No.	Date	Gauge	Type	Dr. wh. dia.	Cyl. dia.	Cyl. stroke	Boiler psi	HP	Weight	Notes
2 (*Isobel*)	AE	1875	1921	4'8½"	0-4-0ST							
	AP	3730	1896	4'8½"	4wWT							
	AP	11087	1924	4'8½"	4wWT							
8 *The Blue Circle*	Bg	621	1919	4'8½"	0-4-0ST							
2 *Lark*	HC	708	1904	3'0"	0-4-0ST	2'0½"	9"	15"				
Southam	HC	D604	1936	4'8½"	0-4-0DM					120		
Southam No. 2	HC	D625	1942	4'8½"	0-4-0DM					120		
West Baldwin	HE	758	1901	3'0"	0-6-0ST	2'4½"	9"	14"				
Cunarder	HE	1690	1931	4'8½"	0-6-0ST	3'4"	14"	20"				
	HE	2837	1944	1'11½"	4wDM					20		
No. 1	JF	20684	1935	3'0"	2-4-0DM	2'6"				100		
No. 2	JF	20685	1935	3'0"	2-4-0DM	2'6"				100		
	JF	4110008	1950	4'8½"	0-4-0DM							
	JF	4220008	1959	4'8½"	0-4-0DH							
Eagle	KS	756	1901	3'0"	0-4-2T	2'0"	7½"	12"	160		9t.	1
Hawk	KS	1213	1914	3'0"	0-4-2T	2'0"	7"	12"	160		6t.13¾c.	
	KS	4266	1922	2'0"	0-4-0ST	1'8"	6"	9"				
No. 2, ex 8	MR	984	1918	1'11½"	4wPM					20	2t.10c.	2
	MR	1899	1919	1'9"								
	MR	1908	1920	1'11½"	4wPM					20	4t.	3
	MR	2127	1922	3'0"	4wPM							
No. 2, ex 8	MR	2154	1921	2'0"	4wPM					20	2t.10c.	
	MR	2261	1923	3'0"	4wPM							
	MR	3657	1924	1'9"	4wPM					20	4t.	3
	MR	3794	1926	1'9"	4wPM					20	4t.	3
	MR	5917	1936	1'9"	4wDM					32/42	5t.	
	MW	1146	1890	4'8½"	0-6-0ST		12"	17"				
	MW	1972	1919	4'8½"	0-6-0ST		12"	18"				
	MW	1995	1920	4'8½"	0-6-0ST		12"	18"				
	MW	2047	1926	4'8½"	0-6-0ST		14"	20"				
	OK	4547		2'6"	4wPM							
	OK	4621	1931	2'6"	4wPM							
	OK	20178		1'11½"	4wDM							
	OK	20227		1'11½"	4wDM							
Gamecock	P	678	1897	1'9"	0-6-0ST	1'8"	7"	10"	160		7t.10c.	4
Niras	P	785	1899	1'9"	0-6-0ST	1'8"	7"	10"	160		7t.10c.	4
Jurassic	P	918	1901	1'9"	0-6-0ST	1'8"	7"	10"	160		7t.10c.	5
5	P	947	1903	4'8½"	0-4-0ST		10"	15"				6
Jurassic	P	1008	1903	1'11½"	0-6-0ST	1'8"	7"	10"	160		7t.10c.	5
Neozoic	P	1119	1906	1'11½"	0-6-0ST	1'8"	7"	10"	160		7t.10c.	7
Liassic (1)	P	1216	1909	1'11½"	0-6-0ST	1'8"	7"	10"	160		7t.10c.	7
Triassic	P	1270	1911	1'11½"	0-6-0ST	1'8"	7"	10"	160		7t.10c.	7
Mesozoic	P	1327	1913	1'11½"	0-6-0ST	1'8"	7"	10"	160		7t.10c.	5
No. 9 *Whitby*	P	1505	1918	4'8½"	0-4-0ST							
Liassic (2)	P	1632	1923	1'11½"	0-6-0ST	1'8"	7"	10"	160		7t.10c.	7
3 *Eagle*	P	1654	1924	3'0"	0-4-0ST	1'8"	7"	10"	160		7t.10c.	8
4	P	1663	1924	3'0"	0-4-0ST	1'8"	7"	10"	160		7t.10c.	8
6	P	1720	1926	3'0"	0-4-0ST	1'8"	7"	10"	160		7t.10c.	8
	RH	168437	1933		4wDM					28		
	RH	172334	1935	2'6"	4wDM							
	RH	172336	1935	2'6"	4wDM							
	RH	172337	1935	2'6"	4wDM							
	RH	172342	1935	2'6"	4wDM							
	RH	183427	1937		4wDM					12		
	RH	221618	1943		4wDM					48		
	RH	221619	1943		4wDM					48		
No. 20	RH	281290	1949	3'0"	0-6-0DM					100		9
No. 21	RH	281291	1949	3'0"	0-6-0DM					100		9
5	RSHN	7387	1948	4'8½"	0-6-0ST		14"	22"				
No. 4	RSHN	7413	1948	4'8½"	0-6-0ST							

Loco ID	*Maker*	*No.*	*Date*	*Gauge*	*Type*	*Dr. wh. dia.*	*Cyl. dia.*	*Cyl. stroke*	*Boiler psi*	*HP*	*Weight*	*Notes*
12, ex *2*	S	6255	1926	3′0″	4wVBT	2′6″	6¾″	9″	275		7t.5c.	*10*
13, ex *1*	S	6256	1926	3′0″	4wVBT	2′6″	6¾″	9″	275		7t.5c.	*10*
3	S	6257	1926	3′0″	4wVBT	2′6″	6¾″	9″	275		7t.5c.	*10*
No. 9 Craven	S	9556	1953	4′8½″	4wVBT				275	100		
	S	9559	1953	4′8½″	4wVBT				275	100		
No. 6	S	9564	1954	4′8½″	4wVBT				275	100		
No. 8	S	9565	1954	4′8½″	4wVBT				275	100		
No. 7 Courtybella	S	9627	1957	4′8½″	4wVBT				275	100		
No. 4	S	10007	1959	4′8½″	4wDH					200	34t.	
	TH	118C	1962	4′8½″	4wDH							
No. 3	TH	164V	1966	4′8½″	4wDH							
	TH	173V	1967	4′8½″	4wDH							
Robinson	WB	1632	1901	3′0″	0-4-0ST	1′7″	6″	9″	140		5t.5c.	*11*
Walton	WB	1633	1901	3′0″	0-4-0ST	1′7″	6″	9″	140		5t.5c.	*11*
Mercedes	WB	1730	1904	3′0″	0-4-0ST	1′7″	6″	9″	140		5t.5c.	*11*
Maudie	WB	1782	1905	3′0″	0-4-0ST	1′3⅓″	5″	7¾″	140		3t.13c.	*12*
Mildred	WB	1844	1907	3′0″	0-4-0ST	1′3⅓″	5″	7¾″	140		3t.13c.	*12*
	WB	2148	1924	1′11½″	0-4-0ST	1′7⅓″	6″	9″	150		5t.5c.	*13*

Makers

AE	Avonside Engine Co. Ltd, Bristol
AP	Aveling & Porter Ltd, Canterbury, Kent
Bg	E.E. Bagulay Ltd, Burton-on-Trent, Staffordshire
HC	Hudswell, Clarke & Co. Ltd, Leeds
HE	Hunslet Engine Co. Ltd, Leeds
JF	John Fowler & Co. (Leeds) Ltd, Leeds
KS	Kerr, Stuart & Co. Ltd, Stoke-on-Trent
MR	Motor Rail Ltd, Bedford (formerly Motor Rail & Tramcar Co. Ltd) 'Simplex'
MW	Manning, Wardle & Co. Ltd, Leeds
OK	Orenstein & Koppel AG, Berlin
P	Peckett & Sons Ltd, Bristol
RH	Ruston & Hornsby Ltd, Lincoln
RSHN	Robert Stephenson & Hawthorns Ltd, Newcastle-upon-Tyne
S	Sentinel (Shrewsbury) Ltd, Shrewsbury (formerly Sentinel Waggon Works Ltd)
TH	Thomas Hill (Rotherham) Ltd, Kilnhurst, South Yorkshire
WB	W.G. Bagnall Ltd, Locomotive Manufacturer, Stafford

Notes

1	'Skylark' class
2	Originally WDLR 2705
3	Converted to 4wDM
4	'Gamecock' class
5	'Jurassic' class
6	'M4' class
7	'7 in.' class
8	'Cranmore' class
9	'100DL' class
10	'951L' class
11	Baguley valve gear
12	Bagnall-Price valve gear
13	Walschaerts valve gear

Index

Bold type denotes illustration